THE UNCONSCIOUS IN
SOCIAL AND POLITICAL LIFE

THE UNCONSCIOUS IN SOCIAL AND POLITICAL LIFE

Edited by

David Morgan

THE POLITICAL MIND

PHOENIX
PUBLISHING HOUSE
firing the mind

First published in 2019 by
Phoenix Publishing House Ltd
62 Bucknell Road
Bicester
Oxfordshire OX26 2DS

British Library Cataloguing in Publication Data

A C.I.P. for this book is available from the British Library

ISBN-13: 978-1-912691-17-3

Typeset by Medlar Publishing Solutions Pvt Ltd, India

Printed in the United Kingdom

www.firingthemind.com

Everything ends in the same way. With death. But before there was life, hidden beneath all the babbling and noise. Silence and feelings. Excitement and fear. The spare, unsteady splashes of beauty.

—*From* La grande bellezza (The Great Beauty)
directed by Paolo Sorrentino, 2013

We never know how high we are
Till we are asked to rise
And then if we are true to plan
Our statures touch the skies.

—*Emily Dickinson, "We never know how high we are", 1176*

Front cover image

August Landmesser, the man who refused to salute

This photo was taken during a ceremony that was attended by Adolf Hitler himself. Within the picture a lone man stands bravely whilst everyone else obeys the power of the crowd and national hysteria by saluting and paying allegiance to the Nazi Party and Adolf Hitler.

August Landmesser defiantly shows his disapproval. It demonstrates the protest of a single person in an authentic way. It is a symbol for me of the courage to stand out against cruelty and fundamentalism. Others who inspire us in these complex times could be Sophie Scholl and the White Cross, Nelson Mandela, Martin Luther King, Rosa Luxembourg, Jesus of Nazareth, Rosa Parks, or Marielle Franco, to name a few of my inspirations. We need great leadership at these times, otherwise the falseness of those who lead through bigotry and hate will triumph.

When going into exile from Vienna, before he was granted safe passage, Freud was paid a visit by members of the Nazi Party and was asked to write a reference to his persecutors attesting to their good conduct. He accepted, writing sarcastically, "I would recommend the SS to anybody!" Needless to say, his ignorant and humourless protagonists did not perceive the joke.

Contents

Permissions

The following have been reprinted with permission.

Chapter Two: The democratic state of mind by Christopher Bollas was originally published in: Bollas, C. (2018). The democratic mind in: *Meaning and Melancholia: Life in the Age of Bewilderment* (pp. 79–92). Abingdon, Oxfordshire/New York, NY: Routledge. Copyright © 2018 Christopher Bollas. Reproduced with permission of the Licensor through PLSclear.

Chapter Four: Europe in dark times: some dynamics in alterity and prejudice by Jonathan Sklar was originally published in: Sklar, J. (2019). *Dark Times: Psychoanalytic Perspectives on Politics, History and Mourning.* Bicester, Oxfordshire: Phoenix. Reprinted with permission of the publisher.

Epigraph at the start of Chapter Four: Europe in dark times: some dynamics in alterity and prejudice by Jonathan Sklar. From *Selected Poems* by Anna Akhmatova, translated by D. M. Thomas. Published by Martin Secker & Warburg Ltd. Reprinted by permission of The Random House Group Limited. © 1985.

Chapter Seven: Inflammatory projective identification in fundamentalist religious and economic terrorism by David Morgan was originally published in: Morgan, D. (2017). Inflammatory projective identification in fundamentalist religious and economic terrorism. *Psychoanalytic Psychotherapy, 31:3*: 314–326. Copyright © 2017 The Association for

Psychoanalytic Psychotherapy in the NHS, reprinted by permission of Taylor & Francis Ltd, http://www.tandfonline.com on behalf of The Association for Psychoanalytic Psychotherapy in the NHS.

Verse from "Country Life" by Show of Hands within Chapter Seven: Inflammatory projective identification in fundamentalist religious and economic terrorism by David Morgan. Reprinted with permission of Firebrand Music / Show of Hands Ltd.

"Refuge" by J. J. Bola within Chapter Seven: Inflammatory projective identification in fundamentalist religious and economic terrorism by David Morgan. Reprinted with permission of the author.

Chapter Ten: Reflection or action: and never the twain shall meet by R. D. Hinshelwood was originally published in: Hinshelwood, R. D. (2017). Reflection or action: And never the twain shall meet. *Psychotherapy and Politics International, 15:1*: e1401. Copyright © 2017 John Wiley & Sons, Ltd.

Acknowledgements

The Political Mind Seminars at the British Psychoanalytical Society have now been running successfully since 2015. They consist of a series of ten seminars presented by colleagues from the British Society with one or two expert external contributors.

I became increasingly interested in exploring the role of the unconscious and the political mind after the events of 9/11. I sat in my consulting room feeling overwhelmed by the horror traumatically unfolding. I felt helpless but thought perhaps psychoanalysis could provide some insight into what was happening in the USA on that day and elsewhere in the world.

What grievances with the West and what basis in religious fundamentalism could lead to this apocalyptic event? Freud in *Civilization and Its Discontents* was pessimistic about man's inhumanity to man and the tendency to obviate anxieties around life and death through war and power.

Similar feelings arose around the enormity of climate change and the terrible loss of life with immigrants drowning in the Mediterranean. I felt our lives, our allies' lives, and, indeed, everybody's lives were being bombarded by events that were difficult to comprehend and that turning a blind eye was dangerous and inhuman.

There is always something to be said for just concentrating on the microcosm of the consulting room and helping each individual patient develop internal resilience through understanding his or her internal world within the security of the analytic setting. This extends to the families, workplace, and beyond. This is revolutionary in its way and I know that sometimes there is criticism from colleagues who feel that psychoanalysis is over-extending its remit when used to attempt to understand the wider world and the social unconscious. However, the consulting room can become a psychic retreat in itself when we are confronted by events that threaten our lives, our loved ones' lives, and the people we care for in our work. There has been a real hunger for psychoanalytic understanding from those attending the seminars. The content of the presentations has been very varied and the quality superlative. Each evening has attracted between 60 and 120 attendees, including a solid group of regulars who have come to all the seminars, plus new people every year.

This book is representative of the seminar series and I hope readers find the ideas helpful. We all need help in these complex times and understanding the unconscious is helpful.

I am extremely grateful to all who have provided their talks and time to this venture. I have been so impressed with the quality of the presentations and their capacity to engage with a wide range of political opinions and audience participation.

I would like to extend my appreciation to Marjory Goodall and recently Harriet Myles and Natasha Georgiou without whose help this venture would not have been possible. I'm grateful to Roger Holden whose technological expertise and demeanour make things run so smoothly.

I would particularly like to thank Ruth, Freya, William, Alex, and Leo; without them, the world would be a much less interesting and more difficult place to be.

My thanks to the late John Berger; an inspiration in politics, art, and how to live.

I would also like to thank Luisa Alexa Passalacqua Carenati who has guided me with her editorial skills and intellect through this process.

About the editor and contributors

Dr David Bell is a training analyst and supervisor of the British Psycho-analytical Society who served as its president from 2010 to 2012. Bell is a consultant psychiatrist in the Adult Department at the Tavistock and Portman NHS Foundation Trust, where he was director of postgraduate training for many years and leads a specialist service (the Fitzjohn's Unit) for the treatment of patients with enduring and complex problems. He was the 2012–2014 Professorial Fellow at Birkbeck College and is currently an honorary senior lecturer at University College London. He lectures regularly on political issues including the historical development of psycho-analytic concepts (Freud, Klein, and Bion) and the psychoanalytic understanding of severe disorder. For his entire professional career, he has deeply involved himself in interdisciplinary studies (the relation between psychoanalysis and literature, philosophy and socio-political theory). He has written numerous papers and chapters in books/monographs, edited two books, *Reason and Passion* and *Psychoanalysis and Culture*, and written one small book, *Paranoia*. He is also one of the UK's leading psychiatric experts in asylum and immigration.

Christopher Bollas is a fellow of the British Psychoanalytical Society and the Los Angeles Institute and Society for Psychoanalytical Studies. He is an honorary member of the Institute for Psychoanalytic Training and Research in New York.

He has been in clinical practice for fifty years and received his clinical trainings in both the United States and Great Britain. He was a graduate of the Psychoanalytic Psychotherapy Training Program at the University of Buffalo (1972), and received an MSW from Smith College in 1973. He trained as a psychoanalytic psychotherapist at the Tavistock Clinic in London and qualified in 1978. He also trained as a psychoanalyst at the Institute of Psychoanalysis in London and qualified in 1977.

He was the first non-medical psychoanalyst to serve on the London Clinic of Psychoanalysis (1979–1983); visiting professor of psychoanalysis at the Institute for Child Neuropsychiatry, University of Rome (1978–1998); director of education at the Austen Riggs Center in Stockbridge, Massachusetts (1985–1987); professor of English literature at the University of Massachusetts (1983–1987); and Vorhees Professor at the Menninger Clinic.

He has lectured widely in Europe, the USA, South America, Australia, Japan, Israel, and Singapore and gave a keynote speech to the International Psychoanalytical Association in Boston in 2015. He has published numerous books, from *The Shadow of the Object: Psychoanalysis of the Unthought Known* (1987) to *When the Sun Burst: The Enigma of Schizophrenia* (2016). His books have been translated into more than ten languages. He is a citizen of both the USA and the UK. He lives in Santa Barbara, California where he maintains his private practice.

Professor Josh Cohen is a psychoanalyst in private practice, and professor of modern literary theory at Goldsmiths, University of London. He is the author of *Spectacular Allegories* (1998), *Interrupting Auschwitz* (2003), and *How to Read Freud* (2005), as well as numerous reviews and articles on modern literature, philosophy, and psychoanalysis, appearing regularly in the *Times Literary Supplement*, *The Guardian*, and *New Statesman*. His latest book, *The Private Life*, was published by Granta in 2013, and addresses our current raging anxieties about privacy through explorations in psychoanalysis, literature, and contemporary life. Josh's next book, *Not Working*, was published by Granta in 2019, and a book on the therapeutic power of literature will be published by Ebury in 2020.

Dr Renée Danziger is a psychoanalyst in private practice. She is a fellow of the British Psychoanalytical Society and an honorary senior lecturer at University College London. She teaches at the Institute of Psychoanalysis and at the British Psychoanalytical Association, and is a training analyst for the British Psychotherapy Foundation's child psychotherapy training. Her doctorate is in politics, and for many years she worked as a social scientist with a special interest in political powerlessness, and in HIV/AIDS policy issues.

Fakhry Davids practises full-time as a psychoanalyst. He is a training analyst of the British Psychoanalytical Society, honorary senior lecturer, Psychoanalysis Unit, University College London, board member, Partners in Confronting Collective Atrocities (www.p-cca.org), and author of *Internal Racism: A Psychoanalytic Approach to Race and Difference* (Palgrave Macmillan, 2011).

Steven Groarke is Professor of Social Thought at the University of Roehampton. He teaches at the Institute of Psychoanalysis in London, is an Honorary Senior Research Associate at University College London, and a training analyst of the Association of Child Psychotherapists. He is a member of the editorial board and reviewing panel, respectively, of the *International Journal of Psychoanalysis* and the *British Journal of Psychotherapy*. He currently works as a psychoanalyst in private practice in London.

R. D. Hinshelwood is professor emeritus, University of Essex, and previously clinical director, The Cassel Hospital, London. He is a fellow of the British Psychoanalytical Society, and a fellow of the Royal College of Psychiatrists. He authored *A Dictionary of Kleinian Thought* in 1989, and *Clinical Klein* in 1994. A long-time advocate of alternative psychiatry, he was a founding member of The Association of Therapeutic Communities in 1974; and in 1980 he founded, with colleagues, *The International Journal of Therapeutic Communities*. He was involved in the Psychoanalysis and Public Sphere conferences in the 1980s and 1990s, and he has contributed each year to the Psychoanalysis and Political Mind Seminars. He has been a member of the Labour Party for fifty years.

Dr Roger Kennedy worked as a consultant family psychiatrist in the National Health Service at the Cassel Hospital, Richmond for nearly thirty years and was an honorary senior lecturer in psychiatry at Imperial College, London. Since January 2011 he has held an appointment as consultant child and adolescent psychiatrist to a multidisciplinary private clinic—The Child and Family Practice, now at 60 Bloomsbury Street, London, as well as maintaining his long-standing private psychoanalytic and psychotherapeutic practice in Twickenham.

He has extensive experience of providing courts and social services with expert opinion on multi-problem families as well as in private law cases. He is acknowledged as a leading expert in the field, and has published many papers and several books, including *Child Abuse, Psychotherapy and the Law* (1997), *The Elusive Human Subject* (1998), *Psychotherapists as Expert Witnesses: Families at Breaking Point* (2005), *The Many Voices of Consciousness* (2007), *Couch Tales* (2009), *Psychic Home* (2014), and *Tolerating Strangers in Intolerant Times* (2019). He sees adolescents, couples, and families for therapeutic work, and offers assessments for children and parents. Dr Kennedy can offer consultations to local authority workers dealing with complex families, and their departments.

Dr Kennedy is also a training psychoanalyst of the British Psychoanalytical Society, and was its president from 2004 to 2006. He has an extensive psychoanalytic and psychotherapy practice for adults, has many years' experience of teaching and training in the therapy field, and is often involved in presenting at conferences both in the UK and abroad.

Dr Kennedy is president of the charity Community Housing and Therapy, a unique organisation that offers residential treatment for the mentally ill and help towards independent living. He is also a fellow of the Royal Society of Arts, a charity which encourages the development of a principled, prosperous society and the release of human potential.

Dr Ruth McCall is a fellow of the British Psychoanalytical Society, supervisor and training psychotherapist for multiple British psychoanalytic psychotherapy trainings, and several years a tutor for the MSc in psychoanalytic studies, University College London. Ruth has a special interest in hysteria and psychosomatic disorders, and lectures on Freud's and Winnicott's work. Her initial career was in television documentary productions, and now she broadcasts and works in private practice in London.

David Morgan is a consultant psychotherapist and psychoanalyst fellow of the British Psychoanalytical Society. He is also a training analyst supervisor at the British Psychoanalytic Association, and a lecturer recognised nationally and internationally. He co-edited *Violence, Delinquency and Perversion* (2007) and authored many publications and chapters, most recently "Inflammatory Projective Identification in Political and Economic Terrorism" in *Psychoanalytic Psychotherapy* (2018), as well as "The Return of the Oppressed", a speech given at the Warsaw EPF Conference (2018). He is currently a director of Public Interest Psychology Ltd as well as a member of the IPA committee on Humanitarian Organisations. He is the chair of The Political Mind Seminars and of Frontier Psychoanalyst, a radio broadcast series on Resonance FM.

Michael Rustin is professor of sociology at the University of East London, a visiting professor at the Tavistock Clinic and at the University of Essex, and an associate of the British Psychoanalytical Society.

He has a long-standing interest in psychoanalysis and its relation to politics. His books include *Researching the Unconscious: Principles of Psychoanalytic Method* (2019); *Reading Klein* (with Margaret Rustin (2016)); *The Kilburn Manifesto* (edited with Stuart Hall and Doreen Massey (2015)); *Social Defences against Anxiety* (edited with David Armstrong (2015)); *Reason and Unreason* (2001); and *The Good Society and the Inner World* (1991).

Dr Jonathan Sklar, FRCPsych, is an independent training analyst, and fellow of the BPAS working in full-time private practice. He was a member of the board of the IPA (2015–2019), and has been a vice president of the European Psychoanalytic Federation (2007–2011). He was consultant psychotherapist and head of the Psychotherapy Department of Addenbrooke's Hospital for twelve years. He taught "Ferenczi and Contemporary Psychoanalysis" on the MSc psychoanalytic studies at University College London and has taught psychoanalysis regularly in Cape Town, Chicago, and Eastern Europe. He is the author of the following books: *Landscapes of the Dark: History, Trauma, Psychoanalysis* (2011, Karnac), *Balint Matters: Psychosomatics and the Art of Assessment* (2017, Karnac), *Dark Times: Psychoanalytic Perspectives on Politics, History and Mourning* (2018, Phoenix).

Philip Stokoe is a psychoanalyst in private practice working with adults and couples, a fellow of the Institute of Psychoanalysis, and an organisational consultant, providing consultation to a wide range of organisations since he qualified in 1983 at the Tavistock Centre. He was honorary visiting professor in mental health for three years at City University, where he is helping to set up a radically new way to train mental health nurses based on psychoanalytic principles. He worked as a consultant social worker in the Adult Department of the Tavistock & Portman NHS Foundation Trust between 1994 and 2012 where he was the clinical director of the Adult Department from 2007 to 2011. He has developed a reputation as a successful teacher and has taught and written about the application of psychoanalysis in a wide range of settings: supervision, leadership, groups, organisations, ethics, borderline disorder, adolescence, residential work, working with victims of sexual abuse, psychological services in the National Health Service, couple relationships, and politics. He has a particular interest in human creativity as it relates to the development of the mind and the central role of curiosity and interest. His early experience as an actor has left him with an abiding interest in theatre, art, and cinema.

Sally Weintrobe is a psychoanalyst who writes and talks on how to understand what underlies our widespread disavowal of climate change. She edited and contributed to *Engaging with Climate Change: Psychoanalytic and Interdisciplinary Perspectives* (2012). Her current work is on the culture of "Uncare", a culture that—she argues—works to sever our felt caring links with the environment and with each other. She is a fellow of the British Psychoanalytical Society (BPAS), a chartered clinical psychologist (BPS), and a founding member of the Climate Psychology Alliance (CPA).

Foreword

This excellent book is a must for analysts and for readers interested in understanding our troubled world in a contemporary frame. David Morgan, its editor, tells us that the book is an outcome of the successful series of Political Mind Seminars given at the British Psychoanalytical Society since 2015. This initiative is really auspicious. The success in managing to bring together a group of psychoanalysts for a prolonged period of time, who were able to sustain the enthusiasm to discuss the effects that very painful situations of the contemporary world have on our subjectivities, is highly remarkable.

The whole world, in its different cultures and diverse geographies, is suffering the impact of unequal opportunities, intolerance of differences, violence, fanaticism, and vulnerability in childhood.

The book studies in a broad arc subjects that include the democratic state of mind, fanaticism, right-wing populism, neoliberalism, and terrorism, amongst others. It also includes the feminist perspective and the moral dimension of climate change.

The core of this publication is, as the title indicates, the attempt to find the unconscious axis of these problems. The book achieves this and in doing so, challenges a pervasive sense that not only exists in the psychoanalytic realm but has also extended to the whole of society: that those who are interested in politics deserve, at the very least, mistrust.

As every end is a new beginning, let us go to the moving quote at the beginning of the book about "the spare, unsteady splashes of beauty" even when we face death. This is the point in which aesthetics and ethics could meet. Starting from Freud's "The Uncanny" we could quote Rainer Maria Rilke, who in the "Duino Elegies" says "For Beauty is nothing but the beginning of terror which we are barely able to endure …". He seems to allude to how the poet, the artist, and even the analyst with his gaze approach chaos or look at themselves in chaos.

From these perspectives, we can say that the contact with beauty is always essentially conflictive, because it is a mask that suggests and reveals at the same time as it conceals. Beauty is always a veil through which one can sense chaos. The aesthetic experience implies brushing against the veil itself, a semblance of the essential mystery.

Going back to the issue of the close relationship between ethics and aesthetics, this book shows that psychoanalysis has to take an ethical stance when confronted with the dehumanisation tendency in our contemporary world.

Virginia Ungar, MD
President of the International Psychoanalytical Association

Introduction

David Morgan

Political and ideological turmoil in the current and the last century has been certainly influenced by the effects of economics, revolution, and endless battles for power and supremacy. These events are also experienced by each human being in the most personal way, leaving deep emotional scars and trauma. Each individual's experience is multifaceted and reflects a transgenerational history that has profound influence on future generations that underpins themselves and their families, involving both the individual and the social unconscious.

If we think of poverty and how its after-effects are felt by future generations, distant memories of loss, trauma, and anxiety over survival continue to reside in the unconscious. This early shadow falls on future generations. So political turmoil is also a crisis of human relationships as well as economic and social convulsion.

The greatest dreads that can impact upon the individual such as anxiety, fear of persecution, and fragmentation of the self, occur in every era, but it is only in the last century with the work of Sigmund Freud that these psychological states of mind became a systematic field of study. Why this occurred is of great interest, but to my mind it meant that mankind had evolved (at least in Western Europe) to the point where survival and anxieties around it became subjugated for the first time to thought that was not "pie in the sky" religious, but a deep understanding of human intrapsychic experience.

This does not in any way suggest that religion and philosophy do not have their own profound wisdom, but to my mind, psychoanalysis does contribute something unique and that is the role of the understanding of the unconscious and how actions are often impelled by this unknown influence.

In *Group Psychology and the Analysis of the Ego* (1921c) Freud states,

> It is true that individual psychology is concerned with the individual man and explores the paths by which he seeks to find satisfaction for his instincts; but only rarely and under certain exceptional conditions is individual psychology in a position to disregard the relations of this individual to others. In the individual's mental life someone else is invariably involved, as a model, as an object, as a helper, as an opponent, and so from the very first individual psychology is at the same time social psychology as well—in this extended but entirely justifiable sense of the word.

If we are to learn from history rather than as it seems driven to eternally repeat it, we must understand what impels us to continue to repeat destructive actions that could lead to our demise.

To my mind this is an evolutionary and revolutionary development that is the understanding of the unconscious, which could contain the potential to divert humankind from the inevitable self-destruction Freud so cogently describes, that we do seem intent on repeating and enacting. If we think of how we dispose of waste materials, using the earth as an endless container for all we cannot use … The infantile mode of relating is so obviously paramount here: it is somebody else's responsibility or another generation's task to deal with our shit.

It was actually Freud not Marx who highlighted that the motive of human society is in the last resort economic: the need to work has meant we have to repress pleasure and gratification, in the interest of working, to survive, as opposed to doing nothing or pursuing our instinctual gratifications at the expense of all else. He described this as the repression of the pleasure principle in the face of reality, what he described as the reality principle, for example, I am writing this at the end of a long pleasurable holiday and the awareness of forgoing the gratifications of pursuing pleasure for the daily need to work is casting its shadow.

Repression, however, is an important achievement of humankind; we sublimate desires to achieve a more socially valued state of existence and it is civilisation that arises out of this.

However, too much repression and we become sick. Marx explored the impact of labour on social relationships, class, and politics. Freud looked at the impact labour had on the mind or psyche of the individual and through extension, the group and society.

The repression for Marx was political. For Freud, the unconscious was how we managed this repression and we were no more aware of it than we are aware of the social processes which determine our lives that Marx brought to our awareness. The main reason for this repression is that humankind is conscious and we are very vulnerable when we are born; unlike animals we take years to stand on our own two feet and are very dependent on our caregivers. Without this care we would die. We are also born with an inherent awareness of the reality of death.

It is getting the help we need to manage this reality of our vulnerability at different stages of development, oral, anal, genital, oedipal that we begin to accept the reality principle and give up our narcissism (fear of not surviving) and need for instant gratification. For example, oedipally we have to find our own relationships rather than incestuous ones. We must move from infantile auto-eroticism to adult relating. This is the first mental and emotional work that prepares us, or fails to prepare us, for the task of adult work and life. Many leaders like Donald Trump and others who behave like infantile children are clearly emotionally immature, but have been compelled to get into positions of power.

Freud's view of humanity was pessimistic; he saw us dominated by a desire for gratification and an aversion to frustration. The apotheosis of this is the death drive, a struggle to return to nothingness, a prelapsarian Eden before we had the frustration of knowledge and limitations.

This may sound conservative but he was also convinced that modern society had become tyrannical in its repressiveness. Freud's contribution to political thinking therefore cannot be underestimated. He questioned the origin and structure of society in *Totem and Taboo* (1912–13), exposed illusions and dogmas in *The Future of an Illusion* (1927c) where he says if a society has not developed beyond a point at which satisfaction of one group is based on the suppression of another, it is understandable that those who are suppressed should develop an intense hostility towards a culture that does nothing to alleviate this inequality.

In *Civilization and Its Discontents* (1930a) he challenges "civilised sexual morality" as the origin of "the nervous and mental illness of modern times". In *Group Psychology and the Analysis of the Ego* (1921c) he analyses the concepts of leader, crowd, and power. He wrote about Bolshevism in the *New Introductory Lectures on Psycho-Analysis* (1933a) and described the foundation of a people in *Moses and Monotheism* (1939a).

In his theory of the superego, Freud ascribed values, ideals, and imperatives associated with morality and society to the psyche. He suggests that sexual (life) drive and death drive, coupled with the instinct for mastery, is a determining factor of existence in society, politics, and the individual.

Political thought—as in Machiavelli, Hobbes, Marx, Weber, and others—intersects and illustrates many of Freud's ideas. For example, the radical rejection of all forms of illusion, the will to lucidity based on a flexible rationality, the dismantling of connections within communities, and the emphasis on the autonomy and responsibility of the individual subject. This is not to say that psychoanalysis has not been criticised.

At times, psychoanalysis has been seen as a form of social control forcing individuals into arbitrary notions of normality. This has been particularly strong in the work of Thomas Szasz (1978) but has tended towards a critique of psychiatry and a medical model that rather dominated American psychoanalysis. In fact, Freud demonstrated how polymorphous and flexible the notion of norm is.

Freud was also accused of being concerned with the individual only, substituting psychological answers for social and historical influences, when it was, as I think he saw it, always a subtle interaction between the individual and social pressures.

However, Freud did not reduce his invention only to an important method of healing mental disorders. In his work, he has also focused on important works that addressed fields that were external to knowledge of the individual unconscious, and politics was included in his work when he addressed issues such as civilisation, law, or the libidinal foundations of leadership.

This scope of the unconscious theory on political matters has not been overlooked by the following generations. In fact, some schools of thought have been impacted directly by Freud's work, or even by its consequences and reinterpretations. The explicit approach between contemporary political theory and psychoanalysis got its first inspiration from the Frankfurt School: Herbert Marcuse, Max Horkheimer, Jürgen Habermas,

Theodor Adorno, and Walter Benjamin. Hannah Arendt was not an aficionado of psychoanalysis but her political philosophy certainly resonated with psychoanalytic thinkers of today.

One of the richest traditions that has arisen from Freud's writings is a form of political psychoanalytic work engaged with the question of happiness and how it affects whole societies, for example Reich and the Frankfurt School of Adorno, Horkheimer, Habermas, and Marcuse. These theorists attempted to explain some of the perceived omissions of classical political theory such as Marxism by drawing answers from other schools of thought such as psychoanalysis and sociology. A synthesis of the work of Kant, Hegel, Marx, Freud, Weber, and Lukács, they were concerned with the conditions that allow for social change and the establishment of rational institutions.

Walter Benjamin, who is associated with the Frankfurt School, also wrote about themes of culture, destruction, Jewish heritage, and the fight between humanity and nihilism, making significant contact with post-Freudian psychoanalytic thinking.

Hannah Arendt, although opposed in some ways to psychoanalysis, through her writing on the Holocaust, Eichmann, and totalitarianism explored intellectual history as a philosopher, using events and actions to develop insights into contemporary totalitarian movements and the threat to human freedom presented by scientific abstraction and bourgeois morality.

In what is arguably her most influential work, *The Human Condition* (1958), Arendt differentiates political and social concepts, labour and work, and various forms of actions. She then explores the implications of those distinctions. Her theory of political action, corresponding to the existence of a public realm, is extensively developed in this work. Arendt argues that, while human life always evolves within societies, the social part of human nature and political life has been intentionally realised in only a few societies as a space for individuals to achieve freedom. Conceptual categories which attempt to bridge the gap between ontological and sociological structures are sharply delineated. While Arendt relegates labour and work to the realm of the social, she favours the human condition of action as that which is both existential and aesthetic.

In the *Origin of Totalitarianism* (1951), she examines the roots of communist and Nazi dictatorships, demonstrating that totalitarianism was a "novel form of government", different from other forms of tyranny in that it applied terror to subjugate mass populations rather than just political adversaries. She conceived of a trilogy based on the mental activities of thinking, willing, and judging. In *Life of the Mind* (1977–1978) which concerned the discussion of thinking, she focuses on the notion of thinking as a solitary dialogue between oneself. This leads her to introduce concepts of conscience—an enterprise that gives no positive prescriptions, but instead, tells one what I cannot do if I would remain friends with myself. Arendt is widely considered one of the most important political philosophers of the twentieth century and now she has influenced many of the parts in this volume.

Frantz Fanon was an enormously important psychiatrist, philosopher, revolutionary, and writer from the French colony of Martinique whose works are influential in the fields of post-colonial studies, critical theory, and Marxism. As an intellectual, Fanon was a pan-Africanist concerned with the psychopathology of colonisation and the human, social, and cultural consequences of decolonisation. In his important book *Black Skin, White Masks* (1952) and other seminal works, he applies historical interpretation and the concomitant underlying social indictment to understand the complex ways in which identity, particularly blackness, is constructed and produced. In the book, he applies psychoanalytic theory to explain the feelings of dependency and inadequacy that black people might experience. This for me has been a profound use of psychoanalytic theory to understand racism and colonial fascism that continues in the work of Fakhry Davids in this book and Frank Lowe (2014) at the Tavistock Clinic with his important *Thinking Space* on race and racism.

Franco Fornari, in his great work *The Psychoanalysis of War* (1974), shows us that war and violence develop out of a "love need": our wish to preserve and defend the sacred object to which we are attached. "Nations", of course, are the sacred objects that most often generate warfare. Fornari focuses upon sacrifice as the essence of war; this astonishing willingness of human beings to give over their bodies to the nation state.

Herbert Marcuse is probably the parent of modern psychoanalytic and political thinking. He particularly develops the idea of alienation in which capitalism exploits humanity, turning people into commodities. In *One Dimensional Man* (1964), Marcuse writes, "People recognise themselves in their commodities finding their souls in their cars and hi-fi, the market creates false needs and false consciousness, geared to consumption integrating the working man entirely into the capitalist system." His thinking is particularly apposite when we see the current effects of neoliberalism on society making welfare, education, and health secondary to profit. In *Eros and Civilization: A Philosophical Inquiry into Freud* (1955), he proposes a non-repressive society, attempting a synthesis of the theories of Marx and Freud exploring the potential of collective memory to be a source of disobedience and revolt and point the way to an alternative future.

There was also the generation of French intellectuals of the sixties and seventies, among them Félix Guattari, Georges Bataille, Gilles Deleuze, Jacques Derrida, Jean-François Lyotard, Louis Althusser, and Michel Foucault, all of whom take up their essays and criticism in the possibilities of thinking with and against psychoanalysis. Political thinkers like Cornelius Castoriadis, Ernesto Laclau, Norbert Elias, Slavoj Žižek, and Zygmunt Bauman—all these writers put the psychoanalysis of Freud and Lacan in the centre of their works. Many of these writings would be impossible to be properly understood without psychoanalytic knowledge.

Alain Badiou (2018), another important French political philosopher influenced by psychoanalysis, says that it has recently become common today to announce, for various reasons, the end of the human species as we know it, threatening categories, such as trans-humanism and the post-human rise to the surface or, symmetrically, a return to animalism, but they obscure the real danger to which humanity is exposed today, namely, the impasse into which globalised capitalism is leading us.

It is in reality this social form, and it alone, which authorises the destructive exploitation of natural resources, linking it to the pure notion of private profit.

That so many species are threatened, that the climate is out of control, that water is becoming a rare treasure—all of this is a by-product of ruthless competition between billionaire predators and that scientific progress is anarchically subservient to marketable technologies. Badiou (2018) states that for four or five millennia, humanity has been organised by the triad of: private property, which concentrates enormous wealth in the hands of very slender oligarchies; the family, through which fortunes pass through inheritance; and the state, which protects both property and family through armed force. It is this triad that defines the Neolithic age of our species, and we are still there—indeed now more than ever. Capitalism is the contemporary form of the Neolithic and its enslavement of technologies by competition, profit, and the concentration of capital only brings to their apex the monstrous inequalities, social absurdities, warlike massacres, and deleterious ideologies which have always accompanied the deployment of new technologies under the historical reign of class hierarchy. The real question in our time, Badiou states, is the possibility of a methodical and urgent exit from the Neolithic. The Neolithic being a thousand-year-old order, only valorising competition and hierarchies, and tolerating the misery of billions of human beings, must be overcome at all costs, he says, lest those wars are unleashed of which the Neolithic has since its appearance fought like those of 1914–1918 or 1939–1945, with their tens of millions of victims, only this time with many more. For Badiou, it is a question of proposing that a non-Neolithic social organisation is possible, which is to say: no privatisation of property which must be common, namely the production of all that is necessary for human life; no family of heirs, no concentrated inheritances; no separate state protecting the oligarchies; and no hierarchy of work. Capitalism he says is only the last phase of the restrictions that the Neolithic form of societies imposes on human life. It is the last stage of the Neolithic. Slajov Žižek has probably been one of the most prolific if idiosyncratic writers in recent years. His ideas would need a separate book to do them justice. However, I feel he argues that the state is a system of regulatory institutions that shape our behaviour; its power is purely symbolic and has no normative force outside of collective behaviour. In this way, the term *the law* signifies society's basic principles, which enable interaction by prohibiting certain acts. Political decisions have become depoliticised and accepted as natural conclusions. For example, controversial policy decisions (such as austerity and reductions in social welfare spending) are presented as apparently "objective" necessities.

Although governments make claims about increased citizen participation and democracy, the important decisions are still made in the interests of capital. The two-party system dominant in the United States and UK produces a similar illusion.

The real political conflict is between an ordered structure of society and those without a place in it. The postmodern subject is cynical towards official institutions, yet at the same time believes in conspiracies. When we lost our shared belief in a single power, we constructed another of the other in order to escape the unbearable freedom that we faced. It is not enough to merely know that you are being lied to, particularly when continuing to live a normal life under capitalism. For example, despite people being aware of ideology, they may continue to act as automata, mistakenly believing that they are thereby expressing their radical freedom. As Žižek states, although one may possess a self-awareness, just because one understands what one is doing does not mean that one is doing the right thing or anything.

His books: *Living in the End of Times* (2010), *Violence* (2008), *Did Somebody Say Totalitarianism?* (2001), *The Parallax View* (2006), and many others contribute enormously to politics and psychoanalysis.

As we can see Freud's estate was particularly vast and rich for political thought and influenced many clinicians, but also important revolutionary figures. Currently, one can say that Freud and psychoanalysis define ways of thinking politics within the political theory.

Joel Kovel, an American psychoanalyst and academic, has probably through his writings been one of the most radical psychoanalytic thinkers there has ever been. His works have included: *Against the State of Nuclear Terror* (1982), *History and Spirit* (1991), *In Nicaragua* (1986), *Overcoming Zionism* (2007), *Red Hunting in the Promised Land: Anticommunism and the Making of America* (1994), *The Age of Desire* (1981), *The Enemy of Nature* (2002), *The Radical Spirit* (1988), and *White Racism* (1970). I think I speak for many when I say he was a shining light in this area. His conversion in later life to Christianity was a surprise to us all. In a personal communication, he stated that he "found it compelling to invoke Christ as an inspiration to humanity in a form that he felt theory could not achieve".

Also, from the American psychoanalytic tradition there has been the important work of Dr Vamık Volkan such as *Blind Trust* (2004) and *The Need to Have Enemies and Allies: From Clinical Practice to International Relationships* (1988) among many other works. Volkan's research focuses on the application of psychoanalytic thinking between countries and cultures, individual and societal mourning, transgenerational transmissions of trauma, and the therapeutic approach to primitive mental states. He developed unofficial diplomacy's "tree model", described "linking objects" and "linking phenomena" of perennial mourners, and observed "chosen traumas" and "chosen glories" of societies. He has used his ideas in work with the United Nations, particularly in Cyprus and Turkey. Similar interventionist work has been undertaken in the UK by Lord John Alderdice who has used his training in psychiatry and psychoanalysis in his work with the Northern Ireland peace process and other frontiers of political conflict. His groundbreaking work is represented by many papers including a chapter in the next volume of The Political Mind, *A Deeper Cut: Further Explorations of the Unconscious in Social and Political Life.*

In the UK there has been a major contribution to the field from a Jungian perspective from Andrew Samuels who was the prime leader in this psychopolitical area a long time before anyone else. In his seminal work

The Political Psyche (1993), he showed how the inner journey of analysis and psychotherapy and the political convictions of the outer world such as market economy, environmentalism, nationalism, and anti-Semitism influence the individual and added an international survey into what analysts and psychotherapists do when their patients/clients bring overtly political material into the clinical setting. As a pioneer of psychopolitical, gender, and sexuality issues, he has made a contribution that has been a remarkable one, particularly in the early years when his was a lone voice in a rather resistant psychoanalytic environment. I do think we owe a lot to his initiatives in this field.

Another Jungian analyst, Coline Covington in her book *Everyday Evils* (2016), provides an important contribution when she looks at the evils committed by "ordinary" people in different contexts—from the Nazi concentration camps to Stockholm Syndrome to the atrocities publicised by Islamic State—and presents new perspectives on how such evil deeds come about as well as the extreme ways in which we deny the existence of evil.

Other important contemporary authors have been Jessica Benjamin, who has written widely on feminism and gender and who more recently contributed articles and thought to the Israel/Palestine conflict, as has Professor Jaqueline Rose—again from Birkbeck University—in *The Question of Zion* (2005) and who has also contributed very importantly to feminist and gender studies. Susie Orbach in the UK has been at the forefront of psychoanalysis and feminist thinking.

Also from the UK, there has been Juliet Mitchell's seminal work on psychoanalysis and feminism (1974) and David Bell's look at culture through the work of Hanna Segal (1999) establishing how Hanna Segal's approach provides a clear focus to psychoanalysis and culture. David Bell has also contributed a great deal to the political debate through his own talks and papers such as "Primitive Mind of State" (1996), and on the subjects of the National Health Service, neoliberalism, and Hannah Arendt.

Hanna Segal herself contributed a great deal to thinking about the dangers of nuclear power. She explored the relationship of war to the contrast between the paranoid and depressive positions in Kleinian thought, highlighting the usefulness of the role of an identified enemy in warding off the subjective pain of depression in *Psychoanalysis, Literature and War* (1997). Segal continued her lengthy examination of the relationship between psychological factors and war in this work on the symbolic significance of the events of 9/11.

Michael Rustin has been very active in the fields of psychoanalysis, mental health, and welfare, developing research methods to explore the study of unconscious mental life. In his important book *The Good Society and the Inner World* (1991), and in *Reason and Unreason* (2001), he addresses his concern with the social and political relevance of psychoanalytic ideas, and with their use in the understanding of cultural phenomena.

Fakhry Davids's *Internal Racism: A Psychoanalytic Approach to Race and Difference* (2011) is a seminal work on racism from a psychoanalyst.

Jonathan Sklar has also contributed recently to the understanding of the profound effects of trauma in the socio-political realm in two seminal works, *Landscapes of the Dark: History, Trauma, Psychoanalysis* (2011) and *Dark Times: Psychoanalytic Perspectives on Politics, History and Mourning* (2019). These are important contributions to the understanding of how trauma if not symbolised and mourned is repeated in future generations.

Other contributions to the field have been from academia, in particular Stephen Frosh and his colleagues at the department of socio-political studies at Birkbeck University, as also Professor Robert Hinshelwood and colleagues at Essex University in the department of psychoanalytic studies.

Psychoanalyst Daniel Pick at University College London in his *Psychoanalysis and the Age of Totalitarianism* (2014) (written with Matt Ffytche) provides a cogent exploration of this important area that is once again re-emerging as a dangerous tendency in right-wing populism as an antidote to the complexities of immigration and economic uncertainty.

Robert Young was one of the first thinkers through his radical "Free Associations Press and Human Nature" series and their related conferences, to begin to explore these areas. The unifying thread of Robert Young's research, political activities, writing, and clinical practice has been the understanding of human nature and the alleviation of suffering and inequality. His work has largely been interdisciplinary, seeking to promote unity in how we think about nature, human nature, and culture. He has made a huge and relatively unsung contribution to this area.

Psychoanalyst Sally Weintrobe's tour de force on climate change, *Engaging with Climate Change: Psychoanalytic and Interdisciplinary Perspectives* (2012), has been a hugely valuable contribution to this neglected area of political and social thinking, addressing what is the most pressing concern of our day.

Joanna Ryan (2017) in *Class and Psychoanalysis: Landscapes of Inequality* explores the hugely important question of class. Joanna Ryan provides an overview in which she looks at the radical potential of psychoanalysis, with its deep understandings of the unconscious, while simultaneously maintaining its status as a mainly exclusive profession which can only be afforded by the few.

She shows how class was clearly excluded from the founding theories of psychoanalysis despite the pioneering work of Reich and others working with the underprivileged and this has left a problematic legacy. This has been compounded by the reduction of psychotherapy providers in the National Health Service, with only a few institutions managing to continue providing psychotherapy, such as the Tavistock and Portman Clinic, Camden Psychotherapy Unit, Maudsley Hospital Psychotherapy Department, and the Cassel Hospital, all in London. Outside of London, a similar picture occurs.

She explores the injuries of class, the complexities of social mobility, and the defences of privilege and illustrates the anxieties, ambivalences and inhibitions surrounding class, and the unconscious way that they may be enacted (Ryan, 2017). I find her work compelling and inspirational, addressing an area that has been neglected, probably due to its uncomfortable truths.

Elizabeth Cotton who writes a blog called "Surviving Work" explores similar issues in her article, "Do you have to be married to a banker to train as a psychoanalyst?" (2017).

As you can see, many psychoanalysts and academics have been inspired to step out of the consulting room to address the wider issues that affect the setting that the people we see and ourselves inhabit. I am aware many analysts do not consider the political world a suitable place for psychoanalysis to venture. I think this underestimates the profundity of our thinking which people are hungry for. The Political Mind Seminars and Frontier Psychoanalyst broadcasts (https://www.epf-fep.eu/fre/news/frontier-psychoanalyst-radio-politics-society-and-the-individual) have demonstrated there is a need for psychoanalytic thinking in these areas. I believe the chapters in this book demonstrate that psychoanalysts can contribute a great deal of valuable understanding to these issues and I hope they will be read by people in the socio-political world as well as interested colleagues.

At the moment, our institutions in the UK that underpin a caring society, such as the National Health Service and welfare system, are currently facing an uncertain future. The same is happening elsewhere. As people become increasingly measured by their economic production and life is based on commodification rather than other values, there is a need to redevelop a culture that preserves the importance of humanity. We should all be working hard to reverse what has become known as neoliberalism with its emphasis on market forces over human love and joy. Psychoanalysis, as you can see in the chapters of this book, makes a valuable contribution to this important endeavour.

References

Arendt, H. (1951). *Origin of Totalitarianism*. New York: Schocken Books.

Arendt, H. (1958). *The Human Condition*. Chicago, IL: University of Chicago Press.

Arendt, H. (1977–1978). *The Life of the Mind*. San Diego, CA: Harcourt Brace Jovanovich.

Badiou, A. (2018, July 26). Capitalism, the sole culprit of the destructive exploitation of nature [translated]. *Le Monde*.

Bell, D. (1996). Primitive mind of state. *Psychoanalytic Psychotherapy, 10*: 45–57.

Bell, D. (Ed.) (1999). *Psychoanalysis and Culture: A Kleinian Perspective*. London: Duckworth.

Cotton, E. (2017). Surviving Work blog. Do you have to be married to a banker to become a psychoanalyst?

Covington, C. (2016). *Everyday Evils: A Psychoanalytic View of Evil and Morality*. London. Routledge.

Davids, M. F. (2011). *Internal Racism: A Psychoanalytic Approach to Race and Difference*. London: Palgrave Macmillan.

Fanon, F. (1952). *Black Skin, White Masks*. Richard Philcox (Trans.). New York: Grove, 2008.

Ffytche, M., & Pick, D. (2014). *Psychoanalysis in the Age of Totalitarianism*. Abingdon, UK: Routledge.

Fornari, F. (1974). *The Psychoanalysis of War*. Alenka Pfeifer (Trans.). Garden City, NY: Anchor Press/Doubleday.

Freud, S. (1912–13). *Totem and Taboo*. S. E., *13*. London: Hogarth.

Freud, S. (1921c). *Group Psychology and the Analysis of the Ego. S. E., 18*. London: Hogarth.

Freud, S. (1927c). *The Future of an Illusion. S. E., 21*. London: Hogarth.

Freud, S. (1930a). *Civilization and Its Discontents. S. E., 21*. London: Hogarth.

Freud, S. (1933a). *New Introductory Lectures on Psycho-Analysis. S. E., 22*. London: Hogarth.

Freud, S. (1939a). *Moses and Monotheism. S. E., 23*. London: Hogarth.

Kovel, J. (1970). *White Racism: A Psychohistory*. London: Allen Lane, 1988.

Kovel, J. (1981). *The Age of Desire: Reflections of a Radical Psychoanalyst*. New York: Pantheon.

Kovel, J. (1982). *Against the State of Nuclear Terror*. Boston, MA: South End.

Kovel, J. (1988). *In Nicaragua*. London: Free Association.

Kovel, J. (1988). *The Radical Spirit: Essays on Psychoanalysis and Society*. London: Free Association.

Kovel, J. (1991). *History and Spirit: An Inquiry into the Philosophy of Liberation*. Boston, MA: Beacon.

Kovel, J. (1994). *Red Hunting in the Promised Land: Anticommunism and the Making of America*. London: Continuum, 1997.

Kovel, J. (2002). *The Enemy of Nature: The End of Capitalism or the End of the World?* London: Zed.

Kovel, J. (2007). *Overcoming Zionism: Creating a Single Democratic State in Israel/Palestine*. London: Pluto.

Lowe, F. (Ed.) (2014). *Thinking Space: Promoting Thinking About Race, Culture and Diversity in Psychotherapy and Beyond*. London: Karnac.

Marcuse, H. (1955). *Eros and Civilization: A Philosophical Inquiry into Freud*. Boston, MA: Beacon.

Marcuse, H. (1964). *One-Dimensional Man*. London: Routledge & Kegan Paul.

Mitchell, J. (1974). *Psychoanalysis and Feminism: A Radical Reassessment of Freudian Psychoanalysis*. London: Penguin, 2000.

Rose, J. (2005). *The Question of Zion*. Princeton, NJ: Princeton University Press.

Rustin, M. (1991). *The Good Society and the Inner World: Psychoanalysis, Politics and Culture*. New York: Verso.

Rustin, M. (2001). *Reason and Unreason: Psychoanalysis, Science and Politics*. London: Continuum.

Ryan, J. (2017). *Class and Psychoanalysis: Landscapes of Inequality*. Abingdon, UK: Routledge.

Samuels, A. (1993). *The Political Psyche*. London: Routledge.

Segal, H. (1987). Silence is the real crime. *International Review of Psycho-Analysis*, 14: 3–12.

Segal, H. (1997). *Psychoanalysis, Literature and War:* Papers 1972–1995. London: Routledge.

Sklar, J. (2011). *Landscapes of the Dark: History, Trauma, Psychoanalysis*. Abingdon, UK: Routledge, 2018.

Sklar, J. (2018). *Dark Times: Psychoanalytic Perspectives on Politics, History and Mourning*. Bicester, UK: Phoenix.

Szasz, T. (1978). *The Myth of Psychotherapy: Mental Healing as Religion, Rhetoric, and Repression*. Syracuse, NY: Syracuse University Press, 1988.

Volkan, V. (1988). *The Need to Have Enemies and Allies: From Clinical Practice to International Relationships*. Northvale, NJ: Jason Aronson.

Volkan, V. (2004). *Blind Trust: Large Groups and Their Leaders in Times of Crisis and Terror*. Charlottesville, VA: Pitchstone.

Weintrobe, S. (Ed.) (2012). *Engaging with Climate Change: Psychoanalytic and Interdisciplinary Perspectives*. London: Routledge.

Žižek, S. (2001). *Did Somebody Say Totalitarianism? Five Interventions in the (Mis) Use of a Notion*. London: Verso, 2011.

Žižek, S. (2006). *The Parallax View*. Cambridge, MA: MIT Press.

Žižek, S. (2008). *Violence: Six Sideways Reflections*. New York: Picador.

Žižek, S. (2010). *Living in the End of Times*. London: Verso.

CHAPTER ONE

Where have all the adults gone?

Philip Stokoe

The title of this chapter—"Where have all the adults gone?"—aims to capture the feeling many have experienced following the UK vote to leave the EU and the election of Donald Trump to be president of the United States. There is an absence of adult functioning among politicians which is intimately linked to a similar state among the electorate, the people. The removal of structures within society which exist to enable countries and governments to look after the people and face reality has led to a release of anxiety about money which has a tendency to plunge us into a fundamentalist state of mind in which truth does not matter, only the certainty of escape from anxiety. This kind of behaviour, and the way that leadership and followership become caught up in something that feels like a hysterical panic, is familiar to those who have made a psychoanalytically based study of individuals, groups, and organisations.

I believe that a particular psychoanalytic way of understanding people in groups and organisations offers a way to understand how society functions which can enable thinking about the relationship between the individual and a large group—an organisation or society—whilst avoiding the most common trap. The trap is the expertise that nearly all human beings have about understanding other human beings: we are very good at reading other people's unconscious. Indeed, this is wonderfully illustrated by our fascination with reality-based television such as *I'm a Celebrity … Get Me*

Out of Here! and *Love Island*. The only unconscious we cannot read is our own, so the pleasure derives from predicting how the characters in the show will interact with each other and seeing how that interaction plays out. The problem is that this skill often misleads us into explaining the behaviour of groups as if it is simply down to the impact particular individuals are having; in other words, assuming group phenomena are essentially about individuals and their personalities. My claim is that it is much more often the other way round, that individuals are unconsciously provoked to express ideas of behaviour on behalf of the group dynamic. Of course, and this is what makes it so tempting to stay with the superficial analysis based on personality, the way individuals become drawn into expressing something on behalf of the group does represent a link to their personality and this will be explored later in the chapter.

In order to describe the processes that go on in groups and the way that individuals are drawn into those processes, I shall first define my understanding of how the conscious mind develops in the individual in a summary of a model of human development.

Development of the mind

We are organised by three drives: *curiosity, love,* and *aggression* (called hate by Bion). These drives enable us to be curious about reality and to relate to it by developing loving concern for others, which means we can:

Form reciprocal relationships
Absorb information
Which we transform into symbols
To enable thought and, ultimately
Undertake decision making.

This leads to the development of a sense of identity: we know who we are. In the developmental timetable, these skills are the consequence of achieving what Melanie Klein (1935) described as the "depressive position". They are achievements of development, not inevitable qualities.

Building on Klein's work, Wilfred Bion (1962) stressed this particularly strongly and added that these achievements require effort or work. Bion accepted Freud's view that "Eros" and "Thanatos" (life and death instincts) were crucial to the development of the mind and he designated them "L" (love) and "H" (hate), but he argued that they couldn't account for important stages of development on their own; he argued that the urge to know was just as important and he gave that the designation "K" and concluded that it is an innate drive. I prefer to call this curiosity. It operates as a constant internal instruction to explain to ourselves what we are experiencing. These explanations take the form of images of ourselves in relation to others or parts of others (which is why this approach is called "object relations").

The discovery that we have such images of ourselves in relation to others preceded the more elaborate description of the development of the mind that I'm referring to, which was largely expressed by Melanie Klein. She was a leading contributor amongst other psychoanalysts following Freud who uncovered the phenomenon that such images accompanied and even organised the emotional encounters with the analyst in the consulting room. They described this "accompaniment of everyday experience" as *unconscious phantasy*.

"Phantasy is (in the first instance) the mental corollary, the psychic representative, of instinct. There is no impulse, no instinctual urge or response which is not experienced as unconscious phantasy" (Isaacs, 1948).

These processes are unconscious, which is why fantasy is spelt with a "ph", but the repetition of explanations, a process that Bion calls "learning from experience", leads to the development of the conscious mind. I would say that these internal images (sometimes described as *imagos*), gradually accumulate and it is this accumulation that creates the conscious mind.

These hypotheses or explanations for what is happening to us can only derive from what we already know. In the light of further experience, we adapt those hypotheses; in other words, we change the internal images. Sometimes, however, these hypotheses do not change in the light of experience. Instead, they become fixed as "unconscious beliefs" and appear as *facts* in the conscious mind. When Ronald Britton was a little boy, another, bigger boy told him that Santa Claus did not exist. It seems that he immediately realised that he had totally assumed that Santa Claus was a *fact*. Now he realised that it was merely a *belief*, not a fact, and beliefs can be tested and shown to be either true or false. Clearly, this one was false. And he wondered what else he had assumed to be a fact, which could turn out to be merely a belief. Since unconscious beliefs are "certain", they protect us from the need to think and, in so doing, they reduce anxiety (Britton, 1998, pp. 12–14).

Fundamentalism, the earliest state of mind

In what follows, I shall refer to the loss of adult capacity as a collapse into the earliest state of mind, described by Melanie Klein as the paranoid/schizoid position. I think that a more relevant term should be the fundamentalist state of mind.

At the beginning of life outside the womb, the baby has no internal defences. We need our defences because they act to damp down our emotional experience. Freud's view was that all stimulus, whether from outside or from within, is experienced through the neural pathways as feelings. The very first thing that the baby does is to find ways to manage the overwhelming experience of those raw feelings and she does this through the activity of K, in the sense that she finds explanations for her experience that also serve to manage it. For example, she explains to herself that the feeling we would call hunger is actually an assault from a dangerous other. Melanie Klein described this in more detail as the baby *projecting* the horrible feeling into an object outside and then *identifying* that object with that horrible feeling. In this way, the baby has invented a defensive process known as projective identification (Klein, 1946). The baby's experience of these horrible feelings is of the worst kind of anxiety, survival anxiety. Fortunately for most of us, the "object" into which this horror is projected (usually mother) manages to survive the experience and, by processing the feelings, arrives at an understanding of her baby's plight and responds accordingly; in this case by feeding her baby. The baby, in turn, feels suffused with enormous feelings of love but, as before, these are too powerful to remain inside and are also projected into the same mother only this time transforming her into an ideal source of love and nourishment. The persecutory anxiety about destruction has been left in the evil hunger monster and there is an answer to all of that terror in the form of this omnipotently yummy mummy.

In these simple acts, something amazing has happened; the baby has created a complete working model of the universe. Split into two separate, emotional locations, total love and total hate, various consequences fall out. Melanie Klein called this a state of mind and gave it the name, the paranoid/schizoid position. I find that a more relevant name for it is the fundamentalist state of mind. I shall describe those qualities of this state of mind, but I want to point out that this is the first that we create as we develop. Consequently, it can be described as our default position. Whenever we are made suddenly or chronically anxious, we collapse into this view of the universe. In many ways, it makes sense for our survival because this is not a state of mind encumbered by the need to reflect or to measure one view against another, it is the place of action. It is also the state that Freud described as governed by the pleasure principle.

In terms of the drives (L, H, and K) and the achievements that result from them which I listed earlier, and which are the result of development out of the fundamentalist state of mind and into the depressive position, what does this collapse look like? In the first place, those capacities, which are higher level functions, will be annihilated by anxiety, and the primary drives will be reorganised. In the fundamentalist state of mind, curiosity is diminished, love transforms into the ideal, and hate into evil.

This state of mind has the following basic elements:

It is ruled by the ideal
Its governing principle is pleasure
Anxiety is persecutory and about one's own survival
Language is that of blame
Mental state of choice is certainty
Solutions are all omnipotent
Threat is difference, e.g.
    help
    valuing
    thinking
Relationships are either mergers or sadomasochistic.

I shall expand on this. In the first place, the universe is divided or split into two separate states, *ideal* or *evil* (total love or total hate), therefore the place we will want to be is with the ideal. This will be the place that has no "un-pleasure", in other words we are driven by Freud's pleasure principle. The threat to this isn't just worry, it is the most massive, persecutory anxiety, total destruction. Since the only event that will require a language is a threat to our sojourn with the ideal, then that language will be the language of blame (if I'm in danger of being kicked out of the ideal nest, someone must be to blame). The only emotional or intellectual state that has any existence is certainty; doubt cannot be tolerated, it is the work of the devil. All problems are resolved through identification with the ideal, therefore such solutions are omnipotent. There is only one threat, difference, because there is only one danger, being dislodged from that nest. This doesn't arise as an issue until there is someone different around because that immediately raises the question, "Which one of us is with the ideal?" We will be made aware of difference, that is to say, a challenge to our comfortable position of certainty and omnipotence, by a variety of experiences of which I single out three as prime examples.

1) If we are offered help, it means unambiguously that we are not ideal.
2) If someone values something about us, this is not the same as worshipping our omnipotence, so we are again threatened; thinking is predicated on not knowing, so it is absolutely abhorred.
3) As for relationships, we are in the realm of George W. Bush who, after 9/11, constantly made it clear, "If you are not with us, you are against us." Thus the only possibilities are merger or a sadomasochistic struggle.

When this state of mind dominates and we are incapable of functioning at the higher level, based on tolerating "not knowing", it requires us to turn off curiosity because it would only force us to challenge certainty. The fundamentalist state of mind is primitive, it is not adult.

At this point, it is worth spending a few words on the places we go for certainty. First Freud and now neuroscience claim that emotions are our link with the world, both inner and outer, and are more powerful than the more recently developed cerebral cortex. Freud's pleasure principle, which is clearly the organising function of the paranoid/schizoid position, restores certainty by removing "unpleasure".

An organism experiences a stimulation as an impact on itself. The stimulation triggers a feeling. You might say this "perception" stimulates an emotional response, which triggers action. This has the effect of moving away from a negative source of stimulation or moving towards one that stimulates pleasurable feelings. This kind of response has often been called "instinctive" and I think this refers to its location at our most primitive level, in contrast to a much slower system that involves conscious thinking. This is the realm of certainties: pleasure means good, pain means evil; there is nothing unclear in the split universe.

What sorts of things serve to provide certainty in the human mind? Such things will all be characterised by the same quality of "no-brainer". We can offer three types of certainties:

1) Animal "instinctive" reactions like fight, flight, and freeze
2) Unconscious beliefs (which we will discuss later), and
3) The paranoid/schizoid or "primitive" defences.

It is appropriate at this point to say that truth requires the capacity to tolerate uncertainty: being a search, it cannot be conceptualised on the level of primitive function where the first requirement is certainty. Of course, it is possible that something that could be described as true will also be experienced as a certainty and therefore have a place in this state of mind; but if it gains this position it is not because it is true, it is only because it is infused with certainty.

Application to organisations

The question is, what carries out the same function within an organisation as in an individual? If we look at "identity" as the primary task of an organisation, then the other qualities—embracing reality, building relationship, absorbing information, and transforming it into symbols—can be linked with love and aggression to form what I call the "shared basic principles", which are the parameters within which an organisation operates. These shared principles are the elements that make up the system of governance in a successful organisation.

Thinking and the ability to make decisions become the hierarchy of decision making. All of this is driven or motivated by curiosity and interest, which creates an attitude within a healthy organisation, which could be defined as a "culture of enquiry", a benign enquiry.

To take these concepts one at a time, the *primary task* is essentially the identity of the organisation, the reason for its existence as it relates to the outside world. Usually called a "mission statement", it has to be written down, most likely on the company website, so that it can be under constant review, because things change and a healthy organisation is concerned about its relevance to the current conditions. Yet, attention to it will immediately arouse anxiety.

Next is *shared principles*. These provide the parameters for the work, for instance, financial, ethical, practice, and attitude. These factors must be held in mind by any part of the organisation (usually the board) whose function is governance. All of which creates the "personality" of the organisation, which is held together by a shared commitment to a benign enquiry.

Finally, the *hierarchy of decision making*. This is the equivalent—in biology—of the circulation of blood. In an organisation, this corresponds to the circulation of authority and accountability, which creates effective decision making and activity. It begins with a leader ("the boss") who delegates decision making to a subordinate ("the manager") who, in turn, delegates decision making to a lower-ranking subordinate ("the operative"). In this way, authority is passed down the line. Organisations are designed from the top down, answering the question, if this is the task, what resources do I need to accomplish it?

In the course of engaging with the work (on behalf of the primary task), the operative will experience "anxiety" both from the engagement itself and from the "clients". In exchange for the authority to make decisions, each person in the system has a duty to account to the next level up for how he or she has progressed. Thus, the operative accounts to the manager and the manager accounts to the boss. This provides the pathway by which anxiety is passed up the line. It is the hallmark of a functional or healthy organisation that anxiety is allowed to be passed upwards and authority downwards. This is because anxiety is always a coded form of communication, usually the most important sort of information (see Figure 1).

To define this a little more precisely, if we focus only on the line of account-ability (Figure 2), the encounters that are highlighted with black circles will be the location where accounting takes place. If we can approach them from the perspective of a benign enquiry, then we will have created the organisa-tional equivalent of "thinking". These are usually in the form of meetings between the manager and his or her "direct report", informed by the primary task and shared principles and providing a space for thinking. Without these structures, the organisation becomes rigid, uncreative, and, finally, toxic.

Figure 1. Circulation of authority and account.

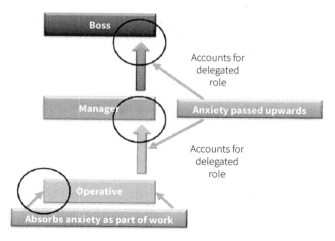

Figure 2. Line of accountability.

Just to be clear about the difference between thinking in an individual and thinking in a group: in the individual, thinking is what happens when the reception of a stimulus (either from outside or inside the individual), which is always in the form of a feeling, is firstly transformed, through a process that Bion called "alpha function", into a symbol. The symbol can now be played with in the mind so that it acquires meaning, which will stimulate, through association, related concepts that can lead to a "response". This process is primarily unconscious, although we develop the skill to imitate it consciously and it is the conscious version that we usually describe as "thinking".

In a group, stimulation will be picked up by members in their own way and the two processes, alpha function and playing with the symbols, require sharing of the feelings (in the first place) and symbols (in the second). In other words, thinking in a group is always a form of conversation.

What the organisation must do

These structures, which are essentially the healthy circulation, and encounters between people that preserve communication and decision making, must be positively valued and embraced by the organisation and rigorously protected because they will be the first things to go under stress. In this respect, the organisation mimics the individual. Within the latter, in the face of sufficient anxiety, "thinking" and "facing reality" are abandoned and replaced by paranoid/schizoid functioning, where certainty replaces thinking and belief replaces curiosity—which would lead to investigating reality. In the organisation, a disrupting level of anxiety will evoke a procedural system to replace thinking and an accompanying powerful belief system replaces investigation.

The impact of anxiety is not the only reason for the organisation carefully to protect and maintain these functions that serve to face reality and thinking. The ordinary process of *work* will lead to a distortion of the system. I think of this as entropy, the second law of thermodynamics which says that everything tends to collapse into chaos. Where there is awareness that this is bound to happen, the process of *account* becomes the place where these failings within the system can be identified and healed.

It is not difficult to see that the divergence from healthy functioning involves the disabling of curiosity and interest ("K"). K is essential to the maintenance of a functioning system but it is vulnerable to anxiety. When K is disabled, the individual or the organisation will fall back upon "belief" (see Ron Britton) and, in particular, "*unconscious* belief" which registers in the conscious mind simply as "fact".

The individual in the group

How does the individual end up representing or "allowing" these processes of dysfunction in groups and organisations?

The individual has a conscious and an unconscious. Part of the individual's unconscious might be described as a "hook" that is essentially a vulnerability; the part of us that Jung described as "the healer's wounds" (1966, pp. 115–116), in other words, our emotional and psychological injuries. Bion called this *valency* (1961, pp. 116–117). Although, to be accurate, he only used this term to refer to the individual's tendency towards one of the specific group defences which he described in that book. Later authors have developed the term to describe our unconscious predisposition to particular defensive behaviours or attitudes. Now it is time to look at the individual as part of a group.

Figure 3 represents the "group consciousness". Clearly, this very statement implies another level of group functioning that we might describe as the "group unconscious". This has been called the "shadow group", which is a good name because it is certainly a reflection of the individuals forming the group consciousness (see Figure 4).

Group conscious

Figure 3. The group conscious.

The shadow individuals are organised by a process called the "group dynamic", which will be described later in the chapter. The group dynamic is the process that provides the unconscious momentum for the group behaviour and preoccupations. This is not to suggest that there is an unconscious process occurring in a group that is in some magical way independent of the individuals' unconscious. There will be some form of unconscious communication between the individuals to lead to certain behaviours. The point is that, for the purposes of describing how groups seem to function, the notion of a group unconscious provides a very useful working model.

How do the individuals shown in the "group conscious" section of the illustration become connected to their shadows in the group unconscious? This takes place through a connection between the shadow and the valency of the individual (the "hook"), which results in the individual being pulled into performing a role on behalf of the unconscious life of the

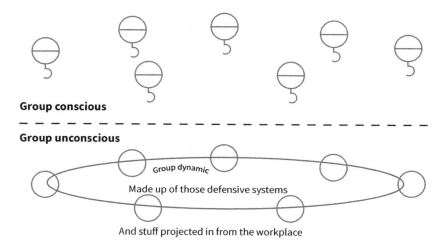

Figure 4. Group conscious and unconscious.

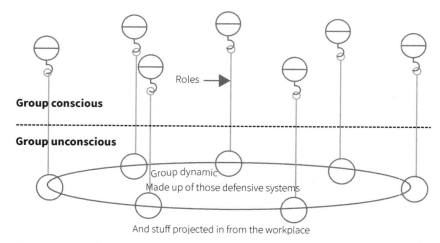

Figure 5. Group dynamic and roles.

group (see Figure 5). It is an important skill in understanding groups to be able to recognise the roles that individuals are drawn into playing. The roles tell us about the unconscious preoccupation of the group but the fact that individual human beings occupy these roles can present us with a problem. Much more often than not, the individual concerned is quite unconscious of being drawn into a role. Indeed, we are all more likely to believe, and to claim, that such thoughts that we express are spontaneous or independent of unconscious influence. This is why a group facilitator, pointing out that a particular group member has just expressed an important preoccupation on behalf of the group, will often be told by that group member that, on the contrary, those views are entirely his or her own construction. It is this phenomenon, our resistance to recognising the unconscious impact on our thinking of group processes when tied to the importance of valency, that leads to the ubiquitous symptom of group dysfunction; the group's total pre-occupation with individuals and their personalities.

We are all pulled into roles through our valencies. For example, suppose that in the shadow group, probably as a result of projection from a particu-lar client, one shadow member is identified with anger (one could say that this represents a split in the projecting client), and another shadow member is identified with submissiveness or a victim (again, a split in the project-ing client). Now, it is as if this shadow group looked upwards at the valen-cies of the individuals forming the group consciousness in order to discover appropriate hooks. Lo and behold, there is a valency for anger in one of the individuals and a valency for submissiveness in another. Immediately, these are linked to form the shadow group and those two individuals will find themselves filled with those feelings; the one with anger and the other with something submissive or dependent or fearful. It is even quite likely that these two will find themselves in a conflict; in which case the basic assumption mode known as pairing will start to happen.[1] Then everybody else links to the group dynamic through their own valencies and the whole thing starts to spin in a predictable way (see Figure 6).

This is the way in which an individual becomes "caught up" in representing some aspect of the group dynamic by being drawn into a role. If there isn't a system that allows these processes to be noticed and thought about, the group will become controlled by them. At this point, the state of mind changes. Bion would say that the group has become organised around *avoiding anxiety*. Without a capacity to think, the group suffers the same collapse into a more primitive state of mind that happens to an individual in similar circumstances, the collapse that I referred to earlier as the "paranoid/schizoid" state of mind.

In order to understand how these ideas might be conceptualised in the context of society, I shall focus on the impact of the neoliberal ideas first imposed on the Western world by Margaret Thatcher and Ronald Reagan in

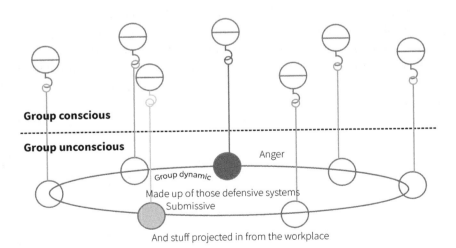

Figure 6. Valency in a group.

the form of the free market. To do this, I shall develop an idea first presented by Professor Michael Rustin.

The free market fallacy

In his paper "The Referendum and the Crisis of Neoliberalism in Europe" (2016), Rustin uses the motto of the French Revolution and, subsequently, the logo of the French Republic, to make the case for the way that the free market policy led to the destruction of important constituents of a balanced society. The logo shows the three elements considered vital to a just society: *Liberté, Égalité, et Fraternité*. We can rearrange these terms into a favourite shape for psychoanalysts, the triangle, and translate into English, *Liberty, Equality, and Fraternity* but I should like to make a further alteration and turn fraternity into *social care*. The reason for this will become clear below. It is my view that these concepts represent a societal equivalent to the mission statement and the shared parameters of the organisation. They exist in a dynamic tension (see Figure 7).

Liberty represents freedom of thought. Equality is the aim to ensure that all citizens (as the US Declaration of Independence puts it) are created equal but it also implies that a just society attempts to monitor and maintain a pressure towards equality. Fraternity or, as I have written it, social care, links to equality and is the commitment to look after our neighbours. It is the organisational expression of loving concern, a direct representation of the "loving drive". The attitude of care and social concern is one of the most important indications of a civilised society and it is an expression of dignity. However, these three are held together in constant tension; too much

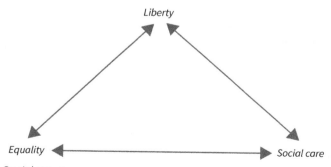

Figure 7. Social structures.

freedom destroys equality and social care, too much equality restricts free thought and ambition, and too much social care can inhibit the development of individual and societal resources (cf. Winnicott's famous dictum that the art of parenting is knowing how much to frustrate the child). Since this "triangle" represents the scaffold or structure for a healthy society, we can be absolutely sure that it will be under attack as soon as anxiety is aroused. According to my theory of organisations, these structures need to be artificially and transparently protected.

As we shall see, under the free market neoliberal agenda, these structures were both removed and redefined. First, let us outline the basic assumptions underlying neoliberalism and the free market as defined by Friedrich August von Hayek (1899–1992) and subsequently by Milton Friedman (1912–2006).

This is an excerpt from Alan Pratt's "Neo-liberalism and Social Policy" where he defines three key assumptions that underpin neoliberalism:

> *Methodological individualism*, which asserts that everything can be understood as and reduced to the level of the individual—this is encapsulated in Thatcher's widely quoted assertion, "There is no such thing as society, only individuals and families";
> *Rationality*, embodying the belief that individuals always act both rationally and in their own self-interest; and
> *Market supremacy*, the notion of the market as the ideal location in which calculative, rational, and well-informed individuals can engage in exchanges. Neoliberals argued that low taxation and minimal state intervention in the market would generate wealth which would "trickle down" from the rich to the poor, avoiding the need for any redistribution of income by the state. (2006, pp. 12–13)

If this is the case, the neoliberal free market makes the mistake of equating the freedom to use capital with human freedom of thought and turns liberty into the symbol for this concept. The problem, as Thatcher and Reagan realised when they took these ideas into the principles for their approach to government, is that society's structures that protect equality and social care restrict the full release of liberty. This required a systematic dismantling of the welfare system. We know, from the release of Cabinet papers (Travis, 2016) that Thatcher was convinced that the whole welfare system had to be dismantled, including the National Health Service (NHS). She was stopped

in this latter part of her plan by a Cabinet meeting in 1982, where a paper out-
lining how to dismantle the NHS was met by, in the words of Nigel Lawson,
"the nearest thing to a Cabinet riot in the history of the Thatcher administration". This led to a different approach in which the welfare state, something
about which there had been a "post-war consensus" among politicians from
all parties (Addison, 1975), was subtly denigrated, so that, instead of it being
something to be proud of, it provided a free rein for scroungers. In the course
of the release of the free market, all three of those principles were renamed.

Renaming

Liberty became the freedom to accumulate wealth; equality was renamed, in
a denigratory fashion, "envy", often referred to as the politics of envy; social
care, with similar vicious denigration, became the nanny state. In this environment, "love" is perceived as weakness, whereas aggression is admired
under the title "competition". But what of "curiosity"? This is now described
as *enquiry*, but enquiry no longer carries any sense of a benign opening
up of thinking; enquiries are to be avoided because they are an attack. The
best example of this is the National Health Service in the United Kingdom.
Its main task is to provide treatment for illness and the mechanism we use
for this is to make a careful, concerned, and thoughtful enquiry into the
patient's symptoms. And yet, at the top of the organisation, there is a clear
culture, expressed time and time again, the aim of which is to avoid enquiries. So often, where there has been a catastrophe, like in Mid Staffordshire,
the actions of the board and executives were motivated more by the need
to avoid an investigation, usually into its management of finances, so that
minor details, like the consequent damage to patients, was ignored (The Mid
Staffordshire NHS Foundation Trust Inquiry, chaired by Robert Francis QC,
March 2010, The Stationery Office). To use the original distinction, enquiry
turns into inquiry.[2] It is clear that enquiries are held to be dangerous to the
organisation. Thus curiosity, which would be the means to restore some reality, renamed as enquiry is perceived as something to be avoided at all costs.

Psychoanalytic critique of the free market

In the light of what was explained in the previous paragraph, we can now
take into account a psychoanalytic critique of the theoretical base for the
neoliberal free market. The model that I am referring to is variously called

the "Tavistock model" or the "group relations model" and it is based on more than sixty years of research in large groups and organisations (Stokoe, 2010; Trist & Sofer, 1959). This is an approach to understanding group and organisational phenomena theoretically based on an amalgamation of psychoanalytic and open systems theories. Experience was gained from two sources, consultation to groups, teams, and organisations, and the experiences collected from group relations conferences. These events are run by a team of consultants under a conference director over several days. Each day consists of a meeting of the whole conference and then other group activities, some in the form of a confidential reflection in your home group; others involve forming new small groups and engaging with other, self-formed groups usually in the service of investigating whatever seems to develop about the unconscious preoccupation of the conference. The task of the conference is usually to study something to do with organisations, leadership, followership and so on, and these activities are set up in the service of pursuing that enquiry. However, the normal structures of an organisation are absent. This allows individuals to experience directly the raw emotions of being part of a group or series of groups. It would be fair to say that a group relations conference is an experiment into group and organisational functioning.

So these two approaches, direct consultation to actual organisations and the experiment of a temporary organisation (the conference) have resulted in a mass of information about how people actually function in groups and in an organisation. It is from this material that I make the following analysis of the truths of the neoliberal claims.

The first of those three claims that the neoliberals hold to be justifications for the free market approach can be represented as: "Everything can be understood as, and reduced to, the level of the individual." Experimental evidence demonstrates conclusively that, as soon as structures are removed, the individual is lost in the group dynamic. The same point was made when I tried to demonstrate above that the release of liberty leads to the destruction of important structures in society and creates a state of mind which is similar to that of the group relations conference.

The second neoliberal claim is that individuals will always act both rationally and in their own interest. But when the individual is subject to group dynamics, this does not apply. An example of this phenomenon occurs during conflict. Freud described this phenomenon in his only contribution to the theory of groups, *Group Psychology and the Analysis of the Ego*, pointing out that soldiers will behave in the most extraordinary way as long as they have a leader providing them with the direction required by the group dynamic. As soon as you remove the leader, the individual members of the group become aware that they are in danger and they run away.

A soldier cries out: "The general has lost his head!" and thereupon all the Assyrians take to flight (Freud, 1921c, p. 97).

To put it succinctly, the individual's self interest is easily lost in the context of a group, particularly where a leader will take on the functions of facing reality and making decisions; the best way to demonstrate this is when those conditions are suddenly lost and the group cohesion collapses, leaving individuals to perceive the truth about their predicament.

The third claim of the neoliberals is that the market will generate wealth which will trickle down from the rich to the poor. In fact, anxiety will be conceived of in terms of the current agreed task, in this case the accumulation of wealth. This is the most important dynamic effect of the free market: the anxiety, which in the fundamentalist universe is always about *my* survival, is symbolised by wealth. Of course, no amount of wealth makes this fear of being robbed go away. As a result, we are moved into a world dominated by anxiety about money and the solution to the underlying sense of terror is to have enough money. Yet accumulation of money does not lead to a feeling of safety (because the dominant anxiety of the fundamentalist state of mind, which is survival anxiety, has now been renamed money anxiety). Instead, wealth merely increases the terror of being robbed. So, whatever position you hold in society, you never have enough money, and anxiety is always experienced consciously as financial.

Unconscious beliefs

Unconscious beliefs and preconceptions seem to populate current Western or first world society. If the beliefs that distort our view of reality are unconscious, what are their conscious representations? Just as with the individual, we might describe these as rationalisations or conscious explanations for behaviour and attitudes; we must treat them as symbolic of the underlying beliefs and preconceptions and defences. So, it is not that they are exactly untrue; rather, they are representations of a truth that requires interpretation.

There are some common themes that have been identified in the phenomena of Brexit in the UK and Trump in the US in the years 2016–2019.

One of these is the hatred of the other usually expressed in racist or sexist terms. Another theme is that of a deviant or tyrannical authority that has taken away the basic human rights from a significant part of the population, a form of disenfranchisement. And finally, a sense of deprivation or disqualification, a feeling of loss and disadvantage: a large part of the population felt they had been abandoned to their fate.

The imagery that accompanied both Trump's campaign and that of those in the United Kingdom who wanted to leave the European Union seems well captured by the popularity of zombie movies, in which an increasingly diminishing population of "normal" people are overwhelmed by swarms and swarms of zombies, who continue to increase in numbers.

But why is this such a powerful and ubiquitous image? At this point I am grateful to my colleague Fakhry Davids for his concept of "the internal racist" (2011). His claim is that this is an innate unconscious concept; more like what Bion (1962) would call a "preconception", and that it was important to have this concept "hard-wired" in our minds as we evolved; he describes it as a repeating mechanism informing the way we create a "sense of ourselves".

First, we create a sense of "I" amongst others: it is a sort of equation, me not you; then, we define ourselves in terms of gender, male not female; and finally, we identify with our "in-group", so that we are part of a particular tribe, rather than another tribe. He argues that we all create a defensive organisation; in the context of the fundamentalist state of mind, dominated by paranoia, we create an arrangement in which we are located in one place, distinct and separate from racial/ethnic others: Us, not a threatening You. This internal and very primitive defensive organisation serves to locate us with our family/tribe of origin, which was in our survival interests once upon a time. So, from early on, we all carry an image of a group of strangers that threaten our survival. So we are terrorised by the image in the zombie films of being overwhelmed by aliens. Similarly, Hollywood supplies the answer to such fundamentalist terrors, superheroes.

In the context of society, the removal of regulations or structures that either protect or express the "higher level" functions of facing reality, gaining information, thinking, caring, and sharing, inevitably lead to a collapse into a fundamentalist world. A world in which thinking cannot be conceptualised, only denigrated. Truth and lies cannot be distinguished and what is required is the sound of certainty. In this world the required certainty evokes primitive concepts or ideas like the threat of the stranger. Other concepts that carry the same emotional weight of certainty can also be evoked but I want to turn to another feature of this state of mind which is the way that anxiety is experienced. In the individual and in a group plunged into the paranoid/schizoid state of mind, the dominant experience of anxiety is about survival; it is life and death, nothing less. If anxiety is symbolised, then that symbol will become the same thing as the anxiety because, in the fundamentalist state of mind, symbols cannot be understood as symbolising something. In the words of Hanna Segal (1957) they are treated as a "symbolic equation", meaning that they are experienced as identical with the thing symbolised; money *is* life or death.

Going back to the context of the triangle described above, the world created by the removal of the adult capacities represented by equality and social care leaves only the symbol of liberty, which has become *money*. When anxiety about survival transforms into anxiety about wealth, nobody escapes. Every level of the population will remain frightened about their financial situation. Because wealth has come to symbolise the basic anxiety of the fundamentalist state of mind that is survival, and this is the most profound anxiety that we can experience, it means that money is held to be absolute, and without any discussion, the most important matter that there is. This applies just as much to those who have loads of money as to those who have none. The evidence for this phenomenon with the former was commented on daily during the US presidential elections by Bernie Sanders, whose policy was to stop the continual movement of wealth into the accounts of the already wealthy. I am suggesting that this shows that no amount of wealth feels enough and that is a classic indication of an unconscious fear or anxiety. Those who have very little or no money spend an enormous amount of time worrying about how to make ends meet. Thus everyone is horrified by an image of having no material wealth.

How else would you define or understand the way that governments rushed to support the financial institutions that had created the 2008 crash? Hence a staggering increase in inequality.

The consequence of a shared fear about money is indicated by the statistic about the inequality in the US. According to the paper by Emmanuel Saez and Gabriel Zucman (2014), 0.01% of the population own as much wealth as the bottom 90%. In the UK, the statistic is that 0.1% own as much wealth as the bottom 90%. The UK is the third most unequal country in the world after the USA and Sweden!

Let us return to the definition of the paranoid/schizoid state of mind to understand what it looks like in the context of this sort of society, which we shall call the "post-free-market state of mind". We can define this state of mind in this way:

Ruled by the ideal, which becomes wealth
The governing principle remains pleasure, which means the avoidance of pain
Anxiety, which is really about survival, has now been symbolised by money; only the quality of symbol has collapsed into a concrete and certain fact, a "symbolic equation"
The language, which is the language of blame, is expressed as denigration
Mental choice is certainty, which has absolutely no connection with truth
Solutions sound all omnipotent
The threat is difference (diversity?), symbolised by foreigners
And relationships are either mergers or, much more often, sadomasochistic.

It is easy to see that, given the opportunity to turn against the oppression, people vote to leave. In the UK, the source of oppression was taken to be the European Union, so they voted Brexit. Of course, the tragedy in both Brexit and Trump is that these votes don't stop the neoliberal march: even the collapse of the banks did not accomplish that; quite the opposite, they allowed the real powers (the financial world) to continue to dominate, while the dispossessed lost even more. In fact it was worse than that. In the UK, many who voted to leave Europe were the casualties of the Thatcher, free market approach to industry, namely to let the market decide. They were the workers in the coal mines and in the steel works whose industries were closed down and they were told to retrain and look for work. They were abandoned in this endeavour and then they watched what should have been a collapse of the financial industry but this time, bankers and speculators were not told to retrain, they were rescued by the government at the expense of the very people who, in a similar situation, were left behind.

Return of the lost good object

So what hope is there? If we go back to what we know about the development of the human mind, but turning now to how the baby moves from the paranoid/schizoid position to that state of mind which results in those capacities that we emphasised at the beginning, we will soon realise the whole discourse revolves around a fulcrum.

Initially the baby is motivated to rid herself of anxiety about survival by taking food/milk from her mother. As long as mother is there with the food supply, there is no problem. However, a crisis occurs when she is not there. At first the baby can avoid this knowledge, and Freud describes a halfway position in which the baby "hallucinates" the breast and Bion expands on this in his theory of thinking. The point is that, whatever attempt the baby makes to tolerate the hunger (still actually believed to be an attack from the hunger monster), there comes a point at which she has to look at what is really happening. Freud says this is the point at which the pleasure principle gives way to the reality principle. However, I think that this cannot happen unless one accepts that curiosity has the same emotional power as love and hate, for it is curiosity that enables the baby to look at what is really happening and come to terms with it. The baby looks up and sees, not a hunger monster (bad breast) but an absence; baby is suddenly confronted with the agony of the absence of mummy. Of course, this discovery leads the baby to realise his need for her. In this moment, the central anxiety moves from "my survival" to "loss of my mummy" (which psychoanalysts describe as "loss of the good object"). In other words, relating replaces "having"; what is now most valued is "relationships", and no longer "possessions" (like food).

The fulcrum that I was referring to is the turning point from pleasure principle to facing reality and the single drive which will enable that is curiosity.

Using this model of development, we can see that the major cost of society's collapse into the fundamentalist state is the replacement of "valuing relationships" with "valuing material wealth". In the loss of the primacy of relationships, social care is also lost. The individual who has dignity and civility is able to be thoughtful and generous, and we all feel good in the company of such individuals. I think of Nelson Mandela, Desmond Tutu, their Truth and Reconciliation Commission, and Leonard Cohen, whose quiet, humble, and respectful attitude to all around him would have that effect on others.

Conclusion

It seems to me that the resolution of this social crisis must be to find an equivalent to the return of the lost good object. When one takes away social protection for the moral imperative of equality, there is no protection from the unconscious group dynamic that is triggered by anxiety.

Since rationality, thinking, concern, and reciprocal relationships all require effort and all collapse under massive anxiety, might it not be our aim to create an environment in which all have the best chance of maintaining that state for as much time as possible? That would turn the meaning of freedom from the neoliberals' definition: the freedom to use our capital as we want, into the freedom to think. If the structures in an organisation designed to replicate the processes necessary for thinking are the first to be attacked in the face of anxiety, would it not make sense to develop a constitution that protects those structures in society?

We know from therapeutic work with individuals that it is possible to restore the higher levels of functioning and we do this by provoking the return of curiosity, which will enable us to notice that we are "caught up" in something. We have to encourage our politicians to seek to investigate, not to simply hit one form of certainty with another. This is particularly important in the environment that represents the welfare system.

This also implies reclaiming love in the form of genuine concern for others. This does not mean repressing aggression. The latter, under the control of love, allows us to stand up to the processes that aim to destroy the structures that allow for equality and social care.

Challenging the dismantling of the welfare system, which is a sign of higher-level functioning in a civilised society, means challenging the idea that such a massive inequality is acceptable. Since wealth does not "trickle down", a strong government has to "enable" a fairer distribution of wealth with strong taxes aimed at reducing massive differences. Leaders have to model the respect we give to those who have needs and they need to challenge the excesses of individuals who are encouraged by projection from the media and demonstrate a higher regard for care than for wealth.

In the pursuit of this aim, it is helpful to remind ourselves of how the three drives act together to create certain higher-level functions. Combination of love and curiosity provides the internal strength to manage the anxiety consequent on standing against the hatred of thinking and concern; this stimulates the capacity to face reality. The combination of love and aggression allows us to value and seek or provide help. Like the capacity to face reality, this development occurs because the combination of drives enables us to manage the anxiety of tolerating difference.

In this way we might be able to rebuild a structure in society to protect equality, and to rebuild a welfare system, by re-establishing social care. Only by doing this will we seriously provide for the most valuable human freedom, the freedom from oppression through the freedom to think. In this way we open the door to the return of the adults.

Notes

1. I refer here to Bion's descriptions of the way that groups defend against anxiety by unconsciously organising themselves around basic assumptions (BAs). He described three: BA dependence, in which the group seem to believe that finding the right leader will make everything better; BA fight/flight, in which they seem to believe there is an enemy out there that they simply have to decide to fight or avoid; finally, BA pairing, in which the group appear to believe that letting two people fight it out between them will result in an idea that will save them all.
2. While in US English there is no distinction, in the UK "enquiry" suggests a question whereas "inquiry" denotes an investigation.

References

Addison, P. (1975). *The Road to 1945: British Politics and the Second World War.* London: Jonathan Cape.

Bion, W. R. (1961). *Experiences in Groups* (pp. 116–117). London: Tavistock. [Reprinted Routledge, 1989.]

Bion, W. R. (1962). The psycho-analytic study of thinking. *International Journal of Psychoanalysis, 43*: 306–310.

Britton, R. (1998). *Belief and Imagination: Explorations in Psychoanalysis* (pp. 12–14). London: Routledge.

Davids, M. F. (2011). *Internal Racism: A Psychoanalytic Approach to Race and Difference.* London: Palgrave Macmillan.

Freud, S. (1921c). *Group Psychology and the Analysis of the Ego. S. E., 18*: 97. London: Hogarth.

Isaacs, S. (1948). The nature and function of phantasy. *International Journal of Psychoanalysis, 29*: 73–97.

Jung, C. G. (1966). *The Practice of Psychotherapy. Collected Works, vol. 16* (pp. 115–116). Princeton, NJ: Princeton University Press.

Klein, M. (1935). A contribution to the psychogenesis of manic-depressive states. *International Journal of Psychoanalysis, 16*: 145–174.

Klein, M. (1946). Notes on some schizoid mechanisms. *International Journal of Psychoanalysis, 27*: 99–110. [Updated 1952.]

Pratt, A. (2006). Neo-liberalism and social policy. In: M. Lavalette & A. Pratt (Eds.), *Social Policy: Theories, Concepts and Issues* (3rd edn) (pp. 12–13). London: Sage.

Rustin, M. (2016, June 28). The Referendum and the crisis of neoliberalism in Europe. https://www.lwbooks.co.uk/blog/the-referendum-and-the-crisis-of-neoliberalism-in-europe

Saez, E., & Zucman, G. (2014). Wealth inequality in the United States since 1913: Evidence from capitalized income tax data. Working Paper 20625, National Bureau of Economic Research. http://www.nber.org/papers/w20625

Segal, H. (1957). Notes on symbol formation. *International Journal of Psychoanalysis,* *38:* 391–397.

Stokoe, P. (2010). The theory and practice of the Group Relations Conference. In: C. Garland (Ed.), *The Groups Book: Psychoanalytic Group Therapy: Principles and Practice.* London: Karnac.

Travis, A. (2016, November 25). Thatcher pushed for breakup of welfare state despite NHS pledge. Home affairs editor, *The Guardian.* https://www.theguardian.com/politics/2016/nov/25/margaret-thatcher-pushed-for-breakup-of-welfare-state-despite-nhs-pledge

Trist, E. L., & Sofer, C. (1959). *Explorations in Group Relations.* Leicester, UK: Leicester University Press.

CHAPTER TWO

The democratic state of mind

Christopher Bollas

W e associate the birth of democracy, in Athens in the fifth century BCE, with the beginning of democratic politics. The democratic process has, in fact, been traced by some back to much earlier hunter gatherer communities, but when Solon led the establishing of democracy in Greece, he instantiated important new political structures: the right of all free male citizens to vote, the right to hold office, selection by lots and not by favour. There was also the right to express one's view in the assembly, and this reflected the wisdom of including as many points of view as possible in the governing process.

The downsides of this system were obvious. By refusing the right of women and slaves to be part of the democracy, the Athenian polis was deprived of the vitality of crucial differences of gender and race—prejudices that became instantiated as part of the democratic process in the West.

Democracy was complex and time consuming—during times of war, the democratic process would be compromised or even suspended—and it required the group having to bear up under the stress of conflicting views that might be driven by questionable (if not nefarious) aims. But the alternatives—tyranny, oligarchy, monarchy—were considered to be worse. So democracy had in its favour both what it was and what it was not.

The right of each free male to speak his mind meant that, for some, profoundly opposing positions were allowed the space of representation. In so many ways, this axiom—speak what you think, your thoughts will be displaced by the next speaker—has parallels with the experience of the speaking self in a psychoanalysis because, in the analytical space, although the "I" presumes to preside over all of the self's views, in fact, this is a nominal position. The thoughts that cross a mind are diverse and contradictory, with some too heinous to be borne by consciousness. The process is founded on the analyst's pledge of neutrality. He or she will not intervene in such a way as to prevent any ideas from being expressed; on the contrary, the self's minority views, that could so easily be silenced, are urged into articulation. The analytical relationship creates a psychological democracy.

There will be moments when the analysand may find this freedom embarrassing, or shocking, or surprising, but in time it allows consciousness to discover the complex views held by any self, within what analysts term "the internal world". This universe of thought and feeling, which we all have in common, is ordinarily kept a deep, dark secret in the world of human intersubjectivity, but in a psychoanalysis, and within a democracy, the self, or the group, is encouraged to speak without censorship. The citizen of Athens also had the right to be represented. Those who were not elected to attend the assembly and take part directly could still expect to have their views expressed and heard.

For hundreds of years, and especially from the eighteenth century onwards, politicians in Europe would debate the pros and cons of democracy and how it could be institutionalised, in full or in part. In doing this, unknowingly perhaps, Europeans were constructing a theory of both the individual and the group mind as a *representative agency*. A philosophy of government was following and realising a psychic need.

John Stuart Mill was a crucial figure in this evolution and he thought of "the modern mind" as owing a great deal to "the powerful dialectics" of Socrates (1859, p. 44). Mill's vision of liberty (in effect, the democratic process) was dependent upon what he termed "reflecting persons" (p. 8). He wondered why people were capable of "rational opinions and rational conduct" and he concluded that this must be "owing to a quality of the human mind" in which the reflective self seeks the company of others who will subject his own views to opposing ones.

He is capable of rectifying his' mistakes by discussion and experience. Not by experience alone. There must be discussion, to show
how experience is to be interpreted. Wrong opinions and practices
gradually yield to fact and argument: but facts and arguments, to
produce any effect on the mind, must be brought before it. (p. 22)

We see here a preview of the psychoanalytical axiom that the reflecting self
benefits from *talking* and engaging the other in discussion. Mill continues:

Because he has kept his mind open to criticism of his opinions and
conduct. Because it has been his practice to listen to all that could be
said against him; to profit by as much of it as was just, and expound
to himself, and upon occasion to others ... because he has felt that
the only way in which a human being can make some approach to
knowing the whole of a subject, is by hearing what can be said about
it by persons of every variety of opinion, and studying all modes in
which it can be looked at by every character of mind. (p. 22)

Discussing the duties of the listening orator (referring to Cicero), he states:
"The rational position for him would be suspension of judgement ... he
must feel the whole force of the difficulty which the true view of the subject
has to encounter and dispose of; else he will never really possess himself of
the portion of the truth which meets and removes that difficulty" (p. 37).
Mill understood that the listening self had to endure the full weight of the
other's points of view, not simply as cognate phenomena—intellectual
objects—but as powerful emotional experiences. This statement could
easily be the credo of the psychoanalyst who, from his position of neutrality,
must subject himself to the full force of the analysand's emotional life if he is
to understand the unconscious truths embedded in his statements.

Although Mill's listening position is remarkably like that of the psychoanalyst, his interventions tend to be more rhetorical: "These are good
reasons for remonstrating with him, or reasoning with him, or persuading
him, or entreating him" (p. 13). He acknowledges the problems posed by
"prejudices or superstitions; often their social affections, not seldom their
antisocial ones, their envy or jealousy, their arrogance or contemptuous-
ness". However, he argues that such feelings are part of the universal need

to act in "self-interest" (p. 10). This doctrine of self-interest is what today we would term a narcissistic defence: the person projects his own opinions onto others and assumes them to be universal. Any other views are simply wayward or incorrect. Mill writes:

> The practical principle which guides them to their opinions on the regulation of human conduct, is the feeling in each person's mind that everybody should be required to act as he ... (p. 9)

Mill was born in 1806 and died in 1873. His life therefore spanned most of the nineteenth century. His essays on the reflecting self were a considerable step forward in the understanding of how a democracy works.

It is surely no accident that the most important modern work on democracy—*On Liberty*—derived in large part from conversations Mill had with his wife Harriet Taylor Mill just one year before her death. The work embodies his wife's views, providing the vital presence of the female other that allow the mind to expand and deepen the listening process, so salient to Mill's view of democracy. Mill would then proceed in 1869 to write "On the subjection of women", which included his wife's views and which were clearly deeply influential, as well as the comments of his daughter, Helen Taylor, with whom he also collaborated on the work. The Mill family's vision, then—at last bringing women into the writings on democracy—demonstrated his theory in a profound and moving manner, some two thousand years after democracy had originally been established as the province of free male citizens.

The psychoanalyst Wilfred Bion was born in 1897 and died in 1979 and, like Mill, he may be seen as representative of his century. However, as a tank driver during the Great War, Bion had witnessed the savagery of a conflict that challenged Mill's view of the possibility of a democracy that did not take into account the depth of human destructiveness. After the First World War, he trained in psychiatry and psychoanalysis and he revolutionised psychoanalytical theory and practice through his work with groups, described in a series of publications, notably *Experiences in Groups* (1961).

The characteristics valued by Mill—the need of participants in a democracy to speak freely, the value to any reflecting self of undergoing powerful emotions stirred up by the views of others—were certainly shared by Bion. However, in his experiments in "social psychology", when he found himself inside the group mind, he arrived at a troubling discovery: if the psychoanalyst leaves the group members to themselves and declines to provide direction, they will slowly descend into primitive and, at times, highly disturbed states. In other words, minds are easily shut down by psychotic anxieties or primitive needs.

Mill, and others, had observed how democracy reflected the minds of those who took part and they suggested that it required flexible and thoughtful selves. This was an important step towards the concept of democracy, both as a theory of mind and as an observation on mental life itself. In my view, Bion's work, and that of other group psychoanalysts in London, *realised* the preconception that democracy was a recognition of how the mind worked. Without stating explicitly that a group was a democracy, or that it represented the democratic process, this is exactly what these analysts were exploring in the latter half of the twentieth century.

Bion's French biographer, Gérard Bléandonu (himself a group psychoanalyst) wrote of Bion's concept of "leaderless groups": "in effect, it introduced a democratic principle into the process of selection by focusing on communal relational aptitudes" (1994, p. 57). The principle was illustrated by Bion's conviction that the selection of officers should depend on how the individual behaves within a leaderless group, thus opening up potential qualification to anyone.

In *Democracy and Dictatorship* (2015), the Romanian social psychologist Zevedei Barbu followed an ancient tradition—one debated by Aristotle—that democracy required the right sort of citizen for it to be effective. In describing the characteristics of the "democratic state of mind", he suggested that it required "a specific *frame of mind*, that is, certain experiences, attitudes, prejudices and beliefs shared by them all, or by a large minority" (p. 13).

In an essay "The fascist state of mind" published in 1992, I noted that as psychoanalysts regarded selves as "composed of varied parts" the mind is "rather like a parliamentary order with instincts, memories, needs, anxieties and object responses finding representatives in the psyche for mental processing" (p. 197). Under the pressure of what I termed the "fascist state of mind" the "democratic mind" could "lose its parliamentary function and evolve into a less representative order", especially if the unwanted parts of the mind were projected into other objects, "leaving the mind denuded of its representative constituents" (p. 197).

In an important essay at the turn of the twenty-first century, Adam Phillips explored ways in which Bion's groups—and any group process predicated on psychoanalytical assumptions—make us all into "equals"—the title of his essay. He pursues many lines of thought, including the idea that differences between people will make some less equal than others even if, in principle, we have the right to equality.

He suggests that psychoanalysis is a form of democracy—indeed "The aim of psychoanalysis … might be the precondition for democracy" (2002, p. 17). Ultimately, it will reveal the forms of authority embedded in any self, the "anti-democratic voices and urgings and their complex history" (p. 24). This notion derives from Freud's censorship model of the unconscious: even though one wants, and tries, to free associate, a part of the mind steps in to censor and distort what might otherwise have been said.

However, although this censorship does exist, if the analysand keeps on talking, moving from one patch of discourse to another, then whether he knows it or not, he will always reveal patterns of unconscious thinking. But these chains of thought that reveal the narrative of the unconscious do not remain incontestable. A few minutes, days, or weeks later, the self may reveal quite different views. Walt Whitman had a clear sense of the dialectic of the free association of people and ideas in his celebration "Song of Myself". He writes: "Do I contradict myself?/Very well then, I contradict myself;/ (I am large, I contain multitudes)."

Above all else, free associations reveal how full of contradictions we are. Within a group, it is not so much that one person speaks for ideas that are anathema to others, although this may seem to be true at certain points. In fact, all group members speaking for long enough will unconsciously disclose a wide range of views, some of which would offend their conscious mind. Given enough time (and that is one thing that the analytic approach does provide), as they "gossip" about life they will disclose many hidden aspects of the human mind, often unaware, in their light-hearted perambulations, that they are letting the cat out of the bag.

I was trained in Bion groups at the Tavistock Clinic in the early 1970s. At that point, the Tavistock had become the centre of a movement: scores of clinicians from around the world would train there in order to learn how to conduct a new form of group psychoanalysis. Unique to the "Tavi Group" was a particular interpretive approach: whatever any member of the group said at any time was to be understood as representative, in some way, of all members of that group. This axiom was realised through a simple rhetorical position.

A fictional (condensed) example:

Jim:	[breaking down in tears] Bob, I have tried and tried to get you to down in understand me.
Bob:	You are just so thick and rejecting—I feel there's really no point in talking to you.
Analyst:	The group is not sure how to proceed. When one does not feel understood it is tempting to find someone to be responsible for that.
Jane:	I don't feel that what Jim has said is something I would ever have said to Bob.
Analyst:	The group is uncomfortable having to contain all the differing elements of the self, especially angry and distressed ones.

By interpreting in this way, the analyst facilitates the continued representation of the issues being expressed: "I don't feel understood", "People are too thick to bother with", "I can't align myself with aggressive behaviour". Because these thoughts are reworded as a *group position*, nobody is isolated for being in the wrong, or left to fight it out. Jim might feel irked at Bob's irritation, but the analyst's intervention indicates that his feeling of not being understood is an ordinary one, common to all members of the group. In this way, even seemingly extreme states of mind are transformed into bearable ideas that can then be thought about.

One of the functions of the group leader is to hold on to complex situations within the group rather than getting rid of them by smoothing them out. Bion referred to this as the function of the container in relation to the contained, and he maintained that the act of interpretation derived from the analyst's "reverie". This deceptively simple formulation opened up new vistas in technique, emphasising a form of analytic listening that relied on an unconscious capacity in the analyst.

For my part, I found in Bion's methodology a remarkable realisation of working democracy. The idea that any individual speaker was speaking for the entire group was a revelation. The theory did not assume, of course, that anything said in the room spoke for all other members of that group right there and right then; it meant that each member of the group would, at certain moments, experience those same sorts of feelings.

When the group analyst makes what we might think of as a democratic intervention—"the group thinks that ..."—she or he slows the process down, reducing the likelihood of any individual acting upon the violence of impulse. Jim has launched an attack on Bob which, in other circumstances, might lead to a violent encounter, but when it is reworded as a thought that could be voiced by any member, the idea is immediately *democratised*. "We are all in this together."

What we learned, both as participants in Tavi Groups and then as leaders, was that a group included all the elements that make up *Homo sapiens*: all the good things about us and all the bad things would emerge in that room, but no one was to be singled out. There were no saints and no sinners.

Bion's approach creates what D. W. Winnicott termed "a potential space". The group has the opportunity to express and consider any thoughts that arise out of the idea that has been expressed—in our example this might be the idea that we are vulnerable, or anger about feeling isolated and not understood, and as the members of the group pick up each of these lines of thought, they will become ramified into many diverse and divergent associative strands. Over time, these will grow into matrices of associations that this group will have assembled as a result of Jim's distress and Bob's defences against the complexity of group life.

Working in this way, one therefore discovers within the democratic process its therapeutic effect: democratisation disseminates divergent emotions or ideas through many people who will elaborate, contextualise, and render them differently. The eventual accomplishment of understanding will be the work of the group, as it gradually forms its own mind according to psychic democracy, entertaining all the conflicting ideas and feelings experienced by its members.

As a process, I found this deeply liberating, and I found its principles applicable in many ways to work with individuals in psychoanalysis. For example, when discussing toxic parts of the personality, or disturbing ideas, I might say: "A part of you is furious with me and wants to wipe out what I have said, but I have also heard from other parts of you that are wrestling with those very powerful feelings."

I am sure I was also influenced in this by Paula Heimann—my first analytical supervisor, who would ask, in relation to a particular moment in a session: "Who is speaking, to whom, about what, and why now?" This showed me that any mind could simultaneously house many speakers, talking to various others about all kinds of things.

At times, I might liken the mind to a democratic assembly, perhaps using the UK Parliament or the American Congress as extended metaphors. I noticed that no one ever challenged this idea; indeed, it was as if we all knew it to be an appropriate analogy. This existential realisation of the viability of the metaphor confirmed for me the idea that the concept of democracy was as applicable to our internal world as it was to conflicts among groups and nations.

In an earlier essay I argued that we all have a "representative drive": an urge to express our views. This drive arrives out of the jouissance of the infant and toddler over expression and then speech. We might see this drive, so necessary to the self's expression of idiom, as the psychic foundation of the force behind democracy; something that arrives, not because it has been handed down over the centuries, but because it exists within all of us as an intrinsic feature of the need to speak freely.

This has a bearing on the debates over whether certain countries—in North Africa or the Middle East—could ever become democracies. In the Arab Spring, it was striking that people naturally formed groups in which the democratic principle was assumed, even though this had never been part of their political environment. But if we understand this principle as inherently psychologically familiar to us, then it should come as no surprise that even those with no experience of this type of government will choose to form a democratic process.

So, when we think of what is required of democratic government, we are simultaneously conceptualising, not simply a frame of mind, but mind itself. The different dimensions of democracy—as a mental feature of an open mind and as the political expression of government shared by all—re-enforce one another. As Fukuyama (2014) states: "Between 1970 and 2010, the number of democracies around the world increased from about 35 to nearly 120, or some 60 percent of the world's countries" (p. 399). When he asks himself why this is so, he first cites the school of thought that believes "democracy has taken hold as the result of the power of the underlying idea of democracy" (p. 400) and he links this tradition to Hegel, and the view that "the working out of the inner logic of human rationality" (p. 400) naturally leads to the democratic frame of mind.

In my view, the idea that democracy follows from the logic of human reason is incorrect. Indeed, the reasoned self evolves gradually out of an *internal* democracy of many competing ideas that, in the beginning, might more accurately be described as mental chaos.

Eventually—and by "The Age of Reason"—people became more familiar with the idea of the mind's sometimes incoherent cacophony and, though from a somewhat distanced inner perspective, they began to trace the hidden logical features of what had seemed nonsensical. What Freud maintained was that there exist within the chaos of the unconscious "clusters of thought": ideas that, when grouped together, form the basis of coherent views. In time, these unconscious clusters of meaning act as internal force fields (the ancient Greeks saw the mind as an arena through which forces passed, like the wind) that may be objectified, or made conscious. The technique of "free association" showed that a seemingly incoherent sequence of discontinuous ideas would reveal "latent contents" that were governed by an underlying logic of their own. This ramifying network of unconscious thinking required dynamic consciousness in order to be spoken, communicated and understood.

Although, as Freud's theory showed, the unconscious self is inherently democratic, this state of mind may easily be compromised by powerful feelings that evoke other forms of self or group governance. These include the totalitarian position, the moment when a self makes a decision based upon great force emanating from within the personality, or the oligarchic situation, in which a group of people forms a governing mentality, or the monarchical state, when an individual adopts a princely view of the world.

Just as we all know of our internal democratic process, we also know of our totalitarian, oligarchic and monarchical tendencies. They are part of who we are. These frames of mind do not arrive from the outside world, in handed-down texts or ancient laws of governance; they are predicated on structures that exist within our internal world and they are mental and psychological pathways we may take at any time. Whereas the democratic frame of mind will happily house many diverse ideas—"democratic vistas", to quote Walt Whitman was the totalitarian frame of mind will shut down the divergent voices of our inner democracy to follow a narrow, rigid set of views.

Like the Greeks, any group that uses the democratic process will discover that this is hardly a frame of mind suited to quick thinking or immediate action. Those who constructed the US Constitution understood this when, in forming the American democracy, they created a system of checks and balances. It was a laborious process, and they intended it to be this way. They knew that in a country already as diverse and complex as the original thirteen colonies, people would need to represent many conflicting issues of economics, ethnicity, and class. They had to form a government that would neither descend into mob rule (a fear prominent in the eighteenth century mind, given the events of the French Revolution) nor revert to a monarchical system.

The American electorate would continue to be highly diverse, even though some values would be shared in common, but sometime in the early twenty-first century, there was a growing impatience across both party lines and throughout the United States with what was to become known as "the do-nothing Congress". Before the dawn of this century, senators and members of the House would "cross the aisle" and form alliances between differing representatives so that many positions or views could join one another under compromise. The various parties of the Congress strove to understand why other representatives took the positions they did, and with that understanding, as democratically elected citizens, they created laws.

However, after 9/11 and the war in Iraq, and in the face of the remarkable pace of globalisation and climate change (yes, strange cousins these), the sheer complexity of the world bore down upon the citizens of the Western world, especially in the United States. First Al-Qaeda and then ISIS (Daesh) successfully terrorised the West, which quickly lost sight of why these people had taken up arms in the first place. As panic set in, patience with the democratic way of thinking gave way to a fear that America was not properly protecting itself.

The reasons for the arrival of Daesh were complex and understandable, but Americans disconnected Daesh's *raison d'être* from their terrorist actions. Many were probably aware that these people were not simply Muslims; they were Sunni Arabs, displaced by the invasion of Iraq and angry at the Shias' failure to protect them following the invasion. However, by this time America was fed up with the conflicts in the Middle East and they renounced these more complex factors. More to the point, they began to renounce the complexities of thought in general. From a group relations perspective, the subtle dimensions of the picture were no longer being represented in the Congress or in the minds of the American citizens, and the fragility of both forms of democracy—of state and of mind—was to manifest itself in the startling fact that a country that had elected the African-American Obama in 2008 and 2012, could choose Trump in 2016.

The metaphor of the mind as a democracy, with different points of view and with numerous representatives and styles of representing, points, perhaps, to an unconscious dimension in the intentions of the Athenians.

The founding of democracy depended on a process of psychological change that began from within, but the Greeks were able to introduce an organising structure that institutionalised these changes so that the social sculptures of the polis provided freedom for mental representation.

The technological revolutions of the twenty-first century have threatened our capacity to maintain traditional forms of meaning within the fabric of the new industrial world. Democracies have become infiltrated and undermined by powerful but shadowy corporations, many of a totalitarian bent, and political parties and elected representatives have opted for the politics of polarisation rather than the democratic tasks of inclusiveness, discussion, and compromise. It would be hardly surprising if selves were no longer so inclined to exercise a democratic frame of mind.

The evolution of democracy, over thousands of years, is amongst our greatest accomplishments. Although it may come and go according to the emotional state of a person or a nation, the democratic process remains a *potential* in all human beings, even within the most totalitarian self. If we appear to be losing our collective and individual capacity to sustain a democratic frame of mind, we may take solace in knowing that, given the right group conditions, it can return.

References

Barbu, Z. (2015). *Democracy and Dictatorship: Their Psychology and Patterns of Life.* London: Forgotten Books.

Bléandonu, G. (1994). *Wilfred Bion: His Life and Works 1897–1979.* London: Free Association.

Bollas, C. (1992). The fascist state of mind. In: *Being a Character: Psychoanalysis and Self Experience.* New York: Hill & Wang.

Bollas, C. (2010). *The Evocative Object World.* London: Routledge.

Fukuyama, F. (2014). *Political Order and Political Decay: From the Industrial Revolution to the Globalization of Democracy.* New York: Farrar, Straus & Giroux.

Mill, J. S. (1859). On liberty. In: *John Stuart Mill: On Liberty, Utilitarianism, and Other Essays* (pp. 5–112). Oxford: Oxford University Press, 2015.

Phillips, A. (2002). *Equals.* New York: Basic Books.

Whitman, W. (2004). Song of myself. In: *Walt Whitman The Complete Poems* (p. 123). London: Penguin.

CHAPTER THREE

Understanding right-wing populism

Michael Rustin

U ntil quite recently, the dominant frame for understanding the present political conjuncture was the onward march of neoliberalism, apparently unrepentant and uninhibited by the financial crisis of 2007–2008 (Hall, Massey, & Rustin, 2015). Much writing and debate has concerned itself with the consequences and implications of this regime, for inequality (Boushey, Delong, & Steinbaum, 2017; Piketty, 2014), mental health and well-being (Wilkinson & Pickett, 2018), insecurity and precarious employment (Standing, 2011), personality organisation (Rustin, 2014), and austerity and the attack on or attrition of public services.

But in the last two or three years, a further development has taken place which is giving rise to extremely troubling phenomena. This is the rise of radical right-wing populism, and forms of nationalist and xenophobic politics which one thought had become so illegitimate (despite periodic outbreaks such as those of Enoch Powell and Jean-Marie Le Pen) as no longer to constitute a significant political force.

It has become imperative that we understand these developments, their causes and consequences. The rise of right-wing populism has to a degree replaced the domination of neoliberalism as the principal political preoccupation of the present day, even though the grip of neoliberalism on the social and economic system remains strong in many spheres. Trump's nationalist protectionism is contrary to America's earlier commitments to a negotiated world order based on neoliberal free trade principles. In the UK the politics of Brexit are themselves complicated and divided. Many Brexiteers envisage a prospect of extreme deregulation and competition, discounting the "short-term" economic damage this would bring just as Thatcher's programme of austerity and deregulation did in the early 1980s. However, Theresa May's own position seems to be more "statist" and less market-fundamentalist than this, as she signalled when she campaigned to become prime minister,[1] not that much has been seen of this in terms of enacted policies.

The character of right-wing populist movements and their leaders needs its own study and explanation. From a socio-psychoanalytic point of view, Adorno's famous essay "Freudian Theory and the Pattern of Fascist Propaganda" (1951) has some relevance to understanding the way in which populist movements of the right exert their influence over their constituencies. However, the main focus of this chapter is going to be less on the role of political leaders and more on the conditions which have enabled them to gain large-scale support. What is it that explains why movements, programmes, and attitudes which for many decades could only gain a marginal or subordinate place in the European and American political system, are now in some respects its most dynamic force? Why are populations who were previously in the main immune to these appeals, now so responsive to them?

Although the movements of the populist right are not to be equated with Nazism in Germany in the 1930s, it may nevertheless be instructive to consider the conditions for the Nazi advance to power at that time, and see what similarities these bear to present-day conditions.

The psychoanalytic focus I will bring to bear on this question concerns states of anxiety, fear, and resentment, and the circumstances that give rise to these. It is anxiety which seems to be associated with a visible turning away from reason, and with the substitution of fantasies, prejudices, and myths for the more mundane considerations of interests and values on which democratic political debate is usually based. The question is, what are the origins of these present anxieties, against which we can regard the conjuring up of enemies, scapegoats, and magical solutions as kinds of unconscious defence?[2]

In Germany in the 1930s, there were two critical preconditions which created favourable ground for the Nazi advance. The first of these was widespread confusion and anger arising from the Great Crash and ensuing

Depression in the early 1930s, which brought widespread economic ruin. The Nazis did after all propose a solution to this social and financial disaster, which had some success through an expansionist economic programme which included of course major rearmament. The second precondition was the widespread state of anger and resentment which pervaded Germany following the military defeat of 1918, and the humiliations imposed on her at the Treaty of Versailles whose economic consequence had been foreseen by Keynes (1919) at the time. It seems that the victors of the Great War psychologically dealt with its massive sufferings and losses not through a shared experience of guilt and mourning, but rather through the compulsion to assign sole responsibility for the catastrophe which had taken place to the defeated enemy. This relieved the victorious powers of the need to reflect on their own role in these events, and from making reparation for their (at best) misjudgements. Instead they demanded that the Germans and their allies accept blame for what had happened and humiliation in their defeat. Hitler and the Nazis were adept at expressing and exploiting these resentments, and at finding objects other than the German people themselves to whom blame and guilt could be assigned. The designated role of the Jews was to be, in effect, the principal scapegoats for this disaster, and then to become the objects of an exterminatory obsession.

To understand why the populist and authoritarian right has gained such support in recent years, we need to reflect on some comparable circumstances, and on the collective emotions of resentment and anxiety to which these have given rise. The financial crisis of 2007 and 2008 is one central source of this shift, bringing to an end as it has done a period of several decades in which improvements in most people's living standards and opportunities, in many Western countries, had become taken for granted as normal conditions of life. The fact that the responsible holders of power were able to escape their responsibility for this crisis, and to resist the adjustments and reforms which might perhaps have restored the antecedent conditions of prosperity, made it possible for other objects of blame to be constructed by conservative protest movements. The further fact that Western governments were now failing to dominate their erstwhile spheres of influence, and found themselves fighting several unsuccessful wars in the Middle East, was another factor in creating anxiety and resentment. (It should be remembered that the hegemony of New Deal politics in the United States, which had continued even under President Nixon, had been first shattered by the Vietnam War; as should the social divisions which this brought about.) The migration and refugee crisis which has destabilised the politics of Europe, and the emergence of a threat of terrorism which affects the public's sense of security far more deeply than the actual dangers it poses to the vast majority of people, are substantially the consequences of the West's failed military policies. The invasions of Afghanistan, Iraq, and Libya have not led to the establishment of stable governments capable of ensuring security within their borders. The tacit support for military insurrection in Syria, and for the Saudi campaign to suppress the insurgent regime in the Yemen, have been later sources of instability. Even the poisoned relations with Russia, for example in relation to the Crimea and the Ukraine, are largely the consequence of the West's hubristic attempts to gain territorial and strategic advantage from the collapse of the Soviet Union, and of Russia's defence of its earlier sphere of influence.

The larger context of this state of anxiety and resentment is the relative decline of the formerly leading nations and blocs of the West (the USA and the European Union) as a multi-polar world comes into being, and new powers such as China and the oil-rich states of the Middle East challenge the supremacy of the old industrial nations. Trump's trade war with China, and even with Europe, Mexico, and Canada, are a symptomatic response to this situation. The United States' attempts to prevent the acquisition of nuclear weapons by enemies it fears it cannot control are indications of the anxieties and hostilities produced by this state of "downward mobility" within the international system.[3] The British response to this situation has been Brexit, and the illusions and memories of Great Britain as a global maritime power, detached from and sometimes menaced from the Continent, which have fuelled this project. Jacob Rees Mogg's latest comparison of May's projected Brexit settlement with King John's homage to Philip II of Spain around 900 years ago shows just how full of deluded nostalgia this state of mind is (Gilroy, 2004).

Gramsci taught that the authority of governments in complex liberal, market societies depends to a great degree on public consent, on a belief that governments are capable of protecting the well-being of a majority of their citizens. "Western democratic government" is far from wholly democratic, in the sense of conferring equal power on all its citizens. Democracy does not go all the way down in these societies. Especially in the United States but also in the UK (Crouch, 2004), the propertied exercise excessive influence on politics and government, through the agencies of lobbying, the press, advertising, and political funding. But so long as people felt secure, and that they could expect improvements in their lives, the vicissitudes and limitations of democratic government were mostly tolerated.

The appeal of "strong leadership" in so many countries today is related to the loss of public confidence in a liberal democratic political system. (Whether it happens to be inflected to the centre-left or centre-right seems to matter little.) This system's comparative failure has made it an object of distrust and resentment, which have been stirred up and exploited by populist movements, mostly of the right, although at a previous moment also of the left, with Syriza in Greece and Podemos in Spain.

Former communist countries suffered serious social and economic losses as well as gains in civil and political freedom as a consequence of the collapse of the Soviet Union (and of the refusal of the West to support a more gradual and benign adjustment to a post-communist system). The contemporary authoritarian governments of Russia, Hungary, and Poland, and of other states previously part of the Soviet Union are the products of the insecurities and resentments which followed the failure of the regimes which followed the fall of communism. The restoration of Russian national pride and power is an understandable aspiration for Russian people who had experienced the disintegration of the final years of Gorbachev and the succession of Yeltsin and his regime's variety of crony and gangster capitalism.

The divided political culture of the United States

Arlie Russell Hochschild's book, *Strangers in Their Own Land* (2016) has thrown considerable light on the political divisions of Trump's America, and the Tea Party and conservative evangelical movements which preceded Trump's rise. Hochschild became concerned several years ago about the deep divisions of culture that now divide the "red" (Republican) from the "blue" (Democratic) states. These communities appear to inhabit different mental and emotional worlds, with little understanding of one another. Why, liberals asked, would many poor people on the right vote against their own economic interests, for politicians whose policies favour the rich and neither themselves nor the majority of Americans? How could this be explained?

To find out, Hochschild for several years undertook research in Louisiana, which is the second poorest state in the Union. The particular area of her research was enjoying an oil boom which was giving its people a hope of economic improvement but was ruining their natural environment and rendering it toxic to all forms of life. In repeated visits, Hochschild got to know—indeed became friends with—some active members of the Tea Party movement, many (but not all) of whom became enthusiastic supporters of Trump. Her project was to understand how they experienced their world. Although her field research was in just one part of Louisiana, she believes her findings to be representative of a much larger population through the United States, but especially in the South where the largest support for the right is located.

She describes occupiers of a social stratum who feel badly treated and discriminated against by the federal government. Its idealised picture of America is of a ladder of opportunity, in which those who stand in line, waiting their turn, working hard, and maintaining decent families and communities, will eventually receive their just rewards. However, their conviction is that numerous other claimants have pushed in and jumped what they see as a queue. These usurpers of their life chances and opportunities include Hispanics and other ethnic immigrants, blacks (though she found people to be circumspect in their references to this deepest racial divide), and "special interests" (gays, feminists, trans people, etc.) of many kinds. Government, they told her, helps those people, but not "people like us". This suspicion of federal government is strong in spite of the fact that 44% of the revenues of the state of Louisiana come from federal sources.

Hochschild's conservative subjects also felt themselves to be held in contempt by liberals. The white supporters of the Tea Party are in general older and less well educated than liberals and Democrats, and they feel looked down on by them. It is also true that the actual opportunities of poorly educated white people in Louisiana to obtain good quality employment are lower than those of other groups, even at a time of economic growth in their region. In the expanding industries of Louisiana, such as construction and petrochemicals, corporations bring in foreign workers to undertake manual work, and at the higher levels of professional employment locals are rejected in favour of better-educated incomers from outside the state. The employees of the government are seen as another relatively privileged group, whose function is mainly to regulate and interfere with the enterprises of the locals.

Hochschild describes the long history of this "Southern" state of mind or "structure of feeling" whose two critical periods were those of the 1860s, the period of "reconstruction" following the Civil War, and the 1960s. The latter was a period of radical liberal agitation and of an expansion of government intrusion into the South, in response to the Civil Rights movement. It also saw a widespread challenge to conservative American values of religion, patriotism, and the family. (Divisions of these kinds, including over the Vietnam War, destroyed the previous Democrat domination of the South.) Its society was always hierarchical and "vertical" in its orientations—the white poor looked up to the plantation owners as a class to be admired and emulated. Their slaves of course were looked down on and avoided, if sometimes also pitied. So the fact that 1% of the contemporary American population owns such a large a share of the national wealth does not arouse the same resentment and disapproval among Southern white people as it does in the more egalitarian cultures of the North and West. These differences are not merely geographical—there is a national demographic divide which corresponds to the conservative political cultures she found in Louisiana, although the specific resentments of displaced industrial workers in the mid-West are different from those of the rural and small-town people of Louisiana she came to know, sometimes indeed as friends.

Hochschild (1983) did earlier pioneering work on the place of emotions in society, and in particular on the organisation of emotional labour, as a form of exploitation. She described occupations (like those of airline stewardesses and debt collectors) in which the management of feelings for commercial advantage is crucial. She has also written, with Barbara Ehrenreich (2003), about the exploitative organisation of the care of children (one could add the elderly) in which migrant workers from poor countries like the Philippines are brought over to look after the children of well-off Californians while their own children are left at home in the care not of their mothers but of their grandparents. Hochschild's writing has brought together an understanding of the exploitative relationships of the labour process, and its specific implications for women and children. It is thus a descriptively powerful but somewhat discreet synthesis of Marxist and feminist theoretical perspectives.

How emotions are constructed and shared in society is also central to Hochschild's understanding of these opposed American cultures. Shared emotions sustain a "deep story" in the South, and elsewhere on the right in America, of how things have come to be as they are. This narrative about the stalling and even theft of the American Dream, is, she found, very resistant to change.

The particular ability of Trump has of course been to give a powerful voice to these resentments and grievances. The outspokenness and lack of restraint with which he expresses his views are part of his appeal to many conservatives, even as they deeply offend most liberals. Trump's supporters feel that political discourse has long been dominated by liberal assumptions and beliefs, and that contrary opinions have been denied expression. The idea of "political correctness" and the sensitivity to stigmatising language that this requires is experienced as coercive by Trump's following. Thus his utterances have the effect of a release of the repressed.

Hochschild learned to understand and feel empathy with the world view of her subjects. Nevertheless she is at pains, through the findings of documentary researchers, to demonstrate the large gap that exists between the shared beliefs of this conservative community and reality. Their assumptions concerning numbers of public employees (believed to be wasteful and overprivileged) were far in excess of the demonstrable truth. However, such facts have little impact on her subjects' settled convictions, and on the "deep stories" (or "basic assumptions") which organise their view of the world.

A notable aspect of Hochschild's account is the friendliness and warmth of many of her subjects towards her, even though they seemed fully to recognise that that this sociologist, liberal, and lifelong Democrat came to visit them from somewhere quite else. The deep differences of political belief between her and her subjects by no means made communication between them impossible. Indeed, one gains the impression from Hochschild's narrative not only that she in her unusual and empathetic way wanted to understand these "others" and their beliefs, but that some of them were interested in the strange "other" that she represented too. Her entire investigation was made possible by an enduring friendship between two Louisianan women (one of them the mother of one of her Berkeley students) who hold opposite political beliefs.

Epistemic anxiety

I will now describe a specific aspect of the differences and antagonisms between the insurgent culture of conservative populism, and the established liberal consensus. It is known that major determinants of political affiliation and voting behaviour have shifted in recent years, from locations within a stratified order of material advantage, to differences of educational attainment. On the whole, the less educated (who are also those of an older generation) were more likely to vote for conservative populists, and the younger and more educationally qualified more likely to vote for liberals and the left. We have seen this pattern in Britain, regarding Brexit.

The idea of a meritocracy—of a society in which rewards and privileges are assigned in accordance with "merit" and capability—has been seen by some as a progressive vision, the enactment of "equality of opportunity". The programmes of the New Democrats of Clinton and the New Labour of Blair were essentially meritocratic in their vision. They appealed, and offered opportunities, to social strata empowered by enhanced educational opportunities and a society becoming more "classless" in its culture, if little less unequal in its distribution of material rewards. Gordon Brown's denunciation of Oxford University in 2000 for denying a place to Laura Spence, a talented comprehensive school pupil (https://en.wikipedia.org/wiki/Laura_Spence_Affair), was the angriest version of an implicit attack on "old privilege" in the name of "new merit". However, bringing about a more equal access to citadels of privilege such as Oxbridge would probably reinforce rather than diminish the structure of privilege which it represents.

When Michael Young published *The Rise of the Meritocracy* in 1958 he believed he was describing not a utopian future, but a dystopia. Individualised failure, through a competitive educational system, would he thought be more psychologically damaging than the collective or "ascriptive" failures of merely having been born in the "wrong" place or in the "wrong" social class. What we now see is how an entire class of the educationally successful are sometimes perceived by those whom this educational regime has left behind. Conservative populism is in part the revenge of those whom meritocracy has left behind.

It is in part the cultural codes and conventions of the educated and therefore the successful which are resented and attacked by populists. This was always a function of the "popular press". That is, not only to communicate to people in ways that the less formally educated could understand (in itself a democratic purpose), but also to trash forms of communication which were mainly intended to reach a different audience. Populism has given expression to a kind of rage against the forms of speech of the educated, and made it legitimate to attack its basic assumptions and conventions. One of its basic, indeed sacred assumptions, is that facts and reasoned arguments matter, and should be principal grounds for taking a view of making a decision. But we see in current political discourse a striking rejection of this core belief.

Thus President Trump appears to lose no support from his core constituency when he demonstrates his complete indifference to matters of fact and consistency. He lies, changes his mind at will, attacks the integrity of the entire process of public communication ("fake news" is a term which expresses this indifference to the truth), and asks his audiences to take their lead from his emotional state of mind, not from the rationality of what he says.

Post-Kleinian psychoanalytic theory has argued that the desire to know and understand is a drive or instinct as primordial in human beings as the dispositions to love and hate. This idea was first suggested by Freud (1926d), and then greatly amplified in Klein's (1928, 1930, 1931) theory of the epistemophilic instinct. It was fully developed in Bion's (1959, 1962) writings, in his argument that the growth of the mind, or the capacity to think, is a primary developmental achievement. It depends, he proposed, on an early environment of love and care which enables emotions and anxieties to be regulated or "contained", and then transformed into the objects and materials of thought. It seems that this necessary dependence of the capacity for thinking on a containing environment of feeling exists not only in the context of early infant care, but in later contexts of learning too, including those of political life.

I have suggested (Rustin, 2019) that there may be a specific form of both conscious and unconscious anxiety which arises from the experiences of learning and knowing, and in particular from the unavoidably accompanying experiences of not-learning and not-knowing. Learning requires the recognition of what is not at present known as well as of what might become known in the future. It involves a recognition of the inadequacy and insufficiency of the anterior self, as well as of its prospective growth and enlargement. Learning is thus a process of disintegration as well as of reintegration.[4] Anxieties are therefore inseparable from experiences of learning. Where there are anxieties there are inevitably defences against anxiety, both conscious and unconscious. These may take the form of withdrawal from a scene of learning, rejection of the value of its supposed object, delusions about false alternatives to it, and mockery, dismissal, or hatred of the bearers of knowledge.[5] Of course another response to such anxieties is psychological collapse, as we see sometimes in breakdowns among students faced with examinations. Learning is best accomplished when such anxieties remain at a tolerable level. This usually requires that a person's entire sense of worth is not endangered by the trials involved in learning. This is why such experiences if they are to go well depend on there being contexts of recognition and reassurance as well as a necessary element of challenge.

Good educational practices are based on relationships of trust within which the uncertainties and risks of learning can be shared and understood.

The desire to know and learn, and the defences against knowing and learning are most easily understood in the circumstances of individuals, and in the practices of education. But the rise of populism has shown us that these issues are relevant also to the wider scenes of social and political life. It seems that a society in which material security and sufficiency, as well as relative levels of status and power, are primarily legitimised by educational achievement, gives rise to powerful resentments against those whose privileges are so justified. And against the cultural codes and conventions through which their entitlements of merit and desert are upheld. It becomes difficult to conduct political debate through arguments based on reasons and facts (however imperfect such processes always are) if the idea that there is a universal medium through which such arguments can be conducted is itself rejected, as just another kind of imposition of power. This is one of the implicit consequences of the "postmodern" critique of universalism and rationality.

Conclusion

The anxieties and resentments which are at the centre of the appeal of conservative populism and nationalism have several interrelated sources. Declining economic opportunities, and the apparent indifference of governments to the plight of those left behind by economic modernisation and globalisation are examples of these. Competition from migrants where local opportunities seem to be in decline is another—it is notable that in prosperous cities there is much less resentment of immigration and multiculturalism. Rejection of the "educated" cultural codes of the powerful represents, as we have seen, a new kind of rebellion against the established political order. Socialist movements of resistance and dissent saw education as a form of emancipation, and an extended "common culture" (as Raymond Williams, 1958, put it) as a central progressive goal. They sought to broaden and transform dominant cultures and educational forms to make them inclusive, not to dismiss them. It is because occupational and class identifications have become weak, under the assault of neoliberalism, giving rise to insecurity and isolation rather than new kinds of solidarity, that regression to nationalist, ethnic, and racial identifications has been taking place.

Richard Wilkinson and Kate Pickett (2009) have demonstrated through many telling statistical and epidemiological correlations, the connections between inequality and a large number of symptoms of physical ill health and of social ill-being. These correlations are the representation in terms of innumerable forms of exclusion and neglect of the relatively disadvantaged, and the demonstration to them that they are disrespected and disregarded by their society (Rustin, 2018). Only if this is changed, and if an ethos of universal and equal concern for all becomes again a motivating principle for government and its institutions can the rise of populism and the disintegration of the democratic political order be brought to an end.

Notes

1. "This is a different kind of Conservatism, I know. It marks a break with the past. But it is in fact completely consistent with Conservative principles. Because we don't just believe in markets, but in communities. We don't just believe in individualism, but in society ... We don't hate the state, we value the role that only the state can play. We believe everybody—not just the privileged few—has a right to take ownership of what matters in their lives" (Theresa May, speech in Birmingham on July 11, 2016).

2. Armstrong and Rustin's *Social Defences against Anxiety: Explorations in a Paradigm* (2014) provides a review of these debates.

3. There is a contemporary research study on the damaging effects of downward social mobility on individuals (Dolan & Lordan, 2013). Seymour Martin Lipset and Reinhard Bendix argued (1959) that malaise was also experienced collectively when entire social groups experience serious decline in their material circumstances or social status. This "downward mobility" thesis, applied to social classes and nation states, has considerable power to explain the system crises of the present day.

4. This idea relates to Britton's (1998) valuable idea that personal growth depends on oscillations between more stable depressive and more unstable paranoid–schizoid states of mind, these "spiral" oscillations leading to more complex kinds of integration.

5. Julius Caesar dismisses the petitioner on the Ides of March who wishes to warn him of the imminent danger to himself:

Artemidorus:	O Caesar, read mine first; for mine's a suit that touches Caesar nearer: read it great Caesar.
Caesar:	What touches us ourself shall be last serv'd.

| Artemidorus: | Delay not, Caesar; read it instantly. |
| Caesar: | What, is the fellow mad? |

(Julius Caesar, Act 3 Scene i)

References

Adorno, T. (1951). Freudian theory and the pattern of fascist propaganda'. In: A. Arato & E. Gebhardt (Eds.), *The Essential Frankfurt School Reader, Part 1* (pp. 118–137). Oxford: Blackwell, 1978.

Armstrong, D., & Rustin, M. J. (Eds.) (2014). *Social Defences against Anxiety: Explorations in a Paradigm.* London: Karnac.

Bion, W. R. (1959). Attacks on linking. Reprinted in *Second Thoughts.* London: Heinemann, 1962.

Bion, W. R. (1962). *Learning from Experience.* Reprinted Karnac, 1984.

Boushey, H., Delong, J. B., & Steinbaum, M. (Eds.) (2017). *After Piketty: The Agenda for Economics and Inequality.* London: Harvard University Press.

Britton, R. (1998). Before and after the depressive position. In: *Belief and Imagination* (pp. 69–81). London: Routledge.

Crouch, C. (2004). *Post-Democracy.* Cambridge: Polity Press.

Dolan, P., & Lordan, G. (2013). Moving up and sliding down: an empirical study of the effect of mobility on subjective wellbeing. C.E.P. Discussion Paper 1190 (London School of Economics). http://cep.lse.ac.uk/pubs/download/dp1190.pdf

Ehrenreich, B., & Hochschild, A. R. (2003). *Global Woman: Nannies, Maids and Sex Workers in the New Economy.* London: Granta.

Freud, S. (1926d). *Inhibitions, Symptoms and Anxiety. S. E., 20*: 74–176. London: Hogarth.

Gilroy, P. (2004). *After Empire: Melancholia or Convivial Culture?* London: Routledge.

Hall, S., Massey, D., & Rustin, M. J. (Eds.) (2015). *After Neoliberalism? The Kilburn Manifesto.* London: Lawrence & Wishart. https://www.lwbooks.co.uk/soundings/kilburn-manifesto

Hochschild, A. R. (1983). *The Managed Heart: Commercialization of Human Feeling.* Berkeley, CA: University of California Press.

Hochschild, A. R. (2016). *Strangers in Their Own Land: Anger and Mourning on the American Right.* New York: New Press.

Keynes, J. M. (1919). *The Economic Consequences of the Peace.* London: Wilder Press, 2018.

Klein, M. (1928). Early stages of the Oedipus complex. Reprinted in M. Klein, *Love, Guilt and Reparation and Other Works 1921–1945.* London: Vintage, 1997.

Klein, M. (1930). The importance of symbol formation in the development of the ego. Reprinted in M. Klein, *Love, Guilt and Reparation and Other Works 1921–1945*. London: Vintage, 1997.

Klein, M. (1931). A contribution to the theory of intellectual inhibition. Reprinted in M. Klein, *Love, Guilt and Reparation and Other Works 1921–1945*. London: Vintage, 1997.

Lipset, S. M., & Bendix, R. (1959). *Social Mobility in Industrial Society*. London: Routledge, 2018.

Piketty, T. (2014). *Capital in the Twenty-First Century*. London: Harvard University Press.

Rustin, M. J. (2014). Belonging to oneself alone: The spirit of neoliberalism. *Psychoanalysis, Culture & Society, 19*: 145–160.

Rustin, M. J. (2018). The causes of inequality: Why social epidemiology is not enough. *Soundings, 68*: 94–109.

Rustin, M. J. (2019). Epistemic anxiety. In: R. Gipps and M. Lacewing (Eds.), *The Oxford Handbook of Philosophy and Psychoanalysis* (pp 687–708). Oxford: Oxford University Press.

Standing, G. (2011). *The Precariat: The New Dangerous Class*. London: Bloomsbury.

Wilkinson, R., & Pickett, K. (2009). *The Spirit Level: Why More Equal Societies Almost Always Do Better*. London: Allen Lane.

Wilkinson, R., & Pickett, K. (2018). *The Inner Level: How More Equal Societies Reduce Stress, Restore Sanity and Improve Everyone's Well-being*. London: Allen Lane.

Williams, R. (1958). *Culture and Society*. London: Chatto & Windus.

Young, M. (1958). *The Rise of the Meritocracy 1870–2033*. London: Penguin, 1961.

CHAPTER FOUR

Europe in dark times: some dynamics in alterity and prejudice

Jonathan Sklar

> *In the fearful years of the Yezhov terror I spent seventeen months in prison queues in Leningrad. One day somebody "identified" me. Beside me, in the queue, there was a woman with blue lips. She had, of course, never heard of me; but she suddenly came out of that trance so common to us all and whispered in my ear (everybody spoke in whispers there): "Can you describe this?" And I said: "Yes, I can." And then something like the shadow of a smile crossed what had once been her face.*
> —Anna Akhmatova, 1 April 1957, Leningrad, *Requiem* (p. 67)

Today's Europe, with its recent explosion of immigration, bringing the mass death of children and adults on our shores, invites a return of the repressed and the blaming of the *Untermenschen* for our difficulties. Our remembrances of history as recent as the 1930s, and the link between austerity and blame, are leading to a wholesale diminution of our humanity. Facts have become no longer recognised—most apparent in the recent Brexit referendum and the presidential election in the US—as have the views of those with expertise. Right-wing political movements regularly brush aside criticism, or any inconvenient knowledge, as being of no value. Such things occurred in the 1930s and made possible the rhetoric that stoked the rise of fascism.

Against the backdrop of these events, I want to examine states of freedom in mental life. This will involve examining states of fundamentalism in twentieth-century society, along with some of their specific impacts, in particular on psychoanalysis and psychoanalytic societies. I will then turn my attention towards alterity—the problem of the other—and how we might understand the massive attacks on migrants entering and living in our worlds, as well as the impact of these attacks on citizens.

The examination of impediments to social freedom has parallels with the process of developing states of mental freedom, in both analysis and the analyst, that exist in the unconscious mind—that is, freedom from the stickiness of our personal histories, freedom within the society that trained us, and freedom from the often unspoken depths of our European culture. Such complex matters include the need for the analysand to find new ways of expression, both in relation to him or herself and in relation to the other, and so to no longer follow the old tramways of habits laid down by personal histories, which can become caught up in and repeated by the transference dynamic.

In another order, these matters include the question of how best the analyst can develop his or her personal practice of psychoanalysis in a place that may be hostile to such a project. This latter situation unfortunately seems to be becoming more prevalent, certainly in the National Health Service in the UK. Here, I have observed psychodynamic therapy to be virtually wiped out. In its place, low-cost "quick fixes" to get people back to work, regardless of the longer-term efficacy or suitability. The government publically pledges its support for mental health issues. Yet its proposed reforms for improving mental health care have been damned by two select committees as lacking ambition and failing to take into account the needs of the most vulnerable groups (Busby, 9 May 2018). The government provides money for adolescent psychiatric services that is not ring fenced and is often redirected to general resources. Waiting times for a young person to be seen for diagnosis as well as treatment is very lengthy. It is in this environment that the mental health professional must try to find a way to work effectively.

Another central aspect that this discussion must examine is the theory and practice of psychoanalysis itself, along with its training. They both have their own unconscious tramways.

Yet the very theme of freedom alongside my associated word "tramways" first leads my thoughts to the railway lines crossing Europe that were used for transportation to the death camps in the Second World War. European culture, like the human subject, has never been free of aggression, stretching from medieval times through the Enlightenment and culminating in the world wars fought on our soil in the twentieth century, and this has played its part in the evolution of psychoanalysis throughout Europe. Freud, having lived through the First World War, was faced with trying to understand the mass slaughter of nationals—despite, or due to, their cultural heritage—and decades later, in 1938, he had to flee Nazi Vienna. His sisters did not escape and died in concentration camps. What would it have meant for the future development of psychoanalysis if the Nazis had killed the Father?

Taking these facts into account, how can we think about trauma in the individual without thinking of it in generational terms, as well as in terms of the cultural heritage forming the backdrop to the development of psychoanalysis from within the Austro-Hungarian Empire? One of my key interests is the interface between personal and historical trauma, and in particular the relation of such traumatic substrates with unconscious processes. What we can grasp of the innermost life of the patient and of the world he or she lives in, and by which he or she is so profoundly affected, is also part of a broader picture in which ontogeny—the development of an individual's history—is entwined with specific cultures.

Psychologies of prejudice

In terms of European culture, the continent has continuously struggled with the idea of the stranger coming from the East, ready to pollute and destroy the Western order. Each country, in its particular form, has at some point declared itself as a bulwark against the horde: France with its back to the Atlantic against the Germanic tribes, the Goths and the Visigoths, and the Mongol horde beyond; Spain and Portugal similarly fearing the caliphate expansion, as the successful Muslim invasion created Al-Andalus; and Germany against the atheist Communists in Russia, as well as the impoverished villages of Poland and the Eastern states dotted with shtetl Jews. This history can also be seen through the opposite lens: the Roman legions spreading the Empire far to the east, along with the many crusades invading the Middle East. Throughout such conflicts ran the conviction that it is cities that are civilised (*civitas*), while the wanderer is impure, dangerous, and stupid. Strong boundaries are similarly an essential component of the nation state, advancing the same psychology of us vs them, and of demonising the other; this system having at its core a psychology of prejudice.

In an attempt to counter this tendency, the European Union, despite considerable internal stresses, maintains justice for all of its citizens as its core value, enforcing it in the European Court of Justice and bound by the European Convention of Human Rights. These ethical and democratic structures transcend the boundaries of the nation states of the Union and are a profound answer to each of their vicissitudes and particularities. It is important to remember that they were set up, in particular, as a bulwark against another war in Europe. Yet the still underlying, latent fears and desires that form prejudice towards the other await their return from repression by such structures.

Unconscious prejudicial phantasies can relate similarly to analytic societies in terms of wishes to accentuate particular forms of analytic theory and training. The wish for a widespread development of training that focuses on one method or perspective can neglect the particular analytic sense of the individual treatment. It can thus appear more important for the analyst to hold on to theory, fearing becoming lost or fearing a state of free fall in the face of not understanding something in or from the analysand. Analysis often comprises finding and sustaining hard-won pieces of knowledge, wrestled from the unconscious, that act as a psychic pointillism or patchwork, slowly connecting in some way as the creative act of the analysis.

Widening the analytic lens so that we can examine such unconscious patchwork with regard to the discipline of psychoanalysis in the European region, we can note present-day concerns, in the current climate of quick fixes and business solutions, about its very survival as a form of treatment. Yet by looking back in history, we can see that psychoanalysis has often had the unstable status of being an unwelcomed other. Indeed, Freud's fear was that it could be attacked and demoted if the scientific community, as well as the Nazi state, perceived it to be a Jewish theory. He never let go of the worry that the eruption of the workings of unconscious life (through psychoanalysis) had occurred within a dialectic that entailed their return to a state of repression—especially if it came to be perceived as having a negative influence in society. This was, in part, the focus of Freud's concern with apostasy among some of his followers.

Knowledge of the unconscious does not have to lead to its subsequent destruction in society, however, despite programmes now abounding that demand quick changes in symptomatology following external modelling, such as the positivistic thinking of cognitive behavioural therapy (CBT), or the impact of an early and fragile positive transference. One positive result of these superficial tendencies is that it is difficult now to really destroy psychoanalysis. Its status is too present, delineated especially by the fact that it is worth attacking because it still exists, albeit as an underground subject.

Some scars in European psychoanalytic societies

It is important to acknowledge that European analytical societies, including those formed around the birth of psychoanalysis, have often emerged, either sooner or later, from profound historical traumas—events that, for many of us, remain part of our own lifetimes. These histories constitute our psychosocial cultural tramways and they can exist in states of repression, or can sometimes, through a reckoning with history, allow the emergence of a new order.

The many years that populations were under rigid control systems (such as in Nazi Germany, Communist East Europe, and racist South Africa) have had their impact—lasting effects of things that could not be spoken or expressed, either in the family or on the streets, without the enormous fear of the network of local spies and party members, and so of punishment. These past aggressive political controls were essentially ways of bullying the other on a grand scale, and they have deeply penetrated family life, schools, and workplaces, in so doing provoking the development of unconscious ways of coping.

Over the last century, the many countries that have had repressive governments have now seen generations of children grow up in paranoid atmospheres, especially so at home, whereby the practice of keeping silent was maintained so that children would not be able to say anything dangerous about their parents' views when outside. Such protective social mechanisms can become what appear as an "ordinary sensible" paranoia.

In the analysis of candidates who grew up under totalitarian regimes—such as Nazi, Stalinist, or South African—the germ of the paranoia needs to have especial notice taken of it. It is ubiquitous, often silent, and with an appearance of being ordinary. To escape such mental attack, such analysands need to question not only their own history, but also that of the analyst—where he or she has come from, and what their imagined trauma has been. This is to ensure that a conformative transference is not just a passive acceptance of a training control system that might be unconsciously perceived as similar to the old nationalist repressive regime. How would one know that the old regime has been overthrown, unless there is authentic freedom in the analytic consulting room, and not just an assumption that all is well? Paranoia invariably lives out its existence underground, beneath a pseudo-normative false self.

Such important analytic work is conducted not through question and answer, but rather through what became known in South Africa as "truth and reconciliation": a process of searching out and giving description to the traumatic landscapes where so many bodies had been secretly buried, away from the families' knowledge. Totalitarian regimes, and their deep controls embedded in social, political, and family life, still play their parts in the unconscious dynamics of twenty-first-century cultural life, as do the wars within some parts of Europe, including those which have only recently ended, for the time being (although one is still being fought between Ukraine and Russia).

It is the scars from such histories that also run through many European analytic societies. For example, the Berlin Psychoanalytic Institute and the impact of the steady departure of Jewish analysts under Nazism. As Eran J. Rolnik writes, "it was clear from the beginning of Nazi rule that Jewish analysts would not be permitted to remain in the country" (Rolnik, 2012, p. 82). The departure of Max Eitingon, the strong and diligent president of the society, loyal to Freud, was particularly painful, prompting Freud to write on 23 August 1933, to Ernest Jones, that "Berlin is Lost" (ibid., p. 83). Felix Boehm, Eitingon's successor, struggled to maintain the survival of the Institute as an environment in which Jewish and non-Jewish analysts could work together, holding it up as an anomaly in Nazi Germany, yet, at the same time, working hard to ensure that psychoanalysis was kept free from any direct link to Judaism (ibid., pp. 89–90). This inevitably caused tensions in the international psychoanalytic community, one particularly incendiary incident being the Institute's response following the arrest of the young Jewish analyst Edith Jacobson, whose ties with Communist resistance had been discovered by the Gestapo (ibid., pp. 88–89).

In reaction to the ensuing international criticism, Boehm explained his decision not to come out in defence of Jacobson in terms of his attempts to dissociate the Institute from both Judaism and political resistance (ibid., pp. 88–89). His attempts at maintaining the Institute as an island in which Jews could still practise did not survive much longer, however, and by 1936 it was annexed to the German Institute for Psychological Research and Psychotherapy (ibid., p. 90). This was the so-called "Göring Institute", its director Matthias Göring being the nephew of Field Marshall Hermann Göring.

Here, Boehm, Göring, and Carl Müller-Braunschweig, along with a further fourteen non-Jewish members of the Institute, went on to develop a significantly altered form of "psychoanalysis" that was compatible with Nazi ideology (the Institute's one surviving copy of Freud's works was locked away in a cupboard known as "the poison cabinet") (ibid., p. 90–91).

As Rolnik concludes,

> German psychoanalysts did not display unusual resilience in standing up to the regime's demands. The Berlin Psychoanalytic Institute fell victim to the official Nazi policy of anti-Jewish discrimination at a relatively early stage. (ibid., p. 91)

In truth, the original psychoanalytic societies of Berlin and Vienna were destroyed and replaced, as if seamlessly and unnoticed, by monsters that covered over the gap.

It is worth noting here that Freud was well aware of the profound impact that Nazism and its anti-Semitic policies were having on every aspect of life, and that he dedicated a major part of his late writings, in *Moses and Monotheism* (which was written in 1934, revised in 1936, and then published in 1938), to analysing the foundations of anti-Semitism. In the first preface of this book, he describes Nazism as "a relapse into almost prehistoric barbarism" (Freud, 1939a, p. 54). It is likely that Freud's powerful description here refers to the Nazi use of power to severely limit and curtail the lives and careers of Jews. Seeing that the surface propaganda was an illusion, he faced the truth of the attacks that were occurring. As Freud wrote in a letter to Romain Rolland: "A great part of my life's work has been spent (trying to) destroy illusions of my own and those of mankind" (Freud, 4 March 1923, p. 346).

The impact of the discrimination, anti-Semitism, and intimidation of Nazism has lasted long after its defeat. In March 2018, the European Psychoanalytical Federation (EPF) held its annual conference in Warsaw. At the same time, the right-wing government was bringing in legislation to criminalise any assertion of Polish involvement in the Holocaust or other war crimes occurring under the German occupation of the Second World War. This created a profound sense of anxiety in advance of the conference. Many analysts even preferred not to attend. Others felt the opposite, however: that in the face of such anti-Semitism, they must attend, specifically in order to stand up to the corruption of Polish ideology. With a similar mindset, I realised that it would be valuable to one day hold a conference titled "Psychoanalysis and Anti-Semitism". This would defiantly counter the historical anti-Semitic attacks on the "Jewish science" of psychoanalysis, which have not diminished to this day (even Freud fell into this perception, holding Jung in such high esteem partly because he was not Jewish).

At the conference, I read the next chapter of this book as a lecture, including the material about anti-Semitism in Poland. There was clearly a great deal of anxiety in the conference about what might or might not be spoken about, and, while I did not think I would be arrested for my remarks in the middle of a conference in Warsaw, this phantasy was tangibly present.

Near the end of the conference, I attended a large group discussion about the meaning and feeling of meeting together in Warsaw. Around 100 analysts sat in a large spiral for 90 minutes and spoke their thoughts. Many expressed their sense of the dead rising from the ground, evoked by the areas still empty and covered with rubble that are parts of the destroyed ghetto; by the horrors written on the tombstones of the old Jewish cemetery; and by the two parts of the ghetto wall that remain standing. The chill was palpable.

Towards the end of the discussion, I spoke of my great concern about the rise of totalitarian states of mind in governments in Europe, the US, and elsewhere, and said that I found the return of Nazism very frightening. I then asserted that it is essential that analysts draw attention to how the mental states of cruelty, sadomasochism, perversion, and identification with the aggressor—which we know and work with in our consulting rooms—can also pervade society. To my horror, not a single colleague responded to my remarks and I was left isolated and alone with my concerns. I later realised that the room was filled with fear—not of the past but for the future—and that the roomful of analysts were unable to process their group affect. The scars are still with us today.

The fall of the Berlin Wall and contrapuntal listening

With the fall of the Berlin Wall and the reopening of Europe from East to West and West to East, the continent has an increased historical and cultural heterogeneity, as we must now take account of the impact of totalitarian regimes on countries that lived behind the Iron Curtain. As a result, analytic training has become much more complex.

Without doubt, Europe has been the leading arena for the development of new analytic societies. Young people suddenly finding themselves in a position with the freedom to think outside of the old regime's rules were at once attracted to psychoanalysis as a place to begin to think freely and to ascertain the damage that had been done to their self, their family, and their culture. Many new analytic societies thus soon formed in Eastern Europe following the collapse of Communism, making treatment available where it was once proscribed.

In conjunction with this, forms of organisation and meeting in the EPF have become part of something profound with regard to negotiating difference—first, acting as ways of breaking down the sense of a large, monolithic organisation into more manageable and approachable resources, but, critically, second, enabling a realisation that no single analytic training contains the truth of analysis. Learning the many ways of approaching the patient is a great antidote to the narcissisms of both small and large differences, and so these regular meetings outside particular analytic societies are an essential resource for the future development of analysis in a growing and complex region.

What we have been establishing with these approaches is a new form that is not only about learning more about the complexities of psychoanalysis but that also allows us to begin to listen "contrapuntally"—a musical term adapted by Edward Said to describe a way of creatively negotiating and discriminating between what can often be profoundly divergent ways of understanding both theory and practice. This type of listening implies that the barrier to recognition, often a result of ignorance, or of ignoring that which we do not imagine of the other, becomes something to be faced, confronted, and argued against within a facilitating environment. It also implies that profound cultural differences can be noticed and explored.

Such listening attempts to overcome what we do not imagine of the other—that which is consequently unavailable for us to process and integrate into understanding. Prejudice relies on stereotypes of otherness, which appear to demand that we know things of the other that are not true. To form patches of truth requires the breakdown of prejudicial unconscious phantasies that can be deeply held constructs, passed down the generations like unprocessed childhood trauma—doing to and being done to ad infinitum.

We can note similarities here between the way that rigidities and prejudices can be passed on in both analytic societies and wider society, and the way in which systems of mothering can be passed on down the generations. In relation to the baby within the particular dyadic culture that the mother brings, the mother's history of being mothered, as well as *her* mother's history of being mothered, can be rigidly encased as a transgenerational unconscious system. Of course, this can be a benign environment that nourishes development and appropriate separations. Yet even the mother who is unable to be other than an identificate of her own negativistic mother might find, in conjunction with her baby, a new dyadic culture in early formation, allowing the development of what Michael Balint called a "new beginning". This possibility of new beginnings applies equally to the contexts of wider society and analytic societies, in which there is the same requirement for the collapse of a previously internalised regime that is tough, unquestioned, and fixed.

In psychoanalysis, different theories are different forms of perception, each deserving appropriate understanding and respect. Nonetheless, some positions impede the spirit of analytic neutrality and interfere with free association, in doing so blocking access to a wider range of analytic ideas. What might be called an ethics of listening applies: in our listening to the conscious and to the unconscious, to work both with analysands and with colleagues. To acknowledge the many differing concepts of mind and relationships in psychoanalysis is a further application of the ethics of listening.

In the EPF, there are not only many types and theories of analytic training and clinical practice, but also many languages spoken and heard. I see it as a crucible where these ideas might be developed into a new European analytic dialogue that, in its openness, would be truly in the spirit of Freud's legacy. The capacity to speak together ethically is the best way of preventing authoritarianism in our analytic practice, in our analytic societies, and in our future European history.

To take a brief example, we can consider the difficulties of listening to a colleague describing their own clinical work using a theoretical frame that might differ considerably from our own. To listen only within a singular theoretical construction might well—through its ideas, its direction of the treatment, whether it uses or does not use regression, and whether it has or does not have a historical-developmental understanding—profoundly impact on how one hears the other. This is arguably an ethical problem, as it requires a particular type of listening that is similar to the analyst's listening to the analysand, with evenly suspended attention, not knowing where one is or where one is going. If one listens to the other's clinical material only through one's particular theoretical frame, it is possible to miss the clinical meanings—for instance, only privileging material through the here-and-now transference, which might not be the reporting analyst's position.

It might well require relinquishing a particular knowledge of theory that has become part of one's unconscious mindset, in order to be able to meet the other in the discourse.

Of course, it can be so much easier to invoke one's own theoretical stance to attack the work of the other and to avoid having to think in a different way. Analytic societies can get into a habit of suspending thinking and opting for a simpler, political solution—one wrapped up as disdain for a differing analytic theory. In such matters, colleagues can become cruel to fellow members with a differing theoretical leaning, and societies can split. In order to throw another light on this matter, I want to quote from the 1995 Nobel Prize lecture by Seamus Heaney, who writes of the need to find an appropriate balance of contradictory positions:

> The need on the one hand for a truth telling that will be hard and
> retributive, and on the other hand, the need not to harden the mind
> to a point where it denies its own yearnings for sweetness and trust.
>
> (Heaney, 1995)

This describes the requirements for a contrapuntal world, of words that need to be spoken and longings that must be recognised, a world that might be thought in terms of Ferenczi's "elasticity" (his expression of the analytic concept of tact), holding the tensions, as they differ from time to time, both in analysis and within society. A certain amount of elasticity is required to listen beyond the preconceptions of one's own theoretical frame to make chains of associations possible beyond an early crystallisation of what one thinks one knows. Humble free association is part of such an elastic position that need not harden the mind.

Totalitarian language and political deceit

Totalitarian language is forged in opposition to such an openness and flexibility of thought; it has a particular meaning that must be adhered to, even if it is evidentially incorrect. This is the antithesis of the Freudian invention, which allows the multiplicity of understandings within speech and writing to be noticed and expressed. Under totalitarian regimes, an unconscious master–slave mentality, such as that which governed the Berlin Institute's conformity to Nazi ideology, seeps into language, as George Orwell clearly noticed. Words can often express their very opposite, and repressive, totalitarian regimes abuse this elasticity to pervert and police their subjects' perception and communication of reality. Such systems, the surveillance within them, and the resulting atmosphere of paranoia, can develop in an environment of cascading political lying.

In this context, it is alarming to witness today's politicians reducing complex discussion to often false sound bites, feeding them to the people, who accept them willingly. Brexiteers argue that payments to the EU, totalling millions each week, could, post-Brexit, be directed solely towards saving the National Health Service—blatantly obscuring the fact that a large proportion of those millions is already spent within the UK, with the EU directing back much of the UK's gross payment to meet other funding needs. And right-wing politicians flaunt their supposed concern for the poor, for the health service, and for universities, while simultaneously cutting financial resources in order to apparently balance the budget, affirming that this destruction of hard-won resources in healthcare and education, and the erosion of the savings of ordinary citizens, is good for us. Meanwhile, David Cameron's Brexit legacy is one that weakens and diminishes the European project at a time when standing together would be the intelligent response to the consistent and murderous attacks taking place in many European countries. This political atmosphere of lies and deceit has led to a sense that we can believe what we like, as long as it is not an expert opinion, and so homespun ideology has become the superior currency.

Trauma, mourning, and monuments

In contrast to these tendencies of control, deceit, and linguistic rigidity, within a master–slave mentality, psychoanalysis offers a path towards truth and reconciliation, and away from paranoid discourses towards alterity. The development of the ability to tolerate the other, without allowing domination, and at the same time as recognising complexity, is the modern heritage of psychoanalysis.

In psychoanalysis lies the potential for freedom. This includes the possibility of attaining a more mature position that recognises the vitality of mourning. Creative separation, together with mourning, is a necessary element in the development of the parent–child relationship. The analyst–patient relationship, through unconscious communication, enables this to take place beyond and despite trauma. Where there has been substantial trauma and deprivation, the analytic situation is one that entails the possibility of new formations, which require a bedrock of trust. This can lead to a sense of reparation that sometimes needs to come from the analyst, as a humane and free other—someone who can not only think and understand outside the tramways, but who can be alive outside of them.

Such new formations can also be possible in a traumatised analytic society—for example, if it is able to struggle to mourn its specific historic confrontations between colleagues, rather than surrendering to years of low murmurings of discontent. Attempts at mourning in larger society include the erection of symbols, often statues for remembrance, in either prominent or less obvious positions, but these can often exist for glorification or political dissemination, or can stand "as if" they represent an invitation to remember, and there can be a similar elision of mourning within an analytic society.

Given the traumas of European history and the often intolerant matrix of beliefs maintained within analytic societies, working between societies and countries is bound to touch upon questions of mourning, and can also provide a space for it to be expressed. If such difficult psychic processes, born of all our different but convergent histories in the twentieth and twenty-first centuries, cannot be reflected in the thought and practice within our analytic societies, then where else? This was the central question that international psychoanalysis had to face when returning to Germany for the first time following the Second World War. It was given particular consideration at the 34th International Psychoanalytical Congress in Hamburg in 1985. What value could psychoanalysis have if the analytic community could not face such profound difficulties?

To give an example in which working across boundaries brought about a consideration of mourning, in June 2010, at one of the EPF annual clinical meetings, I was involved in organising a weekend seminar for recently qualified analysts, to take place in Warsaw. Twenty-eight colleagues from analytic societies all over Europe attended and presented clinical analytic material in small groups to a panel of training supervisors. The location was evocative. On the first evening, many of the group enjoyed being in the beautiful, Old Town square, which was completely rebuilt in the post-war reconstruction. They did not realise that this old centre, seemingly so well-kept and ancient, was in fact a deception. A quarter of the city had contained the Warsaw Ghetto, which was totally razed during the 1943 Jewish uprising. In the following year, most of the central parts of the city were also razed during the Polish resistance partisans' uprising against the

Nazi occupation, before the Red Army advanced into Warsaw. Eighty-five per cent of the city was demolished. Following the war, in the early 1950s, the city was lovingly recreated, Canaletto's famous views of the original city being used as the main reference.

In this process of complete reconstruction in Warsaw, we can read the societal and cultural equivalent of the way in which an individual's trauma can be covered up, suppressed, and then detached from any possibility of understanding, such that it can be viewed only from outside as a façade. Unaware of the history, the visitor delights in the perfectly reconstructed medieval environment. Yet what is this Disneyesque reconstruction, which hardly shows any link to the city's real past? The enjoyment of the repaired centre indicates a necessity to not remember, a need to be beguiled by the surface pleasures in sight.

In the centre of the Old Town, outside the castle, is a small photo of the site in 1945 showing almost nothing of this vast building; only a forlorn gateway with its right-hand corner just a tottering thin pile of bricks. Nothing else is standing. A sea of rubble—a horrid and eloquent metaphor of what had happened here earlier... Time has now moved on. The castle and square are fully reconstructed, ignoring what occurred there in the Second World War. This has a symmetry with the neurotic individual who must repress that which cannot be known, because knowledge is apparently too terrible to be made manifest. Knowing the destruction that has occurred means that what one gazes upon holds within its view that which was wiped out. It exists in the negative shadow of what we see before us, as it is this absence that subsists as the trace of the destructive order. In relation to psychosis, Freud describes that "the delusion is found applied like a patch over the place where originally a rent had appeared in the ego's relation to the external world" (Freud 1924, p. 151). Similarly, this European city has applied "a patch over the place where originally a rent had appeared" to cover the absence. Its citizens, and perhaps its visitors, cannot bear to contemplate the tear in their own past, and in their own population, unless courageous mental work is undertaken.

Such patches of architectural memory can be found all over Europe, the only partly recognised signs of a missing history in many important landscapes. In many Spanish cities and towns, for example, there are streets named "Calle Judia" ("Jewish street"); the only remaining signs that Jews once lived there, before their mass expulsion under the Alhambra Decree of 1492, ordered by Queen Isabella and King Ferdinand. All other traces of that history have been completely wiped out. It has not been easy to build the edifices that enable us to mourn our bloody European heritage and provide an atmosphere to facilitate such mourning (see Young, 1993). Germany has had a long journey on this path, from the Mitscherlichs' important book *The Inability to Mourn* in 1967, which analysed the failure of the German people and German society to acknowledge the crimes committed in the name of National Socialism, to the Berlin of today. Alexander Mitscherlich's earlier book, with Fred Mielke, *Doctors of Infamy: The Story of the Nazi Medical Crimes*, when first published in 1949, so inflamed much of society that large numbers were bought up by the German Medical Society in order to suppress it. This society, of course, has its own horrific history—that is, the Nazi medical experiments in many concentration camps, and in particular those conducted by Dr Mengele on twins.

Among the Berlin monuments that exist to remind citizens of the totalitarian past, there are two that strike me as being of particular interest, although perhaps only one of them is truly significant or effective in this context. The first is at Bebelplatz, the site at which, on 10 May 1933, the Nazis burnt 20,000 books, including works by Freud. Today, there is a line written on a plaque in the square, taken from Heinrich Heine's 1820 play *Almansor*: "*Das war ein Vorspiel nur; dort wo man Bücher verbrennt, verbrennt man am Ende auch Menschen*" ("That was only a prelude; where they burn books, they will also ultimately burn people"). The plaque is accompanied by a monument by Micha Ullman consisting of a small glass window set flat into the cobblestones and looking deep underground into an empty library with rows of bare shelves. Evocative, certainly, yet as one walks away from the site, to any distance, it becomes invisible. The ordinary passer-by is not even aware that it is there, so the event is certainly remembered, but only if one is standing in just the right place. The dictum "out of sight, out of mind" occurs to me. If one is aware, prior to visiting, of the destruction that occurred here, or if one just happens to come across it, then it can have a powerful effect. But it is a monument that is easy to ignore.

The second monument is by Peter Eisenman. Commemorating the Holocaust, it consists of 2,711 concrete slabs near the Brandenburg Gate. This is a public work, not hidden away but daily in the sight of all who pass by it in the very centre of the city. It points the way unequivocally and unavoidably to that which is known and needs to be seen, a constant confrontation with destruction, in this way playing an essential part in the regeneration of national soul and spirit. The prose of Anna Akhmatova in the epigraph at the start of this chapter bears testimony to daring to be able to describe that which is so painful, nearly too painful for us to bear bringing it, in words, into the present. And yet, it can be done.

Dissonant landscapes

We can relate this question of historical trauma, and how it is either registered or refused by the mind, to the analytic process. All crises, historical and personal, are both endings and beginnings. In time, the existence of a crisis allows for the development of thoughts both of the origins of the crisis and of how it might end. There is always something unpredictable about this, as well as potentially unsettling—even radically so. To take a metaphor, the apparently simple commencement of a Beethoven symphony can evoke an unconscious expectation, not just of its development, but also of how the composer will be able to dare end what he has created. We find that great works often end in a dissonant way in relation to our milder, more humdrum expectations, exposing the listener to the shock of another, different resolution. Similarly, free association contains the potential for a radical edge that can move us further and further away from the neat narrative hedgerows of conscious life. In doing so, it allows us to find a dissonant landscape, and not necessarily the one we might have tried to creep towards. With understanding, free association can place us at such cardinal positions; we then have to try to understand where we are. These places are different from those where we want to be or desire to be, and indeed often from where society demands that we be. We may be finding shards of an unthought, unspoken traumatic vista, emerging from the analysand's past like a haunting.

This is the reason why all totalitarian regimes detest the possibility of thinking for oneself: because it allows one to break away from the group narrative and the control system of abuse. Again, we can draw an analogy with the role of the analyst in their enabling of free associations that reveal traumatic material deep under the surface. Some analysands can act in a similar way to a dissident in the ranks, breaking free from the dominant, known rhetoric of family life. Issues of dominance and passivity are a common facet of family life, spread around the various players. The analyst is unconsciously expected to play a double role, on the one hand quietly part of that old regime, while on the other being in a separate mental place—one that enables them to notice and help either create or accept a disturbance from the fixity that has hitherto ruled the family and their individual mental states. This process is never easy. It would be wrong to view the end of an analysis, or the end of this chapter, as offering a simple resolution: "all's well that ends well". Psychoanalysis does not deliver cures. However, its instruments do enable the possibility, if we are brave enough to examine the contents of Pandora's box, of finding hope in knowledge.

"Confusion of Tongues" and the splittings of the mind and society

The mourning of historical trauma, however, like all mourning, requires authentic knowledge of what took place, and that the trauma is openly known about, engaged with, and understood. In an attempt to understand, then, let us turn to one of the things from Pandora's box: the problem we all have with the other, around the concept of alterity. For this I want to go back to the arguments between Freud and Sándor Ferenczi in the early 1930s, coinciding with the rise of Hitler, and domination by totalitarian politics.

Freud feared a rejection of his core ideas of unconscious life, especially of the base that he had established in the unconscious oedipal phantasy. Ferenczi, however, while always a Freudian and accepting the unconscious phantasy structure of the Oedipus complex, was also concerned with those many patients who had experienced an environmental deficiency through an early infantile trauma. He felt that these patients required a new technique to deal with the pre-oedipal loss of basic trust, and other concomitant issues.

In a paper concerned with such early traumas, "Confusion of Tongues between Adults and the Child" (1933), Ferenczi shows in a radical way the structure of abuse between the adult and the child. It describes the biphasic attack on the child, beginning in a guise of playfulness that excites the child, desirous of the attention of the grown up, who grooms the way for a sexual assault that may end in penetration. By this point, the child is at best confused, at worst in pain, and Ferenczi describes how the child can protect him or herself from the impact of the attack—an attack on both trust and the body—by a split in the ego. "That is not really happening to me, just to my body." Or the child can look intensely at the pattern of the wallpaper or the curtains in an attempt to separate themselves from what is happening in the room. The child becomes lost and missing as a deep defence from the pain of the onslaught. However, Ferenczi now brings out the other, arguably worse, trauma: the adult repudiating what has just occurred, often telling the child, "It is only your imagination," or saying, "Look what you made me do—it's your fault," and "Don't tell anyone our secret—if you do, nobody will believe you." This even more vicious, second assault is now on the mind of the child. Reality is attacked and the child is detached from anyone who might help and listen, told that they will not be believed. They are invited to understand that it is really all an incident about nothing. This is an attack on thinking—on reality—and it invariably leaves the victim alone, hurt, and confused, and with severe difficulties regarding basic trust.

All this deals with the subject of paedophilia in a way that, when the paper is read for the first time, feels contemporary, despite having been written in 1933. It helps us to understand the psychology of splitting in the defence of the ego, pursued at the cost of forming an internal state of alienation and a carapace in the child's character, leading to great fear in the child, and then adult, around trusting in the world and in relationships. Anna Freud developed Ferenczi's ideas further, describing an additional mechanism of defence resulting in an identification with the aggressor (see A. Freud, 1936). This is the common history of many paedophiles, often having been abused as children themselves.

We can apply the same dynamic steps to understanding the attacks on alterity with anti-Semitism, Islamophobia, racism, misogyny, and homophobia. For instance, a group of colleagues are meeting together and suddenly one tells an anti-Semitic joke, in the knowledge that one of the group is Jewish. Everyone but the Jew may laugh, and he might feel helpless at being, at that moment, not part of the group, unless he tries to signal with laughter that he is part of it. Perhaps he becomes angry about the cruel and crude stereotyping, and, being an adult, he might well decide to speak up. If he protests, the anti-Semite can quickly riposte that it was only a joke, nothing was meant by it, and the Jew is just oversensitive. Here we can see the second attack, as in paedophilia, where the evidence in front of the victim is dismissed as not being real. The attack continues to proceed with the idea that the Jew is just too thin-skinned. This has a further meaning, that there is no anti-Semitic attack, only that he (a Jew) has a problem with humour. It is a double attack that, as with the child, leaves the victim in a state of alienation from the group.

This unconscious dynamic also plays out in racist and homophobic attacks where the victim is insulted and then informed that they took a wrong and unintended meaning. Such victims are told that any racist or homophobic meaning is the product of their own misunderstanding, and so, far from being a victim, they are in fact the architects of their own difficulty, and, furthermore, are not like "us", who can understand jokes and are adult enough to not misunderstand what is being said.

In 2012, fascist Serbian football supporters, watching an under-21s match between Serbia and England, pelted a black English player with bananas. When the racist implication that the black man was a monkey was objected to, there was incredulity from the Serbian fascists at this thought; their joke was only a bit of fun. They said that those who had thought of the implied racism were the true racists, not those throwing bananas—furthermore, they had no sense of humour. In this case, the English team stood by and defended their comrade, and so he was not left alone; the desire to attack alterity and the true nature of the racists was thus revealed.

We can see that the behaviour of the group has a profound significance—that is, whether they join in the attack or stay quietly neutral, as if it is nothing to do with them, or whether a critical number stand up with the victim against the double attack. Racism, anti-Semitism, and homophobia do not work in an atmosphere in which the premises of the attack are strongly rejected. In such cases, the attackers come under scrutiny for the first time and cannot hide in the group. Nor can they pervert the group into identifying with them in their attack.

To consider another case, in Paris, January 2015, the murder of French journalists by Islamist terrorists, in response to their satirical depictions of Muhammad, and then two days later the killings of Jews, caused an eruption of outrage. In this aftermath, a sense of "us" vs "them" began to percolate through the drama. Rather than understanding that the attack was carried out by a small cell of terrorists motivated by contempt and hatred for French and Western society, this reaction allowed the attack to succeed in causing further splits between Muslim French citizens and how they were perceived by non-Muslim French citizens, as if all were capable of killing in the name of Allah. Instead of a group process that brought the country together, there was an increase in anti-Muslim sentiment.

Worse still was the opportunity taken by a few senior Israeli politicians to employ anti-Semitism as a device to demand that all French Jews quickly relocate to the safety of Israel. Here there is a further attack, this time on the French state that apparently cannot guard the lives of its Jewish citizens—the twisted assumption being that Israel is a safe place for Jews, something that has been clearly untrue all the way from the inception of the state in 1948 up to the present. According to the Israeli Prime Minister, Benjamin

Netanyahu, Europe, the terrible place that was the crucible of the Holocaust and that has harboured the continuation of anti-Semitism ever since, no longer deserves to have Jews living there.

In this example, the ripples through society and politics, and between nation states, pile on top of each other, allowing an attempt to gain advantage, following terrible wounds to individuals, communities, and countries, by suggesting that bystanders and citizens should take various sides. In such situations, thinking is necessary to avoid further layers of encrypted and potential trauma being doubled up and intensified—something that the abused child is much more vulnerable to doing.

Of course, we now have President Trump, with his crude stereotyping of the other and continual projections of destructiveness on to a person or people other than himself and his administration. The "alt-right", the Ku Klux Klan, and Nazi groups have consequently found their voices, empowered by the Trumpian dystopic vision and its profound capacity for lies. Trump's attacks, which encourage his supporters to further vilify individuals or groups, have the same structure as the double racist attack of the fascist Serbian football fans. Yet it seems that Trump has an additional capacity to mesmerise by taking a grossly oversimplified, untruthful position that is so off-centre that the listener has to continually rethink what is being said. This is a form of unbalancing the other, including his staff; he alone is above the fray, commenting from the heights of the presidency and invariably causing chaos, which in fact seems to be his goal. His deepening of the poverty of so many people, in a sea of riches for the few, is the recipe for an eruption of anger to be utilised, as in the 1930s, by a regime leaning towards totalitarianism.

Trump too often comments on a situation in which someone has identified and called out a situation, within a society or institution, as anti-other, stating that it is, in fact, that person who is the problem. "It is really your fault as you are the one who is bad since you accuse the other of racism, anti-Semitism, etc." If that person speaks up against Trump's smear, she or he is attacked further. This dynamic can be seen repeated time and time again, and it is partly a result of the identification that people can have with the group, institution, or tradition being criticised. For people who identify with a group as a good object, someone who points to problems of discrimination within it is turned into the problem. This is Trump's attack dog upping his accusatory rhetoric to blame Mexicans, Muslims, the poor, the pope, all of whom can be split off and contained behind a wall of separateness, us vs them, like an excretory process. We treat fellow human beings in the same way that we void shit and piss, getting rid of the "bad stuff" without guilt, as if they were "nothing". This was central to Hitler's Final Solution, the processes of which were oiled by its victims being cast as *Untermenschen*. In this particularly vicious psychology, in order for the many to feel "great again", some groups have to be demeaned and got rid of (in the 1930s, it was Communists, homosexuals, cripples, Gypsies, and Jews).

Remember that Holocaust Memorial Day in the US in 2018 had, for the first time, no mention of the Jews. It is important in cases such as this to understand the importance of words—their inclusions, elisions, and transformations. Similarly, the renaming of a political party is never something meaningless; the policies continuing in the same direction, only under a different name. In March 2018, the French right-wing Front National proposed changing its name to "Rassemblement National". There was already a centre-right party using this name and they issued a legal challenge attempting to block its use by Marine Le Pen's party. However, in the light of the extreme right-wing nature of the Front National, their wish to take the name "Rassemblement National" is particularly disturbing; a party who supported the Nazis operated with that name from 1941 to 1944, their flag and logo resembling the Nazi flag with its swastika. The Front National's attempt at rebranding thus appears to be a return of that which had been repressed.

Psychoanalysis and resisting domination

To speak up against developments such as these requires a certain bravery, whether acting alone or as part of a group, in order to deal with the anxiety of being out of step with the perceived majority. As Frank Kermode says in his famous essay *The Sense of an Ending*:

> This is not, after all, quite the world of those who seek 'the courage to be and strip reality of the protection of myth'.
>
> (Kermode, 2000, p. 132–133)

In analysis also, it is always a continuing struggle for the analysand to find that state of being that is distinct from immersion in his or her primary narrative. Analysis can be an act of freedom against the chains of imposed and self-imposed narratives from family history or unconscious romance, but it also has to struggle against the passive expectation that something will be done by someone else, often expressing itself as the desire for this to be the analyst's function. One of the main themes examined in this chapter is how central these issues of freedom and emancipation are to the analytic process. This centrality is the reason for the explosion of analytic training subsequent to the tearing down of the Berlin Wall (another wall built to separate people), the freedom that came with the collapse of Communism leading many who had lived under its corrupting ideology to desire an analytic treatment—one that would allow them an interior space in the mind in which they could examine the mental damage accrued from living in a paranoid culture. The deep fear for these individuals was their own mental corruption and complicity. Who informed on me and how can I alleviate my guilt for having informed? How can I rebalance my mind to restore my parents' authority, rather than the state's? The need is to purge the poison in the individual's unconscious state of mind after being surrounded by non-stop brainwashing, divested of the capacity to think for themselves. Privacy, confidentiality, and the development of trust became essential tools for many who thus came to appreciate the huge value of psychoanalytic holding, as well as analytic investigation into the impact on citizens of massive state corruption. The developed capacity to mourn such external and internal traumatic states, through nurturing the capacity to free associate, provided minds with the freedom to think. Free association is not just a profound technique advanced by Freud; it is also a formation of mind that is central to developing societies and politics that are creative and free.

This is particularly important in our world today with the recent and continuing global financial crisis exposing the hidden world of selfishness. The other side to the accumulation of great wealth is the severe deprivation of so much of the population. The poor are then blamed as if their poverty is their own fault. Again, the double attack. You are poor—unlike us—and it is your fault. There is always a necessity to find an object to blame, and, in addition to the poor, this can just as easily be blacks, Muslims, or always the ubiquitous Jew. As many European societies shift further to the right, and human values seemingly become polarised into primitive dichotomies of us vs them, the spectre of totalitarianism returns to haunt us all. More than ever, an analytic thinking space is necessary as one form of resisting the lurch into domination, both in society and in family life.

Time and the ending

The timelessness of an analysis also lives in the time that it contains and examines. An analysis is about a beginning, a middle, and an ending. The end is ever-present in the living of our lives, both for the individual and for society, as well as for a particular analysis. Death is a certainty of the condition of being alive, even if for many it remains unknown to consciousness. This needs to be part of any analysis—the imagined deaths of the analyst and of the analysand, and the fusion of these two strands in the end of the treatment. We die and will be in the minds of those we leave behind; similarly, the end of an analysis leaves both parts of the dyad to have in mind, from time to time, "remembrances of things past". The individual runs mythically from moment to moment, while our culture runs in grander aliquots from year to year, across the century, or to the pull of the millennium. In 2010, the International Psychoanalytical Association (IPA) commemorated its centenary, as if the survival of psychoanalysis (and not its often-longed-for death) is contingent upon the magic of reaching 100 years of age (this not incompatible with the idea that psychoanalysis, as a discipline, a *mere* hundred years old, is still a child or adolescent).

It is interesting here to consider Kermode's contrasting of long spans of time, such as centuries, with the insistent ticking of the clock that pulls us along our journey from birth to death. He describes the commencing movement in the sound of "tick" as a humble genesis to the more guttural sound of "tock", a type of feeble apocalypse—the pause being the life in between. In contrast to this narrative structure, with its formulaic direction from then until now, Kermode suggests that we might instead hear the sequence differently, as "tock–tick" (Kermode 2000, p. 45). In this tiny metaphor, Kermode breaks through into dissonance, inviting us to view the seemingly well-ordered sequence as a potentially fractured noise. The "tock" is a more dissonant sound, and so by reversing the sequence, to "tock–tick", that dissonance becomes more prominent, and this reversal is also jarring through its distortion of the familiar order.

Of course, a person's life can be conceptualised in terms of a forward-moving dynamic. Yet, if we are to think about the structure of beginning and ending, and insert the "tock" first, the time interval, despite being the same, carries a very different resonance. It contains dissonance, which is the stuff our patients bring to us when the clock needs resetting, in their perceptions of the dominance of dissonant rhythms in their lives. Tick–tock is a human narrative created to fill the void of time as the clock moves ever forward. However, psychoanalysis has a freedom to mentally escape such shackles and to go backwards when necessary, hearing "tock–tick", in order to re-find lost objects or the history of the patient. This is the value too of *après coup*, or *Nachträglichkeit*, which allows the possibility of going back in time and unconsciously re-evaluating etchings on the mind.

Re-finding lost objects is of course in itself another mythical quest, but it is one in which there can be a rebalancing of what can feel like the magical drive of destiny, such that the individual may realise more responsibility for his or her own causality. This means escaping the groove of a slavish, unconscious drive to continue the life one has grown up with, including its perceptions, misperceptions, and prejudices, as if our character and object relationships have been fixed by the contingencies of life as something concrete that cannot, must not, be altered. Beneath such phantasies that things are fixed for all time resides the fear of "and then what?" What might the individual do with their trauma within a skein of severe disturbances in society, such as totalitarianism, where political lying and attacks on alterity develop a pseudo-normality? What is to be made of life in the empty space without the patch that seems to hold it all together? This is a place where psychoanalytic dialogue can be formative, allowing the concrete patch to be prised away so that a new healing can begin. The free-associative thinking that allows this process can contribute a new dialogue, and a new way to think about political discourse, in doing so opening up the freedom to have an adventure, to be alive in one's life—to think and to be in society—even as the long shadow descends into the dark.

References

Akhmatova, A. (1957). *Requiem*. In: P. Forbes (Ed.), *Scanning the Century*. London: Penguin, 1999.

Busby, E. (2018, May 9). Government's mental health plans to leave hundreds of thousands of children without needed support, MPs warn. *Independent*. https://www.independent.co.uk/news/education/education-news/childrens-mental-health-government-green-paper-education-select-committee-social-care-a8341821.html (last accessed 19 June 2018).

Ferenczi, S. (1933). Confusion of tongues between adults and the child. In: M. Balint (Ed.), *Final Contributions to the Problems and Methods of Psychoanalysis* (pp. 156–167). London: Hogarth, 1955.

Freud, A. (1936). *The Ego and the Mechanisms of Defence*. London: Karnac, 1992.

Freud, S. (1923, March 4). Letter to Romain Rolland. In: E. Freud (Ed.), *Letters of S. Freud, 1873–1939* (p. 346). London: Hogarth, 1961.

Freud, S. (1924). Neurosis and Psychosis. *S. E., 19*: 147–154.

Freud, S. (1939a). *Moses and Monotheism: Three Essays. S. E., 23*: 1–138.

Heaney, S. (1995). Nobel lecture, 7 December 1995. *Nobelprize.org* <https://www.nobelprize.org/nobel_prizes/literature/laureates/1995/heaney-lecture.html> [last accessed 19 April 2018].

Kermode, F. (2000). *The Sense of an Ending: Studies in the Theory of Fiction with a New Epilogue*. Oxford: Oxford University Press.

Mitscherlich, A., & Mielke, F. (1949). *Doctors of Infamy: The Story of the Nazi Medical Crimes* (Trans. H. Norden). New York: Schuman.

Mitscherlich, A., & Mitscherlich, M. (1967). *The Inability to Mourn: Principles of Collective Behavior*. New York: Random House, 1975.

Rolnik, E. J. (2012). *Freud in Zion: Psychoanalysis and the Making of Modern Jewish Identity*. London: Karnac.

Young, J. E. (1993). *The Texture of Memory: Holocaust Memorials and Meaning*. New Haven: Yale University Press.

CHAPTER FIVE

Neoliberalism is bad for your mental health

David Bell

J oel is in his nineties and needs support on a daily basis. For a while Ayesha came and he got to like her and depend upon her. With no warning Ayesha disappeared and was replaced by a different person every day. One day, Raisa arrived looking panic-stricken—"I have seventeen minutes ... is it food or a bath?—I don't have time for both."

My presentation falls into three parts. In the first I will offer some broad considerations as regards the socio-political transformations that have come to characterise our contemporary world; I will then discuss how these changes reach into the way we think about ourselves both ordinarily and as expressed more formally in the academy. Lastly, I will narrow my focus to the consideration of mental health services, namely the quiet catastrophe of deterioration in the theory and practice of psychiatry. But first a housing statement:

All cultures develop their own modes of self-explanation but such explanations, somewhat like symptoms, inevitably conceal as much as they reveal. In this sense psychoanalysis may be well placed to enter into a critical relation with these self-explanations—that is, the forms of consciousness that characterise our age, and which thus present themselves as "normal". This chapter aims then, here following a valuable psychoanalytic tradition, to problematise this apparent normality. In so doing it will examine the kinds of subjectivity it on the one hand generates, and which on the other are necessary to sustain it.

Historical context

In the last thirty years or so capitalism, our world, has moved into a different phase, a profound change in its inner nature, from production of objects, to production of services, and the supremacy of markets which are purely financialised … and so completely abstracted from material objects. This has been accompanied by an increasing penetration (geographic, social, and cultural) of the market form into all spheres of life.

These profound changes express the near hegemony of neoliberalism.

Definition of neoliberalism

Although having roots as far back as 1940 and originally expressing a form of opposition to socialism, neoliberalism went through various transformations eventually becoming the dominant school of political economy in the closing decades of the twentieth century.

Key features include a radicalisation of the (so-called) free market where competition is maximised, free trade achieved through economic deregulation, privatisation of public assets, vastly diminished state responsibility over areas of social welfare, the corporatisation of human services, and monetary and social policies congenial to corporations and disregardful of the consequences: increasing inequality, poverty, rapid depletion of resources, irreparable damage to the biosphere, destruction of cultures, and erosion of liberal democratic institutions.

It might be helpful here to recall Marx's characterisation of a commodity as embodying two distinct values: use value and exchange value (Marx, 1867); the former expresses its unique qualities whereas exchange value refers to not anything material about the object but only its monetary value—as a commodity. The more objects and services are commodified the more their exchange/monetary value takes precedence over their use value. The logic of their management/administration does not need to distinguish the specifties of the object—whether it be cans of beans, portfolios of assets, or psychotherapy treatments. Further, the exchange/monetary value attracts to it a strange near mystical power, which Marx (1867) termed "commodity fetishism"—that is, the monetary value of the commodity is misunderstood as a mysterious concrete quality it possesses, as opposed to the reality that it can only reflect the social relations it embodies.

This ever-increasing commodification of the world reaches deep into the psychology of the person—reformulating personhood, psychological life, moral and ethical responsibility. (I will return to this shortly.)

Perry Anderson captures this well: "[We now have] the saturation of every pore of the world into the serum of capital. With the falling away of ideological opposition, we face a world where, without any victory, the adversary has gone" (1998, p. 21).

This world, then, "of no alternative"[1] manifests a manic triumphalism violently sweeping away anything in its path. The psychoanalyst Hanna Segal (1995) used this term to refer to the unopposed expansion of Western domination once its main obstacle (the Eastern bloc) had disappeared. But my use of the term here refers not to geography, but to culture.

This increasing penetration of the market form into our lived lives, the transformations of human activities into commodities, becomes so pervasive, so naturalised, that we cease to see it—and where ideology coincides with what we take to be "just the way the world is" we have ideology in its purest and deadliest form.

There is a well-known story of two small fish swimming in the water on a pleasant July day. As they go along another larger fish comes towards them swimming in the opposite direction. "Lovely day to be in the water, boys!" he says as he swims by. A few yards further on one of the little fish turns to the other and says, "What the hell is water?"

The point of this story is, of course, that because we swim about in a world of social relations, constructions of self, and so on, we cannot see it for what it is (it is just the way the world is). And perhaps there is corollary—namely, if we ever manage to remove ourselves from this set of relations and view them, so to speak, from the outside, then we may realise just how perverse and unnatural they are.

This new major shift in our culture produces its corresponding consciousness, a "structure of feeling" (Raymond Williams, 1977), which some social theorists have characterised as the postmodern condition of "schizoid" (see for example Eagleton, 1985)—and this term captures well the pervasive hovering existential anxiety expressing a new depthlessness, fragmentation of identity, loss of feeling, and sense of formlessness and loss of solidity; experience is of the moment, relations ahistorical.

As the individual apprehends the world in this new restricted way, as his own activities seem to him to follow/obey a commodity structure, he internalises this phenomenon—and so experiences his very self through the lens of the commodity form.

Perry Anderson describes the postmodern world as one:

> where the typical polarities of the subject run from the elation of the commodity rush, the euphoric highs of spectator and consumer, and the dejection of the nihilistic void of our being. (Anderson, 1998, p. 57)

> In psychological terms we may say that as a service economy we are so far removed from the realities of production and work that we inhabit a dream world of artificial stimuli and televised experience: never in any previous civilisation have the great metaphysic preoccupations, the fundamental questions of being and of the meaning of life, seemed so utterly pointless. (ibid., p. 51)

And, one may add, never have they seemed so necessary.

These "structures of feeling" which have come to dominate our world are both manifest in, and maintained by, various perverse ideological constructions, one of which I will now examine in some depth as its reach is so broad and so deep.

The survival of the fittest; the perversion of Darwin; the myth of the autonomous subject

The claim that the only genuine freedom is the freedom to compete in the "free market"[2] receives ideological support from social Darwinism (a term coined by Herbert Spencer). Darwin did not use the term "survival of the fittest"—"fitness" for him referred not to warlike competition, but to the "fit" between organism and environment.

This perversion of Darwin has infected our thought but we do not recognise it because (like the fish) we live inside it. A scientific description has been corrupted into a kind of moral imperative. "Survival of the fittest"—that is those that survive are the fittest and thus "morally" superior, and those who go down only have themselves to blame. This world filled with hatred and moral righteousness gives external life to our own archaic superego. It becomes a force shaping our destiny, drawing us into the moral abyss of masochism and self-blame. William Davies (2018) captures well some elements of this moral vision, here referring to the Conservative Party:

> Toughness, even pain, performs an important moral and psychological function.
>
> The fear of "moral hazard" produces a punitive approach to debtors, households, firms or national governments, the assumption being that anything short of harshness will produce a downward spiral of generosity, forgiveness and free-riding, eventually making the market economy unviable. Gratification must be resisted. Pain works. Only pain forces people to adapt and innovate. The productiveness of pain is a central conservative belief, whose expression might be economic, but whose logic is deeply moralistic.

This peculiar moralism is closely related to the survivalist mentality that dominates the public sector, which I have discussed in a previous paper (Bell, 1996):

> There are "good" hospitals or schools and "bad" ones. Goodness here refers not to the qualities of the object but to its place in the market; it is assumed that if something that is more popular in the market is "better" than something that is less popular,[3] the "bad" ones will die because they will not get the custom of the mythically empowered consumer, while the "good" ones will survive. The only way the "bad" ones might survive is by transforming themselves and becoming "good", something that is their own responsibility; and they can expect no help from the nanny state to get them out of the mess they have got themselves into!

"Good" and "bad" become, in the transitory shifting nature of the market forces, categories existing only on a horizontal plane—detached from their own history. "Good" must survive; "bad" will go to the wall—and it deserves to. In this primitive world, the marketplace is deified as the only source of human freedom and responsibility.

The trouble is there is something very persuasive about this sort of argument, for it appeals to our wish to live in a simple world of "good" and "bad". The question of an exploration, an understanding of why a particular hospital or school is "bad" (that is, a historical, i.e. vertical examination) does not really arise: it is bad ... because it is bad. Investigation would introduce difficult complexities which go against the simple appeal of "taking your custom elsewhere".

The "free" (neoliberal) market (mis)conceives the world as made up of autonomous subjects serving only their interests, most powerfully expressed by Margaret Thatcher's *cri de cœur*, "There is no such thing as society, only individuals." This is of course an illusion,[4] but powerful social, cultural, and economic forces make it possible for individuals to (mis)perceive themselves in this way.

Freud repeatedly emphasises the biological fact of the long period of infantile dependence that characterises the human animal, the indelible mark it leaves upon us, an awareness that is a continuous source of discomfort. And so the myth of the autonomous individual finds its willing soil in those parts of our nature that hate awareness of this dependence upon others and the complex social organisations that make our lives possible. As psychoanalysts we know there is hardly a more dangerous delusion.[5]

There is close relation between the idealisation of the mythical autonomous subject and the attacks on the welfare state/the public sector: the former provides the ideological justification for the latter.

The hegemonising project of marketisation has always had to deal, in one way or another, with an obstacle that stands in its way, the non-marketised social institutions that we have created that bind people together, providing a structure for containing and managing human destructiveness and a context for collective reparative effort. Apart from their huge economic significance (they are an intolerable block to a lucrative market), they have remained an ideological thorn in the body of contemporary capitalism. In the UK in the 1980s the commodity form entered the NHS with a vengeance, marking a fundamental shift in attitude to dependence upon the state. In the paper referred to above I put it as follows:

> The welfare state does not provide people with the basic necessities of life as part of a duty of state but instead is a mechanism by which people are disempowered, creating in them a helpless state of invalidism. The "have-nots" instead of "getting on their bikes" and competing in the marketplace [like real men], stay at home and whinge for the nanny state to do something for them. (Bell, 1996, p. 48)

Here appropriate state provision is perversely twisted into its contemptuous representation as "nanny".

The primitive morality evinced here has the qualities of an archaic super-ego. Here, I believe, we see enacted on a wide social canvas, the processes Herbert Rosenfeld (1971) termed as "destructive narcissism". Rosenfeld worked with some very tormented individuals who functioned as if they had submitted to an internal propagandistic system that idealises a kind of mad self-sufficiency—it confuses ordinary need and dependence with helpless invalidism, both being viewed with hatred and contempt. He recognised that this process has a kind of inner momentum and is associated with a peculiar excitement. In the guise of offering protection it lures the self into ever more destruction while projecting the hated dependency and vulnerability elsewhere.

Attacks on the welfare state (i.e. attacks on awareness of human need and vulnerability), coupled with the idealisation of the market forces, supported by the delusion of the autonomous individual, produce profound alienation, denial of the role of social values, and contempt for ordinary human vulnerability. The hated dependency is projected elsewhere—onto those on benefits, refugees, "welfare tourists", and so on.

These massive shifts in the way the human world is construed impact upon mental health in a number of distinct ways that are, however, interrelated:

- Transformations in conceptions of personhood
- New conceptions as to the aims/aspirations of psychological services
- The reconfiguration of the workplace (impacting directly on the mental health of the workforce and thus indirectly upon those in their care)
- Cuts to funding and transformation of mental health/psychiatric services.

I will take these in turn.

A major feature of that world which characterises neoliberalism is to be found in its lack of depth. The neoliberal individual, *Homo oeconomicus*, exists on a horizontal plane; his identity is abstracted from its mooring in history and social structure.

And once one has recognised this horizontality one sees just how widespread is its influence and expression. It is no coincidence that this horizontality, the loss of vertical and historical dimensions, has come to dominate our thinking—as the best example of horizontality is to be found in the market itself. For the market, everything is, necessarily, judged on how it is valued *now*—that value may be a prediction of future value but that is only of interest in terms of how it influences *current* value.

As this market form comes to dominate our self (mis)understanding it contaminates our conceptions of personhood. The aim of the individual becomes less thought of as personal fulfilment through social connectedness, toleration of the ordinary unhappinesses of life, as a source of inner strength—a more tragic view—and transforms into the *acquisition of qualities* (such as happiness) conceived as a kind of personal management exercise. One has a set of assets, and management of those assets, that is to say maximising them, is like managing a business portfolio. One's relation to the world here is not defined by social norms and responsibilities to which one must adjust, but rather, the world *is a store of resources* to be used in the service of self-optimisation. This characterisation has a strange resonance to what we normally describe as deep narcissistic/perverse pathology.

The aims of the aims of psychology services

The aims of the aims of psychology services are necessarily deeply affected by this re-construal of individual happiness, as Binkley (2013) puts it (quoted in Sugarman, 2015, p. 109):

> [Happiness] is not a state of being, a relation sustained responsibly with others, but a life resource whose potential resides at the disposal of a sovereign, enterprising, self-interested actor.
>
> We are told to rid ourselves of inherited interdependencies resulting from excessive welfarist social policies of a previous governmentality … we are enjoined to extricate ourselves from a legacy of interdependencies and the misbegotten beliefs that perpetuate them:[6] the importance of mutual commitments, social cohesion, and collective responsibility …

And also:

> … the road to personal fulfilment is paved with the same stones as those leading to success for businesses and other institutions,

namely, becoming more independent and self-sufficient, enterprising, competitive, flexible, adaptable, risk-seeking, less reliant on government support, and oriented toward pursuing self-interest in a society reconceived in the image of a market.

The ideological function here is clear: individual health and misery are configured as exercises in personal risk management and thus sheared away from their deep roots in social/cultural forces that shape us; this individualisation of misery brings in its shadow feelings of guilt and shame, and support the neutralisation of those perceptions that might bring collaborative socio-political understanding and action.

Here those of us involved in mental health (maybe particularly psychotherapists) need to be keenly mindful, for we are under pressure to participate in the degradation of our profession into technologies of control. CBT clearly has an advantage for it can be easily represented as a personal thought management exercise.

The corrosion of dignity of the workforce

Much of this section draws on an earlier paper already alluded to: Jeff Sugarman, "Neoliberalism and Psychological Ethics" (2015).

Sugarman asks, quoting Sennett:

> How do we decide what is of lasting value in ourselves in a society which is impatient, which focuses on the immediate moment? But, as Sennett (1998) observes, (in)flexible capitalism experience drifts in time, from place to place, job to job, and contract to contract. In lives composed of fragments, episodes, instrumental values, and where career is no longer a meaningful concept.

Sugarman (p. 106) also draws from Freeman (2010):

> Life narratives are not merely registers of events. They bestow temporal logic and coherence—ordering the progress of life in time, furnishing hindsight, foresight, and insight, rendering explanations for why things happen, and providing for the integrity of self and identity ... the neoliberal context of employment is perpetually transitional. It demands and exploits a workforce that is global, disembedded, mobile, and flexible. ...

In many sectors, lifelong vocations are being replaced by job portfolios composed of short-term projects and contracts. "Knowledge and skill based on a personal narrative of development degrade into a definable competency—a fragmentation of identity" (Sennett, 1998, quoted in Sugarman, 2015, p. 106).

In this atmosphere of temporariness and cut-throat competition, a sense of vision, of building of services, collapses as the view narrows down to a primitive survivalism. Many National Health Service employees find themselves using the word "survival" every day—"What can we do ... we have to survive." And this survivalist mentality invades all aspects of thinking. Protest about the cutting of resources, or the simplified pragmatic solutions that involve giving up long-held ideals, are quickly squashed, with the question, "Do you, or don't you, want to survive?" Recently, a National Health Service hospital was put under great pressure to increase bed numbers and turnover in order to increase income.[7] As there was no residual space for beds, it was suggested that the nurses' study be turned into a small ward. The study realised a very important psychological function for the nurses: it was one of the few places where they met and relaxed together, away from the constant stress of contact with patients. When one of the nurses complained about the loss of this valuable place, she was immediately asked, in an intimidating manner, as if she was asking for some indulgent luxury, "Do you or do you not want this unit to survive?"

The daily existence of those working in health and education and elsewhere in the public sector is one of constant threat, as they are pressured to meet targets; flooded with the anxiety of survival and forced to sell themselves in a world where the representation of services takes precedence over any actuality, a world where, as Mark Fisher (2009) has so aptly put it, "All that is solid melts into PR."

The digitalised world provides the perfect vehicle for a further major step in the instrumentalisation of our daily life—continuous survey/surveillance. In the public sector staff are flooded with online tasks they are compelled to fulfil, not because of their intrinsic worth but in order that the organisation can register that x per cent of employees have fulfilled the obligatory requirements—non-fulfilment might be punished by a reduction in the organisation's status.

In both public and private sectors every customer is requested to rate the worker. Workers even ask their customers directly to rate them; these ratings are then fed back to the worker through electronic, rather than human structures. Thus the (at least potentially) human relationship between manager/employee is replaced by the online survey—a form of continuous amorphous surveillance from which there is no escape.

This process seems to make an external reality of Freud's (1930a) description of the superego as evincing a kind of inhuman relentlessness, like a terrible internal "panopticon" which is inescapable.

Freud writes: "Civilization therefore obtains mastery over the individual's dangerous desire for aggression by weakening and disarming it *and* by setting up an agency within him … like a garrison in a conquered city" (p. 124).

… and absolute submission is required.

Inevitably, staff are in danger of prioritising the need for good personal ratings over their professional responsibilities. (Health professionals, and maybe particularly *mental* health professionals, have, as a difficult part of their work, the obligation to discuss matters which their patient may wish to avoid, and discussion of such matters may lead to lower performance ratings.)

This atmosphere of threat of punishment (for example through not meeting targets) flows downwards through the system creating severe anxiety at every level … and upwards from the user survey. The professional is thus caught in the middle of a pincer movement.

These surveys and performance assessments, again, exist only horizontally, ahistorically; they are always snapshots, not films.

In many workplaces there is a kind of acknowledgement of the mental suffering caused by these degradations in the workplace, through the provision of staff programmes (via an army of happiness experts) which, however, inevitably serve to support the idea that the solution of the misery is to be found within the individual and thus attention is directed away from its deeper causes. The demand that workers derive real fulfilment from their work, a demand that might bring them together in facing a common problem, transforms into technologies of well-being and happiness.

It is a strange conjunction in history, that just at the point where the wall came down in Berlin and we saw the end of Stalinism, we seem to have created a bizarre combination of a (so-called) free market economy shackled to a Stalinist control through continuous surveillance, performance indicators, and rewards systems, while the workforce keep their sanity with a kind of samizdat culture.

Mental illness and its treatment today

Apart from the impoverishment in the structure and scale of the health services available to them, mentally ill people in England have been deeply affected by these transformations of our sociocultural life. The hatred of ordinary human dependency (a constant of our nature) described above has long been the staple fare of some tabloid papers, but at our current historical juncture this kind of primitive thinking has been adopted by political leaders, giving it a new power. And this mentality can exert a certain bewitching attraction for masses of the population who come to support it, either through identification with it, or by submission, a submission as often as not borne of despair. This binary world of good and bad has seeped into public consciousness on a massive scale as people have gathered behind the conservative slogan of "strivers" (good working people like us) versus "skivers" (parasites who cheat, draining away our precious resources).

At the 2012 Conservative Party Conference, this evocative image was used by the Chancellor, George Osborne.

> Where is the fairness, we ask, for the shift worker, leaving home in the dark hours of the early morning, who looks up at the closed blinds of their next-door neighbour sleeping off a life on benefits? (quoted in *The Guardian*, August 1, 2013)

This whipping up of hatred lives off the illusion that very high levels of financial loss result from false claims, whereas in reality they are of hardly any budgetary significance, thus revealing the purely ideological nature of this movement.[8]

Our inner secret contempt for dependence (our own and others) is here given a wide public canvas; the flames of hatred are fanned. Even those who have nothing objectively to gain from this perverse ideology, those who are legitimately entitled to benefit, nevertheless internalise this scenario and so come to identify with this degraded version of themselves—they believe that the very fact that they require support *really is* evidence of their inferiority and so succumb to viewing themselves through the internalised contemptuous eyes of their oppressors. They see themselves as having failed, as being parasites on society and undeserving, and collapse into despair.[9]

The previously unthinkable becomes quotidian: for example, the imposition of a cap on housing benefits, forcing families to vacate their homes, fuels the sense that they do not deserve to live there. Attempting to turn nurses and doctors into border guards to "catch health tourists" results in acutely ill patients being asked to sign papers guaranteeing payment before being treated, and being informed that failure to pay may result in deportation (even where rights to remain are subsequently granted).[10] And these changes are driven through at such breathtaking speed that it is difficult to remain aware of their massive impact on vulnerable people, and of the erosion of our ordinary sense of responsibility for others.

Those who are mentally ill are peculiarly vulnerable to these broader sociocultural changes. For there is a default position in relation to the mentally ill which requires continuous work to resist, namely that they are responsible for their illness; a position that of course easily fits into the characteristic self-righteousness of the mindset just described. Any economic[11] crisis similarly affects the mentally ill in a variety of different ways which reinforce each other. Unemployment, widening inequality, loss of job security, and economic hardship all cause increased psychological morbidity in the population, and those who are already mentally ill are particularly affected.

Work capability assessments

The work capability assessment (and the various different forms it takes) is an authorised surveillance system aimed at servicing the notion that there are a large number of people who for their own personal gain falsely claim benefits ("the scroungers")—there is no evidence that such a group is of any relevance to the economy of the health service. Mentally ill people are particularly disadvantaged here, as few of those carrying out the assessments have any knowledge of mental illness or any understanding of how the process of assessment so regularly traumatises mentally ill people. I have known a number of patients suffering from enduring mental illness who feel so persecuted by the WCA process that terror of it comes to dominate their mental state. It needs to be understood here that many people who are mentally ill are already, internally, persecuted by a terrible kind of inner self-judgement that relentlessly tells them they are worthless, filling them with humiliation and shame.[12] In this situation, the person needs to find reassurance in external reality that provides some degree of protection/insulation against this inner persecution. But the WCA process itself, and in particular the assumptions which it has come to embody—that those on benefits are trying to get away with something, the whole atmosphere of distrust of claimants—creates an external reality that far from providing reassurance, reinforces these menacing internal processes.

I have known patients with serious mental illness who inform the panel that they are "feeling much better and are ready to work". This is of course not based on any real assessment of their own capacities, but arises from a wish to prove themselves "worthy". However, the panel are quick to accept such statements as it is not in the nature of the exercise to question their veracity, or to discuss them with the mental health professionals who know the patient. Other patients, because they are so terrified, just do not manage to attend the assessment. There are cases of people dying not long after disability assessment had considered them fit for work, including cases of suicide.[13]

Changes in the care of patients with serious mental illness

As regards inpatient care I can best use some of my own experiences to show the contrast between how it was, say, twenty-five years ago, and how it is now. Twenty-five years ago occupancy rates on inpatient wards were about 80%, which is generally agreed to be about right, that is, on a twenty-bed word sixteen or seventeen beds would be occupied. This allowed nurses to have more time with patients, and time for teaching or discussion of difficult issues. Less than a quarter of the patients were detained compulsorily. Patients released from compulsory status always stayed on the ward. This was a crucial period for establishing the vital therapeutic relationships with the staff, as it is obviously very difficult to establish such relationships with patients held against their will.

Patients would stay for a number of weeks or months. They would prepare for discharge by going home for a trial period and then would return to the ward to report to their key workers on how they had got on. And even after complete discharge they would return to meet informally with the staff. The individual would be seen in the outpatient clinic by the same team that had admitted him or her as an inpatient, as it was understood that continuity of care is of central importance—patients feel safer with those who have known them at their worst and share with them a knowledge of their history.

Now the current situation. Bed occupancy rates are very often over 100%, even up to 120%.[14] This means that wards are overcrowded and that the beds of patients on leave (even for one or two days) are immediately taken by other patients, regardless of the impact on the returning patients, who are then moved to vacant beds potentially in other wards or even in other hospitals. Acutely psychotic patients are sometimes given mattresses on the floor. Patients are discharged[15] well before they are ready (partly because of the pressure on beds), and the result is often early readmission.

And instead of only a minority of patients being held compulsorily, the majority of patients on the ward are now in this category. Not only must the few available beds be given to the most acutely ill, but there is even some evidence of patients being held "on a section" simply to ensure they will be given a bed.[16] And as soon as these patients move to voluntary status the pressures to discharge them, to free up beds, are impossible to resist, so that patients are regularly discharged before they can really manage. A BBC *Panorama* programme (broadcast October 26, 2015) gave a disturbing but not atypical picture of a mental health hospital (Barnet). We saw nurses, trying to function under enormous pressures created by the cuts, being ordered by the managers to discharge patients who were less ill (they had long given up the criteria of "well enough") in order to free up beds. This sort of quotidian crisis derives in large part from structural features of the NHS where managers are judged, more than anything else, on their capacity to come in on budgetary target (a budget ever decreasing in the climate of cuts). Where staff or patients draw attention to the human costs, these deficiencies are reframed as resulting from bad management so avoiding the systemic critique.

These factors have very powerful negative effects on the ward atmosphere: wards are overcrowded with acutely psychotic patients. No wonder that patients and psychiatrists try to avoid admissions to this very disturbing environment.[17]

The high intensity of the atmosphere on wards, coupled with the declining capacity to contain this disturbance, creates a toxic environment that of course impacts upon the mental states of the patients.[18] However, deterioration in any particular patient is most unlikely to be understood as related to these systemic causes. Instead, it will be recorded in terms only of the individual factors in the patient—seen as indicating not a need for a more containing environment but for increased medication.[19]

Further, overcrowding and high turnover of patients have a massive impact on the nursing staff. The labour process is intensified, and the space for reflection and carrying out the "emotional labour" which is a crucial part of nursing is compromised, resulting, again, in a lowering of morale and in many cases, burnout.

Nomothetic and ideographic levels of description

The changes in the care of the mentally ill discussed above have inevitably been accompanied by changes in the way mental illness is conceptualised, and perhaps nowhere is this more evident than in the loss of the tension between the nomothetic and ideographic levels of description.

The nomothetic refers to the grouping together of objects that share certain similarities (for example fruits, twentieth-century literature, borderline patients, sonata form, borderline transference), whereas the ideographic gives emphasis to the unique characters of the individual object. So when we talk of "this or that kind" of patient we iron over the huge differences there are between them. However, rational discourse necessitates some degree of nomothetic description.

Psychiatry has in the past tended, at least to some degree, to accept this duality of description. I can remember for example when I was studying psychiatry more that one of my consultants insisted on hearing the patient's history *as a narrative*.

However, in the accelerating impoverishment of psychiatric thought, this tension has been almost lost—that is, there is a pressure to regard patients purely in terms of diagnosis, with pre-prescribed "care pathways" (I have written about this elsewhere, including its sources in the commodification/marketisation of mental health care (see Bell, 2018)).

A core quality of the psychoanalytic approach, in contrast, is to be found in its capacity to sustain this tension, always preserving an emphasis on the ideographic, whether at the level of the individual person or in the detailed discussion of a particular session.

The transformation of day hospitals

Until relatively recently many patients with enduring mental illness were well managed in day hospitals, which provided a non-toxic environment where they could gradually develop interpersonal skills and receive emotional support in a structured environment, this often requiring many months, often more than a year. However, these centres have now been redesignated as "recovery centres". The implication here is that in a quite limited amount of time, measured in weeks, patients can recover from years of mental illness and return to ordinary living. This peculiar model not only bears little relation to the reality of these patients' difficulties, but also creates a tyranny for the staff. The patients are *supposed* to recover, and there are performance targets against which this will be judged: if they don't recover the conclusion drawn is that the staff have failed.

What is missing here is any recognition that a great deal of the care of those with enduring mental illness is more to do with damage limitation and providing forms of support and care, skills which are now much less valued.

The recognition that patients are damaged by institutionalisation has been twisted into a justification for not providing services they can depend upon.[20] Moreover, day hospitals were staffed by teams, usually established over many years and composed of individuals with high levels of skill. But the de-skilling process, driven by financial pressures, results in patients being looked after by well-intentioned individuals who have virtually no experience of working with the mentally ill. The parallel with the reduction of the skill mix already familiar in social care, and now taking place in NHS hospitals, is clear.[21]

In a perverse logic some of these changes in health care are presented as providing the patient with more freedom to choose the services they want. But patients can't choose a service that has been closed. That is, the "choice agenda" serves to make people feel they have more freedom and to mask the fact that they have less.

Marketising the care of the mentally ill

George Monbiot (2016) captures well a paradox of neoliberalism, namely that universal competition which is hailed as bringing a new kind of freedom, relies upon universal quantification and comparison. The result is that workers, job seekers, and public services of every kind are subject to a stifling regime of assessment and monitoring, designed to identify the winners and punish the losers.

As NHS care is increasingly converted into a healthcare market, provision of care is transformed into marketable products with contracts competed for by rival bidders (NHS and private). This fragmentation of care into discrete marketable packages is particularly inappropriate for chronic disorders, and is in this latter category that much of the care of the mentally ill belongs.[22]

In the case of mental illness it means trying to fit every patient into one of twenty diagnostic "clusters", each with a prescribed package of care, with a price attached. Not surprisingly it is difficult and often impossible to categorise mentally ill patients in this way.

What we are witnessing here is an accelerating commodification and instrumentalisation of mental suffering—it is diagnoses that are treated, not people.

These changes also have a profound effect on the morale of the work force—the most crucial element in health care but one which goes largely without mention in policy documents, which focus on various "skill mixes", but never on the people themselves.

Staff manning wards and services without adequate resources, forced to reapply for their own posts, which have sometimes also been downgraded, as bed numbers, and the staff complements that go with them, are cut, are hardly in a position to maintain the "containment"—that is, the capacity to manage the intense and disturbing interactions involved in the care of these patients, and so withstand pressures to act precipitately and to maintain the capacity to think—that is one of the most vital aspects of the care of the mentally ill.

Many consultants spend a significant part of their time discussing not patients but contracts, responding to pressure to get patients into treatment quickly where a contract is "under-performing" (or where there is even a threat that it may not be renewed, with potentially catastrophic consequences for the department's ability to function). Where contracts are "over-performing"—that is, the service is treating more patients than originally contracted for, perhaps because local GPs are satisfied with it and so are referring increasing numbers of patients—there are very powerful pressures to discharge patients from care.

Conclusion

In conclusion I will step back again to the broader perspective. If we accept that humankind is divided in its nature—on the one hand an irreducible urge to destruction, combined with a wish to be drawn into a world of mindlessness, and, on the other, a reparative wish towards the other, desire for real knowledge and understanding of ourselves and his world—then we can ask:

"What kind of social structures might act to contain our destructiveness and support the more creative and reparative wishes; and, alternatively, what kind of social structures obstruct this capacity and serve the opposite aim, fanning the flames of our destructiveness, or draw us into a world of mindlessness.

Crucial here are those social processes that support denial of our nature, the splitting off of uncomfortable aspects and locating them in others, so reducing our capacity for knowledge and thought.

These processes are opposed by those structures that act to limit projection, bring us into contact with our nature, and so promote integration and recognition of our dependence upon others.

My thesis is that the penetration of the market form into all areas of social functioning and consciousness acts to support the narcissistic sides of our nature and lures us into an amoral, ruthless world of one against all. Non-marketised forms of human engagement put a brake on this process. Nowhere is the conflict between marketised and non-marketised forms of life so hotly contested as in the domain of the public services—last remnant of a form of social existence offering an alternative to the market form.

We have taken an extraordinary step backwards in our attitude towards people with mental illnesses. The several hundred thousand people disabled by depression and anxiety, and the 150,000 with psychotic illnesses, unable to cope with normal life, are increasingly being deprived of adequate services and pushed out to fail and suffer again. A century and a half of advance in our understanding of mental illness, and in our sympathy for its victims, is being brusquely jettisoned. What was once supervision and containment degrades into its perverse residue—surveillance.

Zaretsky (1998) has suggested that a major feature of the social consciousness immediately post-war derived from the entry of the feminine into social consciousness—as seen in the foundation of the welfare state and the caring social structures that evolved with it—this is mirrored in psychoanalysis by the ascendance of the work of Anna Freud, D. W. Winnicott, and Melanie Klein who all brought the maternal relationship into the centre of psychoanalytic understanding and social consciousness. It could I think be argued that the current attack on welfare and forms of care is underwritten by a reassertion of a very destructive phallic power bringing a barely concealed contempt for care equated with a degraded femininity (as manifest for example in the term "nanny state".

To marginalise and neglect the needs of sick people in this way would be judged intolerable if applied to the physically ill.

If we are serious about caring for people who are mentally ill we need a lot more than righteous assertions of "parity of esteem" which have no real content. Some basic principles must be reasserted. Resources for these most vulnerable members of the population must be restored. Bed occupancy rates for inpatients need to get down to 80% and patients need to be able to remain voluntarily in hospital long enough to establish therapeutic relationships with staff. Continuity of care must be restored, so that those looking after patients as inpatients continue to look after them in the community. Day hospitals must be reinstated to their original mission of caring for people on a long-term basis, accepting that many of them will need permanent support. Work Capability Assessments, given that their function is purely ideological and does not serve any real material function, should be stopped. But if they are to continue then recommendations for the mentally ill patients must be based on opinions of professionals who have knowledge of psychiatric illness and who have real understanding for their patients' needs. The myth that everyone can and must recover—and in short order—must be dropped. We have to recognise that much of the care of the mentally ill centres upon damage limitation and rehabilitation, but not on cure.

Each of us in our workplaces experiences in microcosm a version of this peculiar world I outlined at the beginning of this chapter. Without realising it we perform conflicts which reflect the tensions and transformation going on in the socio-political world around us. Perhaps nowhere is this clearer than the pressure to dismantle the forms of communal cooperation, the commitment to an idea of public service and social justice, which were part of the founding purposes of the NHS. We witness the daily burden of trying to do our job in an atmosphere of survivalism and projection of anxiety downward which we have to constantly resist … Individuals carry a massive amount of responsibility that seeps into their daily lives, but without the requisite authority.

It seems to me that it is a kind of miracle that we have managed to sustain reasonable morale.

A major task for all of us at all levels must be to try to limit the damage that inevitably results from the destructive processes I have described and support each other in preserving our professional integrity and the values that are so central in our work.

Notes

1. The expression "There is no alternative" (TINA) was a slogan often used by Margaret Thatcher. The phrase was used to signify the claim that the market economy is the only system that works, and that debate about this is over.

2. I have put this term in quotation marks to highlight the fact this freedom is entirely illusory—for the functioning of the market is absolutely dependent on the framework of state provision. This becomes most starkly manifest whenever there is an economic crisis, for example in 2008 when the state bailed out financial institutions in the UK and the US (see also footnote 5).

3. Hence the preference for marketing happiness rather than management of mental pain.

4. That is, it eliminates the reality of the network of social relations that we all depend upon for our very existence.

5. J. M. Bernstein (2010) has suggested that, particularly in the American context, dependency on the state can be tolerated only as long as it is invisible. The state's massive bail-out of the banks removed this invisibility and forced awareness onto the American psyche of this utter dependence on the state. He views the Tea Party movement as an expression of rage at this fact of life, and championing the myth of the autonomous individual as an attempt to deny it. He writes:

   > My hypothesis is that what all the events precipitating the Tea Party movement share is that they demonstrated, emphatically and unconditionally, the depths of the absolute dependence of us all on government action, and in so doing they undermined the deeply held fiction of individual autonomy and self-sufficiency that are intrinsic parts of Americans' collective self-understanding. [Their] great and inspiring metaphysical fantasy of independence and freedom is simply a fantasy of destruction.

6. The phallic quality of this discourse is easily apparent.

7. This material was brought to me as part of a service consultation but I need to protect, for obvious reasons, the confidentiality of my source.

8. As many have noted, this is also a displacement, given that the burden of private debt is of far more significance than public debt. But whereas public debt is a moral category—private debt is a purely practical matter to be managed in the most economic way.

9. The catchword "nanny state" perfectly expresses this perverse logic and hatred of vulnerability.

10. NHS Trusts are since 2017 legally obliged to take measures to prevent those who do not have the appropriate immigration status from receiving treatment. There is no evidence that the treatment of refugees and immigrants who may belong to this category has any significant economic impact—its function is purely ideological, to help prime the sense that there are those (like us) who are entitled and those "like them" who should be left to die. See for example, from the Whittington hospital website, a "Pre-Attendance Form" (https://www.whittington.nhs.uk/document.ashx?id=5950). This hospital may need to ask the Home Office to confirm your immigration status to help it decide if you are eligible for free NHS hospital treatment. In this case, your personal, non-clinical information will be sent to the Home Office. The information provided may be used and retained by the Home Office for its functions, which include enforcing immigration controls overseas, at the ports of entry, and within the UK. The Home Office may also share this information with other law enforcement and authorised debt recovery agencies for purposes including national security, investigation and prosecution of crime, and collection of fines and civil penalties.

 If you are chargeable but fail to pay for NHS treatment for which you have been billed, it may result in a future immigration application to enter or remain in the UK being denied. Necessary (non-clinical) personal information may be passed via the Department of Health to the Home Office for this purpose.

11. I try to avoid the term "financial" or "economic" crisis as these terms serve to support the notion that this is something to do with arithmetic and not politics.

12. In technical language one would say that a very harsh persecuting superego is a very common feature of mental illness.

13. See https://www.google.co.uk/search?hl=en&gl=uk&tbm=nws&authuser=0&q=suicide+after+atos+deemed+mentally+ill+fit+for+work&oq=suicide+after+atos+deemed+mentally+ill+fit+for+work&gs_l=news-cc.3..43j43i53.850.9320.0.9582.57.3.3.51.

14. See http://www.guardian.co.uk/society/2011/jun/20/mental-health-services-in-crisis-over-staff-shortages.

15. See, for example, http://www.mirror.co.uk/news/uk-news/vulnerable-mental-health-patients-forced-2343568.

16. House of Commons Health Committee Post-legislative scrutiny of the Mental Health Act 2007 First Report of Session 2013–14, paras 27-33, http://www.publications.parliament.uk/pa/cm201314/cmselect/cmhealth/584/584.pdf.

17. I have known a psychiatrist faced with the problem of a patient who would agree to be admitted to hospital X as a voluntary patient but not hospital Y (and

the psychiatrist understood why, given the appalling conditions in hospital Y). The result was that the patient had to be admitted on an involuntary basis, that is, under a Section, to hospital Y.

18. There is a vast amount of evidence that psychotic patients are highly sensitive to the emotional intensity of their environment.

19. Arthur Crisp (personal communication) who was professor of psychiatry at St George's Hospital in the 1980s, carried out a very simple and elegant research exercise. He kept a daily record of disturbing events on the ward and showed that the number of such events increased with a regularity as the day of the ward round loomed up and receded immediately afterwards. What this demonstrated so clearly was that although it may have seemed that the immediate cause lay in factors to do with the individual patient, the more important aetiological factor was to be found in this purely social factor.

20. The Care Quality Commission's 2011 Mental Health Survey in the community found that 31 per cent of respondents who needed support from someone in NHS mental health services for their physical health needs said that they had not received support but would have liked it. Some 42 per cent of respondents received care under a Care Programme Approach—an approach which should include support on housing, employment, and financial advice. However, the survey found that 35 per cent had not received any help with finding or keeping work; 27 per cent had not received any help with finding or keeping accommodation; 27 per cent had not been given any help with financial advice or benefits (cited in Mental Health Network/NHS Confederation Factsheet November 2011).

21. The Centre for Health and the Public Interest, *The Future of the NHS: Lessons from Social Care*, October 2013, para 35.

22. Integration across physical, psychiatric, and social services vital for the needs of the mentally ill becomes nearly impossible in a marketised system.

References

Anderson, P. (1998). *The Origins of Postmodernity* (p. 21). London: Verso.

Bell, D. (1996). Primitive mind of state. *Psychoanalytic Psychotherapy, 10*(1): 45–57.

Bell, D. (2018). Introduction: Against the tide. In: Meyerowitz, R., & Bell, D., *Turning the Tide: The Psychoanalytic Approach of the Fitzjohn's Unit to Patients with Complex Needs*. London: Karnac.

Bernstein, J. M. (2010, June 13). The very angry Tea Party. *The New York Times*.

Binkley, S. (2013). *Happiness as enterprise: An essay on neoliberal life*. Albany, NY: SUNY Press.

Davies, W. (2018). What are they after? *London Review of Books, 40*(5): 3–5.

Fisher, M. (2009). *Capitalist Realism. Is There No Alternative?* Southampton, UK: Zero.

Freeman, M. (2010). *Hindsight: The Promise and Peril of Looking Backward.* New York: Oxford University Press.

Freud, S. (1930a). *Civilization and Its Discontents. S. E., 21.* London: Hogarth.

Jameson, F. (1991). *Postmodernism, or, the Cultural Logic of Late Capitalism.* London: Verso.

Marx, K. (1867). *Capital: A Critique of Political Economy.* London: Penguin Classics, 1990.

Meyerowitz, R., & Bell, D. (2018). *Turning the Tide: The Psychoanalytic Approach of the Fitzjohn's Unit to Patients with Complex Needs.* London: Karnac.

Monbiot, G. (2016, April 15). Neoliberalism—the ideology at the root of all our problems. *The Guardian.*

Rosenfeld, H. (1971). A clinical approach to the psychoanalytic theory of the life and death instincts: An investigation into the aggressive aspects of narcissism. *International Journal of Psychoanalysis, 52*: 169–178.

Segal, H. (1995). From Hiroshima to the Gulf War and after: Socio-political expressions of ambivalence. In: H. Segal (1997), *Psychoanalysis, Literature and War. Papers 1972–1995* (pp. 157–168). J. Steiner (Ed.). London: Routledge.

Sennett, R. (1998). *The Corrosion of Character: The Personal Consequences of Work in the New Capitalism.* New York: W. W. Norton.

Sugarman, J. (2015). Neoliberalism and psychological ethics. *Journal of Theoretical and Philosophical Psychology, 35*(2): 103–116.

Williams, R. (1977). *Marxism and Literature.* Oxford: Oxford University Press.

Zaretsky, E. (1998). Melanie Klein and the emergence of modern personal life. In: L. Stonebridge & J. Phillips (Eds.), *Reading Melanie Klein.* New York: Routledge.

CHAPTER SIX

Toleration of strangers

Roger Kennedy

Introduction

The sense of home as the ground of our being, the place we need in order to feel secure, is fundamental. Whatever the nature of the home we seek, the fear of homelessness is never far from that of the sense of being at home. I will argue that a fear of a loss of home, or more fundamentally a fear of a loss of a psychic structure which provides a central core of our identity—a "psychic home" (Kennedy, 2014)—accounts for a certain amount of prejudiced and intolerant attitudes to refugees and migrants; that basic fears about being displaced by so-called "strangers" from our precious and precarious sense of a psychic home can tear communities apart, as well as lead to discrimination against those who appear to be different. However, it is not an easy process for the stranger to become integrated into a new community, and I shall propose that a "tolerance process" is required, involving a number of steps, some of course practical but others more crucially involving psychological shifts from both the newcomers and "oldcomers".

Home and homelessness

If one is to understand the place of homelessness in the human psyche or soul, then Freud's paper on "The 'uncanny'"—*das Unheimliche*, the "unhomely"—is fundamental. The word *das Heimliche* in German can be traced back to what is homelike, what belongs to the house, but also something that becomes concealed, withdrawn from the eyes of strangers (1919h, p. 225). Ultimately, the uncanny is something which is secretly familiar and has undergone repression and then returned from it (p. 245)—hence the double feeling of the strange and the unfamiliar that is indicative of an uncanny experience.

There is an uneasy tension in the modern soul between feeling at home and feeling estranged. This tension is revealed in uncanny experiences, which remind us of the precariousness of our hard-won sense of psychic organisation. Michel de M'Uzan (2005) emphasises how uncanny experiences commemorate a crucial phase in the development of psychic functioning, a moment which brings to the fore the indeterminate nature of identity, when the self becomes "strange" to itself.

The latter point resonates with Julia Kristeva's meditation on the stranger—*Strangers to Ourselves* (1991). She writes that with Freud, an uncanny foreignness creeps into the tranquillity of reason. "Henceforth, we know that we are foreigners to ourselves, and it is with the help of that sole support that we can attempt to live with others" (p. 170). That is, we are *our own foreigners*, strangers to ourselves, divided, and estranged. Psychoanalysis is a "journey into the strangeness of the other and of oneself, towards an ethics of respect for the irreconcilable. How could one tolerate a foreigner if one did not know one was a stranger to oneself?" (p. 182). One could indeed say that in order to listen psychoanalytically at all requires one to abandon the familiar so as to be receptive to the strange and unfamiliar.

Yet it is only with the greatest of efforts at times that we can learn to tolerate both the strange within and the stranger without.

The myth of the stranger as different, strange, weird, uncanny, can make people feel not "at home" with strangers, seeing them as potential threats to identity rather than as potential allies. They bring their own ways of life, their habits and customs, or their "habitus", to quote Bourdieu (1990, p. 53), that is, their durable, transportable dispositions, their feel for their own fields of cultural practice, which may or may not overlap with the fields of practice of the indigenous population. Equally those already at home in their country can forget that the history of many European countries involves waves of mass migration, going back thousands of years. This history reveals how identity is not a fixed entity, but fluid, hybrid, and complex.

Of course, identity matters in immediate and indeed practical ways. For example, if you wish to renew your UK passport, you now have to apply to HM Passport Office, which will authenticate your personal details and confirm your identity as a UK citizen, or not. Having a home is vital to this. Without an address, you cannot really be a citizen. This dilemma was especially poignant after the Second World War. Tony Judt (2005) has charted in his groundbreaking book *Postwar*, how there took place then a massive movement of millions of people, due to the aftermath of the fighting and displacement of communities, the opening up of the concentration camps and also the civil wars that soon took place in what became communist Europe. Not only had there been, as a result of Stalin and Hitler, the uprooting, transplanting, and deportation of some 30 million people between 1939 and 1944, but after the war Europe had to deal with an unprecedented exercise in ethnic cleansing and population transfer. Untold millions were displaced or were refugees. The distinction between displaced persons, assumed to have a home to go to somewhere, and refugees, who were classified as homeless, was one of the many nuances that were introduced by the authorities trying to deal with this trauma, whose legacy remains to this day, marking the European identity. Yet there are places in Europe where this history has either been forgotten or just erased, so that all those wishing to enter European space are lumped together as one threatening entity.

The psychic home

In order to clarify a *psychoanalytic* contribution to the current political and social unrest in Europe, I will look at how the place of a psychic home can add a dimension to the understanding of conflict between people from different geographical areas. I would suggest that having a psychic home, an internal sense of a secure home base, is a key feature of identity. The psychic home provides an organising psychic structure for the sense of emerging identity. Such a home base must be built up from a number of different elements, as with the physical home, which forms its substrate. There are intrapsychic elements but also intersubjective elements, involving the social world.

1) There is the basic structure of a home as a protected and hopefully welcoming space for shelter, providing the core of the internalised psychic home. The physical space of the home has an important function in helping to shape the interior life. One may say that the psychic home has a dual aspect—as both physical and psychical container. The boundaries of the house also have to be seen in context, within a community of

other homes, and within a society. The home must be permeable to external influences, or else it will become the source of unreal relationships, including intolerance *of strangers*, who are perceived as threats to the precarious psychic home.

2) There is already a pre-established intersubjective symbolic space predating the building or setting up of the home. The home-to-be already has a place in the family history and narrative, already situated as an element in a complicated network of relationships. There is a lineage, reaching back generations.

3) The contents of the psychic home, its mental furniture, consist essentially of identifications with family members making up the home's interior. In the secure home, the parents provide continuity over time in their home making, providing a supportive base for the children to eventually leave, and ultimately to build up their own home. A stable psychic home involves individuals being recognised as being autonomous yet dependent, and receiving respect for their identity. For such people, the stranger can be a source of positive curiosity not a threat to their stability.

4) The ordinary home consists of activities; it is not a static or frozen entity. What could be called the "work of the day" (Kennedy, 2007, pp. 246–260) takes place within the home. This refers to significant events, which require thought and/or action.

Thus one can see how the notion of a *psychic home* consists of a number of different and interacting elements, including the physical interior of a home but internalised as a psychic interior. I am suggesting that the basic elements of the psychic home can be seen to provide a way of organising the person's identity, or can be seen as intrinsic to any notion of identity.

The psychic home in psychoanalytic treatment

Like our patients, we psychoanalysts carry our psychic home with us, though it will manifest itself differently. We may not reveal details of our private life to our patients, but we carry our psychic home with us into the session. Our choice of interior design of the consulting room, not to mention the books and any objects, may well reflect the nature of our psychic home; there is an interaction between the subjectivity of the analyst and the interior space where he or she works. An alive psychic home can provide a sustaining space for the analyst, allowing the analyst to cope with the inevitable loneliness of the work.

While the analytic work carries on in separate localities, that of analyst and that of the patient, they do intertwine in various ways, in a dynamic fashion. Sometimes the analyst may find that the psychic home is invaded by the patient, with little space to think or feel; or else there may be a confusion of spaces, with little sense of a boundaried psychic home. These experiences may occur at once or take time to develop through the strange unfolding of the transference and countertransference. A patient comes into our consulting room for the first meeting. We may have spoken to the patient briefly on the telephone, or communicated by email, and perhaps found out a little about the individual, either directly or from a referring colleague. But the fact is, both analyst and patient are strangers to one another in a number of ways, both with regard to knowing about their lives and cultures, but also with regard to their strange inner life. We provide a potential home for the expression of this inner life, for the engagement of the analyst's and patient's psychic homes.

In psychoanalytic treatments, one can see the notion of a psychic home in a variety of ways. Here is a brief example from my own practice.

Mrs X now has a good home, with a stable family, but she never feels secure in herself; she carries around inside some deep anxieties, linked to the experiences of her early life. Her parents split up when she was very young, her mother soon remarried and then the patient was sent to boarding school soon after. Until the analysis, she had never questioned what had led to the break-up of the family, or why she was sent away from home. She carries around quite a fragile sense of a psychic home, afraid of expressing dependent feelings, and quite emotionally inhibited as a person.

She struggled for a long time with the analytic setting. She wanted to come to sessions, but as soon as she arrived, feelings of dread and despair would quickly arise, making, as she said, the couch uncomfortable. She managed her discomfort by a sort of freezing, with her body stiff and immobile on the couch. The analytic setting for a long time thus became a necessary but dreaded place. She would often wonder why she wanted to come, when on entering the consulting room she would feel so awful.

One of the main themes was an almost complete absence of early home memories, particularly after the break-up of her parents' marriage. She could recall losing a precious soft toy, and that her mother took her to an expensive store to replace it, but no substitute was found to be suitable, though she made do with some hard toys. However, bit by bit over the years, some early scenes came to her mind, after we had gone over some of the difficult feelings she experienced at boarding school. There, she often felt lonely, cut off, and not one of the groups. She began to make connections with some of her current fears about intimacy and those boarding school experiences. One session seemed to convey something of a turning point. It was the first time that she had made a stand about coming to her analysis.

She began in a fairly animated way. She was annoyed because at work there was a new computer system, and she had been told that she will have to set aside some full days to learn it. That would mean missing both personal commitments and her analytic sessions. She was angered by her (female) manager who expected this of her. However, she was not going to go along with this and would leave early to come to her sessions. My patient was also annoyed that she herself was made to feel neglectful by not going along with her work's expectations.

I was immediately struck by her making sure she would come to her analysis despite the pressure to miss out.

She was also worrying about a vulnerable client who was angry about having his invalidity benefit removed. She was not sure what he would do to himself. There were also worries about a close family member who was ill and still in hospital.

I said that she was telling me about a number of outside pressures that had to be overcome. She did overcome them when she had decided she would come to her analysis.

She said that in fact her manager was normally reasonable, but what annoyed my patient was that the manager herself was being put under pressure from above but she could not stand up to it. My patient did not want to be the one who made a fuss. She feared both standing out and any retaliation—the latter was a real fear, as someone in the team had in fact been effectively excluded for making a fuss previously.

I said: "You mean, do people make a fuss, or do they have to put up with whatever comes their way?"

This comment made her think of a member of her family who had gone into hospital recently and had to put up with poor treatment and incompetent staff.

(I was thinking, "Do I put up with her or make a fuss? What kind of manager/analyst am I for her? How competent am I?")

She continued—her family member would not find out what was happening to him. Typical for her family, who just gave themselves to the doctors.

I said: "Well, there is a doctor here, and maybe you fear giving yourself up to me."

She agreed. She talked about it being difficult here, with issues of control and power. She has to fit in with the holiday dates I had recently given her. Though she also sees they are reasonable, given the reality of the summer holidays and her own children's school dates. But there is an imbalance of power. She cannot make me say things. She does not know when I will say things. She wants me to say more. She has "zero control" over me. She added that she often had a sense of deprivation here; she felt deprived for much of the time.

After a pause, she said that she was having thoughts about mothers and babies, and all that babies get from their mothers in terms of physical contact and visual stimulation, as much as talking.

I linked what she told me about her own possible early depriving experiences as a baby or young child, with a mother who came and went, and how she could not make a fuss, she had to put up with what she was given, the hard toys for the soft ones.

She said that when I do speak she can feel in contact, and that does give her enough to keep going, but the feeling of deprivation is still often there. So she felt better about being here, even though it was also difficult.

I acknowledged what she had told me and then finished the session.

While of course there were many different elements to the session and to what was going on in the analysis at that time, I would point to the fact that it was a new experience for her to take a stand about her sessions. This did seem to be linked to a developing, if fragile, sense of being more "at home" in the analysis, even though that meant having to experience difficult feelings. Given the fact that home for her was so full of conflict—with a mixture of loss, displacement, and rejection, I did feel this was a significant development.

The dynamics of the stranger

Those fleeing wars, such as the current wave of Syrian refugees, are of course hoping for a safe haven, a place where they can rebuild their lives. One of my main points is that it is not only that such people require practical help, but that there are some fundamental issues concerned with the nature of identity that need to be faced by both the refugee populations and the potential host countries if there is to be the hope of reasonable integration. In particular, there is a complex interaction between the psychic homes of refugee and host. The refugee feels a stranger in a new environment, carrying within his or her own sense of psychic home (however ravaged by trauma), and the host may feel a fear of a loss of a secure sense of a psychic home as a result of being "invaded" and "enveloped" by all these strangers, "diluting" and "contaminating" his or her own culture and sense of community.

In order to understand the place of the stranger in communities, one can look at some key sociological texts, which already point the way towards some resolution of some of these basic tensions. There is a substantial literature on the nature of the stranger, mainly from the last century. The stranger can be defined as a person who tries to be permanently accepted or at least tolerated by the group which he approaches (Schütz, 1944, p. 499). For Simmel (1971, p. 143), the stranger is not the wanderer who comes today and leaves tomorrow, but the man who comes today and stays tomorrow; he is a potential wanderer, who has not quite got over the freedom of coming and going. In the case of the stranger, the union of closeness and remoteness involved in every human relationship is patterned in a particular way—"the distance within the relation indicates that one who is close by is remote, but his strangeness indicates that one who is remote is near" (p. 143). A trace of this strangeness, the elements of closeness and remoteness, enters into even the most intimate relationships (p. 147). Because of their strange intermediate position, neither owning a home within the community nor being totally outside, the stranger can be more objective about attitudes, freer from local prejudices, and thereby, like the psychoanalyst, can be the receiver of confidences.

The stranger can thus be a potentially creative force, a catalyst for change and for challenging the "thinking as usual" approach of the home group. Of course the stranger may also be a significant threat to the home community and even destabilising, and, as I have indicated, this matches current fears about being "swamped" by those wishing to escape wars from outside Europe.

The stranger is thus imbued with a good deal of ambivalence, and may or may not be integrated into the home culture. He may remain in a transitional position, neither in nor out, but for that reason a potential force for change.

Margaret May Wood (1934) made the point that the way that a stranger may or may not be integrated into the home culture will depend upon the social relationships already within that culture. Thus factors which tend to allow integration of the stranger will include similarity of language or the stranger learning the new language, shared values, a lack of affection from the stranger to his or her own country of origin (though that could potentially cause more difficulty if the stranger brings too many resentments), gratitude to the host community if its members make available a new home, owning property and land, and intermarriage. Conversely, a stranger may fail to integrate if these sorts of element are not present.

Bauman (1993) emphasises that strangerhood has become a permanent condition of modern life. The problem of modern society is not how to eliminate strangers, but how to live in their constant company, in a situation of constant uncertainty as to their responses. After all, to live in a modern city, at least in a democratic society, is to be faced by millions of strangers. There need to be spaces, such as cinemas, theatres, and parks, "managed playgrounds", where strangers can meet or pass by without fear of being challenged. This would contrast with totalitarian regimes that demand absolute conformity, where any stranger, any strange behaviour can be seen as a challenge to absolute authority. Even in democratic societies there can be periods when intolerance of strangers becomes an acute problem; the period of McCarthyism in the US in the 1950s being one typical such period. Current Islamophobic utterances reveal that intolerance can always find someone eager to blame strangers for the ills of the world.

Such paranoid attitudes to strangers contrast with the reality of the necessity for close and creative contact with foreign cultures in order for societies to be enriched.

Appiah in his book, *Cosmopolitanism: Ethics in a World of Strangers* (2006) explores the vital importance for the health of societies that they foster a notion of decent living with strangers. He defines cosmopolitanism (p. xiii) as involving having obligations to others that stretch beyond those we have to our family and to our own culture; and that we take seriously the values of others who do not have our beliefs or take part in our practices. Such an attitude contrasts with the *intolerant* totalitarian position, which involves loyalty to only one portion of humanity, often excluding others.

It is no coincidence that people in such regimes have a constant fear that their homes will be invaded. In between there are many other variations, or what Appiah calls a "partial cosmopolitanism" (p. xv), that is, a certain amount of openness to other cultures, with *degrees of tolerance*, while retaining one's own strong tendency to stick to one's own psychic home as a refuge and shelter.

Such texts then point on the one hand to the universal ambivalence towards strangers, and yet also to the need to recognise and overcome such ambivalence if societies are to grow. But one can add that for that process of growth to be achievable, there needs to be attention to the nature of tolerance and intolerance.

The tolerance/intolerance dynamic and the tolerance process

Tolerance is a complex phenomenon, and there is a massive literature on what one could call the tolerance/intolerance dynamic, most of it focusing on social, political, and legal issues, and few looking at psychological tolerance. Much of this literature still owes a considerable debt to the classical writings on mainly religious tolerance as well as Mill's essay on liberty which puts forward the notion of the harm principle—individual liberty must be tolerated unless this conflicts with a potential (and significant) harm to the community. In general, it is proposed that tolerance entails putting up with a person, activity, idea, or organisation of which or whom one does not really approve, at least initially (King, 1976, p. 21). Or it can be seen as an attitude or practice which is only called for in certain social conflicts. As Rainer Forst (2012) puts it, toleration involves conflict:

> The distinctive feature is that tolerance does *not* resolve, but merely contains and defuses, the dispute in which it is invoked; the clash of convictions, interests or practices remains, though certain considerations mean that it loses its destructiveness ... The promise of toleration is that coexistence in disagreement is possible. (p. 1)

Of course this leads to a number of questions such as what kind of conflicts call for or permit tolerance, who are the subjects and what are the objects of tolerance, what kinds of reasons are there for objecting or accepting what is to be tolerated, and what are the limits of toleration in different cases, including how far can the intolerant be tolerated? One can also ask what kind of tolerance is specific to psychoanalysis. It would certainly seem that a psychoanalytic approach to this vast field would indeed involve "tolerance in conflict", or more specifically tolerance *of* conflict and of uncertainty. A psychoanalytic attitude would be conducive to toleration of conflicting viewpoints, at least in theory. Unfortunately in practice, we know only too well that psychoanalytical institutions are awash with intolerance. For that reason alone, it would undoubtedly be worthwhile for psychoanalysts to pay close attention to the tolerance/intolerance dynamic both in themselves and in their institutions. The point is that, as I have mentioned, this is a dynamic; one needs to provide a framework and a willing atmosphere in which conflicts of these kinds can be examined, with no necessarily perfect resolution. The resolution in a sense is in the *processing* of the dynamic. It is hard work.

In order to provide some guide to the vast landscape of tolerance studies, I would suggest that one could summarise the different ways of conceptualising tolerance as follows. It is worth noting that these categories are not rigid and that they usually involve interplay between different positions, and that in a given situation there is usually a mixture of tolerance and intolerance.

1. One can divide the field into *subject* and *object tolerance*. By subject tolerance I mean that one *respects* the other and others as subjects *of* their experience, with agency and capacity for independent judgement. This contrasts with object tolerance, when the other and others are seen as mere objects to be treated as subject *to* those in power. Those that are merely tolerated as objects may be confined in a ghetto or walled off from society in less visible ways, but their object status remains. The degree to which others are treated as subjects will of course vary, providing a complex interplay between subject and object tolerance. In a clinical setting, one could imagine a patient moving from a position of object tolerance to subject tolerance as their capacity to "become a subject" develops (Kennedy, 2007, pp. 180ff.).

2. One can divide the field, as does Forst, into the *permission* or *respect* conception of tolerance. The permission conception is about those in power allowing others, usually a minority, to live in accordance with their own convictions. This would be to accept a minority's minimal demands for freedom of belief and practice, but may be better than nothing, at least for a while. It is a kind of *vertical* tolerance, from top down. With respect

tolerance, the tolerating parties respect one another as *autonomous* persons, as equally entitled members of a community under the rule of law. Clearly this is similar to subject tolerance and is more like a *horizontal* form of tolerance, involving more equal relationships.

3. There is *negative tolerance*, in which one just puts up with a person or persons, while *positive tolerance* involves a willingness to actively engage with and actively accept the other. This is similar to a position of putting up with the other for pragmatic reasons, such as it not being worthwhile to challenge different ideas, beliefs, and practices for reasons of, for example, state security or stability of an institution, as opposed to accepting positively that they have liberty of conscience to hold their beliefs and so on.

4. *Repressive tolerance.* Herbert Marcuse (1965) argued that toleration only masks and cements social exclusion. He urged for the suppression of objectionable views, not their toleration. Wendy Brown (2008) argues that tolerance can too easily hide and sometimes even legitimate violence and the misuse of power by those in authority. Too much emphasis on tolerance can become paternalistic, seeing strangers as "other", as uncivilised, or needing civilisation or needing to be "taught" tolerance; there is an inevitable asymmetry between the tolerant power and the object of toleration.

While such latter views need to be taken account of as an antidote to paternalistic thinking, and it is true that an authority which tolerates could just as easily not tolerate, they would seem to run too much risk of losing something essential in the management of human relations; one has only to see the consequences of living in regimes where tolerance is not tolerated. Pure tolerance may never be achieved, but some tolerance is surely better than none. The point is that there needs to be a *tolerance process*, in which critical thinking and respectful judgement can take place in an atmosphere of debate and reasonably open communication, when issues around what can and cannot be tolerated about different beliefs, practices, and attitudes in people in our own and other cultures, are examined. Dare one say that a "facilitating environment" for such open debate needs to be available?

One could envisage such a tolerance process consisting of the following broad steps:

Toleration is not just to be seen as an end point but requires time to achieve. The very act of going through a process is in itself potentially tolerance promoting. It goes without saying that for this process to even begin, there would need to be an atmosphere of respectful debate and a wish to examine uncomfortable realities, including a natural ambivalence towards the very process itself.

Toleration requires a movement from "object" to "subject" tolerance. As I indicated, I am thinking here of the parallel with psychoanalytic treatment, where the analyst is part of a process of helping the patient "become a subject".

Seeing the other as a subject requires some self-reflection, where otherness in oneself is seen as part and parcel of being human. In Kristeva's (1991) words: "How could one tolerate a foreigner if one did not know one was a stranger to oneself?"

With regard to the specific issue of how such a process may apply to the current refugee crisis, I have suggested that there is a complex interaction between the psychic homes of refugee and host. The refugee feels a stranger in a new environment, carrying within his or her own sense of psychic home (however ravaged by trauma), and the host may feel a fear of a loss of a secure sense of a psychic home as a result of being "invaded" and "enveloped" by all these strangers. The hope is that naming these anxieties can provide a framework for mutual adjustment on both sides, leading not to some perfect solution to the current crisis, but one that affords the hope of some positive way forward.

References

Appiah, K. A. (2006). *Cosmopolitanism: Ethics in a World of Strangers*. New York: W. W. Norton.

Bauman, Z. (1993). *Postmodern Ethics*. Oxford: Blackwell.

Bourdieu, P. (1990). Structures, habitus, practices. In: *The Logic of Practice* (pp. 52–65). Cambridge: Polity.

Brown, W. (2008). *Regulating Aversion: Tolerance in the Age of Identity and Empire*. Princeton, NJ: Princeton University Press.

De M'Uzan, M. (2005). *Aux confins de l'identité*. Paris: Gallimard.

Forst, R. (2012). *Toleration in Conflict: Past and Present*. C. Cronin (Trans.). Cambridge: Cambridge University Press.

Freud, S. (1919h). The "uncanny". *S. E.*, *17*: 217–256. London: Hogarth.

Judt, T. (2005). *Postwar: A History of Europe Since 1945*. London: Penguin.

Kennedy, R. (2007). *The Many Voices of Psychoanalysis*. London: Routledge and the Institute of Psychoanalysis.

Kennedy, R. (2014). *The Psychic Home: Psychoanalysis, Consciousness and the Human Soul*. London: Routledge.

King, P. (1976). *Toleration*. London: George Allen & Unwin.

Kristeva, J. (1991). *Strangers to Ourselves*. L. S. Roudiez (Trans.). New York: Columbia University Press.

Marcuse, H. (1965). Repressive tolerance. In: Wolff, R. P., Moore, B., & Marcuse, H., *A Critique of Pure Tolerance* (pp. 81–117). Boston, MA: Beacon.

Schütz, A. (1944). The stranger: an essay in social psychology. *American Journal of Sociology, 49*(6): 499–507.

Simmel, G. (1971). *On Individuality and Social Forms: Selected Writings*. Chicago, IL: University of Chicago Press.

Wood, M. M. (1934). *The Stranger; a Study in Social Relationships*. New York: Columbia University Press.

Inflammatory projective identification in fundamentalist religious and economic terrorism

David Morgan

Some reflections on projective identification

When I worked at the Portman Clinic, it was obvious that in some violent patients the pain and tedium of being a "have not" from successive generations of "have nots" meant that at some point, their powder keg of loveless emptiness and "have not-ness" would explode into a drive to evacuate their experience into someone else.

This is well illustrated in a quote from Dr Murray Cox in discussion with Mark Rylance the actor. Cox was a consultant psychotherapist at Broadmoor Hospital who on describing a murderous patient, said he had used the phrase, "I needed a life so I took one" (2001). This quote says it all; a profound failure to mourn because there is nothing good enough to allow the process to begin and it leads to an enactment where loss is transferred—usually bodily—into another. A well-known case at the time was an erstwhile patient who had been denied admission, despite his desperate search for help, by many hospitals. When, at some point after all these negative responses to his need, he was refused a light for his cigarette by another man (who appeared to have everything this seriously ill man lacked), he attacked and killed him.

Another well-known case at the time was of a young boy abducted and murdered by two other young boys many miles away from any help that might have intervened. It was clear (as I had some therapeutic involvement with the workers involved with the killers), that they too were psychically dying a long way from any help that might at some point have intervened with the underlying need to enact this horror—their internal horror—on the mind and body of another.

It is difficult not to think of these experiences now when writing this in the aftermath of the recent terrorist attack that occurred on Westminster Bridge, London, apparently by a so-called jihadist, a loner, preyed upon through the internet by manipulative religious fundamentalists who hold a grievance, real or imagined (probably both), towards the West. This awful event ironically overshadowed the funeral of Martin McGuinness, the latterly successful Irish politician, formerly an IRA commander and known euphemistically as the "Butcher's Boy", not solely because his father was actually a butcher. McGuinness was allegedly responsible for not only the death of Lord Mountbatten, but also two young innocent teenagers who were blown up with him and probably several other acts of terrorism on the British mainland.

Lone attackers

Lone attackers like the recent Westminster terrorist are clearly manipulated and used to enact acts of terrorism for interested parties. These individuals are vulnerable men, often with some ongoing history of violence, who are excited to overcome their internal disorders and discomforts through externalisation into others. They commit criminal acts and turn their backs on their families and culture, often leaving the UK or elsewhere for ISIS and imminent death in holy jihad or enacting terrorist atrocities and turning against the societies in which they live to murder and maim their fellow countrymen or others abroad. This so-called radicalisation is still increasing. The International Centre for the Study of Radicalisation at King's College London has estimated that more than 20,000 people from around the world moved to join what they saw as a holy war of jihad, excited by highly subjective interpretations of ever-malleable religious scriptures.

They are different to the foot soldiers and bombers of some organisation such as the IRA, apparently motivated by political ideology and a wish to unite Ireland, although I would suggest that these IRA foot soldiers were again easy targets for leaders to use for terrorist ends, however justified those ends and means were felt to be. The religious fundamentalists offer "pie in the sky" rewards for acts of terrorist atrocities, providing imagined heroic activities as a distraction from otherwise sad or isolated lives. Even genuine political liberation still attracts the zealot often driven to be used as a "pawn in the game".

As one young man I met in a migrant centre said, "Growing up as a po' boy in Staines, working at a telephone call centre? Or becoming a jihadist with a gun, 'a hero in my time', defending my brothers? No contest bruv!" Although it's worth noting that recently it has been disputed that the reward of the many virgins promised in contested religious writings is, in fact, a mistranslation, and should be read as raisins not virgins! A disappointing outcome if ever there was one, even for the most enthusiastic dried fruit connoisseur!

The jihadists are often deeply influenced by a simplistic ideology that aims to establish a caliphate, a return to religious fundamentalism; these are religious beliefs that are, at this time, particularly threatened from the secular West and the infiltration of internet access and other technology. Is it just that religion is under threat and this is a retreat to certainty that these religious fundamental values offer, including the simplistic device of the infidel and unbeliever into whom all badness can be inflamed and projected?

The Welsh terrorist

On a more prosaic level and, closer to my own spiritual home, the depressed and violent young Welsh fire-setter that I saw at an NHS clinic, affronted by my Welsh name and English accent, told me that the "Sons of Glendower", a nationalist group dedicated to burning down second homes in North Wales, were the vanguard of a Welsh resurgence to rid his land (and probably as he said mine) of the foreign invader.

He had a point; my father's village had become a dormitory for holidaying wealthy people from Manchester and London who put little into the village and had caused the pub to go gastronomic, depriving locals of their traditional watering place. As in the song by the folk group Show of Hands called "Country Life":

> ... and the red brick cottage
> where I was born
> is the empty shell of a
> holiday home
> Most of the year there's no

one there
the village is dead and they
don't care.
Haven't been back since the
pub closed down
One man's family pays the
price
for another man's vision of
country life.

Loss of home

Every age has its hopes and fears and one can find individuals who feel threatened by the present and shun the world for the eternal promise of being reunited with some ideal. They harbour grievances and a dream of a return to some prelapsarian state, as in my Welsh fire-setter, of "Welshness", mirroring the dream of a lost Eden, mirroring in a more extreme version the lost caliphate that seems to motivate believers in the Middle East. We are in a profound period of economic crisis where the human industrial system could threaten to destroy all traces of tradition, certainty, and belief, so this regression to a simplistic ideal is understandable.

Mechanisation, industrialisation, urbanisation, and the massification of society take precedence over religious and spiritual traditional values. We take the supremacy of modernity for granted; we can accept it as a natural condition. But for some, these new forces threaten to destroy old value systems and they will behave as if their actual lives are under threat.

You can't defeat an ideology when it feels based on a justified grievance that people's belief systems or actual home or homeland are under threat from the modern world and a wish to regress from the advances of modernity which seems to lack all spiritual awareness and religious observance, except that of materialism. As I heard one quasi fundamentalist say in a group for refugees, "One episode of the Kardashians and I want to get my gun!" However, those of us not taken up with religious and fundamentalist views do not of course see any justification in taking the lives of others, or even attacking their properties, as a valid response to marginalisation. But it is at least an understandable knee-jerk response to the perception of cruel and thoughtless policies that have little awareness of local strife, and this sense of displacement and fear can be manipulated by the unscrupulous fundamentalist leader be it Bin Laden or indeed a less violent (for now) Donald Trump, and in the past Thatcher and Galtieri.

It may, as with my Welsh "keep the home fires burning" compatriot, feel as if it's the only recourse, in a cruel changing world that can ride rough-shod over cherished beliefs and traditions, to resist that change. This is so clearly also a reflection of the individuals' struggle against their own repressive internal regimes that can only find relief through attacks on externalised representations, but to reduce all acts of rebellion and terrorism to this would be facile. It is important to understand the vulnerable lone wolf seeking an exciting method of evacuation of his mental strife into others or even the employed professional soldier doing the same thing at the bidding of his respective masters. However, collectively it may also begin to help us understand why we have become the legitimate target for terrorism.

Psychotic aspects of violence

At the moment, we in the West are in a period of communal violence that can be likened to the most difficult stages of psychotic illness, when the only response is one of containment and trying to minimise the damage. We are now the unwilling containers of these projectiles and we have to understand what we have been perceived to have done to deserve this (Vernon, 2015). What is our valency in this? There appear to be two conflicting regimes at war with each other; religious fundamentalism in the form of a particularly virulent form of Islam, which most Muslims do not of course adhere to; the other an unfettered fundamentalist, neoliberal secular market economics that promulgates a vicious form of social Darwinism; "We are all revolutionary in our shopping habits now," that most of us don't want to adhere to but unwittingly play a part in, and until the arrival of climate change, refugees, soup kitchens, Brexit, and Trump, could remain relatively unaware of. It was hard at the time not to feel that the horrific attack on the Twin Towers was also an assault on the symbol of this secular religion, of a "winner takes all" culture, by a fundamentalist minority, who felt they had the right to enact murderous revenge for the perceived wrongdoings on the part of the West and specifically America.

So now, once safe democratic communities like ours are overtaken by enormous powerful feelings that can overwhelm our capacity to think clearly and act constructively, we are being projected in a way that can lead to retaliation in kind. It is enormously attractive when evacuated into, to just evacuate back and retaliate. As with the psychotic patient, what are being evacuated and relived and put into the body of the other are often experiences that represent the deepest traumas and these traumas can be dealt with through concrete retaliatory primitive evacuation—both by the terrorist and the economically disenfranchised and the victims of terrorism.

Inflammatory projective identification

We, at the moment, are the unwilling container for these explosive attacks, and their aim, perhaps through the process of inflammatory projective identification, is to communicate fragmentation and psychosis into the minds and bodies of us the victims.

"As they pulled the trigger they looked into our eyes saying look at me, look at me," reported a victim at the Bata-clan Ballroom, Paris. The victim forced to face the unthinkable, which are the projected unthinkable parts of the perpetrators, which the perpetrators themselves cannot face within themselves, forcing their victims by proxy to bear fragmentation and fear. Is it traumatic fragmentation that is being communicated, the threat to faith and fundamentalist thinking that is threatened with disintegration in the face of the apparent unlimited freedoms of secularism, with their liberal attitudes towards women and gay people and dogs and the dominance of materialism over spiritual and religious observation?

Ancient regimes

The old certainties that were offered by religious fundamentalism are now under siege from apparently godless thought, and the resulting dreaded horror of uncertainty. Being without the religious or indeed secular certainties (the Nazis and Stalin killed many more people than any religion has managed to do), means that we now have to live in a godless uncertainty. This might indeed be a mature development, but it is very challenging, as it requires a sophisticated move from an externalised superego or authority that keeps us in check, to an internalised individual conscience. After all, the move from an external eternal authority (Allah, God, Jehovah, the Fatherland), to an internal conscience capable of self-regulation and morality, is a road fraught with difficulty. This was something that the biblical entity Moses understood when, faced with his people's worship of the golden calf, it drove him to concoct a superhuman being, who produced the commandments that we follow today, literally putting the fear of God into them. No doubt the golden calf worshippers who remained loyal to their own gods were seen as inferior. The wish always to regress to an ancient regime that offers absolute certainty and to have an infidel, non-believer, to carry all the uncertainty is profoundly seductive. In our own minor way, the regression to Brexit and little England and a *Dad's Army* attitude is a similar, albeit less violent search for certainty in an increasingly complex global economy.

Or is fundamentalist thinking more a violent response by beleaguered communities or people who feel under siege to the perceived unfettered aggression of Western neoliberalism and its God capital, which may include encroachments onto Islamic territories for purely strategic economic gain and the implicit support of despotic regimes providing little economic relief to the poor. Religion and nationalism always provide enormous succour to the hungry; nothing can really salve an empty stomach or deprivation like zealous hatred of another, or a flag to stand under, or a gun to put one's own fear sternly back into another. This is attractive not only at the threatened collective level, to reverse feelings of diminishment and loss, but also for the beleaguered individual frightened of his own mind, and having no other equipment to help manage insight, other than evacuating pain and horror into the other, usually someone perceived as privileged.

Transgenerational trauma

John Alderdice, a consultant psychotherapist and former speaker in the Northern Irish assembly agrees (2005) with the notion of transgenerational trauma going back many generations, particularly when that past is marked by hurt and abuse. The emotional impact in these situations of the past is felt as powerfully today in the present, especially when it has not been acknowledged or understood by anyone. Further, there are few past experiences that have more purchase on the present than those of humiliation. The desire for vengeance and the righting of wrongs can shape an entire life. They also have a particular power to generate violence because of the need to reverse the experience of humiliation that the aggressor is perceived to have inflicted.

A further insight in the victim/perpetrator dynamic is that victimhood often—not always—develops a sadomasochistic quality. The victim grows up in an environment in which the currency of communication is the exchange of pain. It is possible that no other currency of communication can be imagined. Hence, the dynamic can be perpetuated down the generations. Mark Vernon (2015) says if we think we can appeal to rationality, such as "Why can't these people see reason?" we simply and fatally misunderstand what's going on. "The outsider from a stable society regards the damage of communal violence as self-evidently not in the interests of either individuals or the society, and often they feel sure that people can be made to 'see sense'." The insider understands that this view fails to appreciate the weakness of such rational argument in the face of profound violence. "The terrorist has a profound need to make the perceived aggressor feel the humiliation that they felt." This is like the patients I mentioned at the beginning who feel driven to evacuate pain, loss, and humiliation into the other.

Socio-economic explanation

A different explanation has been put forward and that is a socio-economic one, in particular, the idea that terrorism has to do with poverty. To some extent it does; people who enact these attacks, the lone wolves, are often people at the lower end of the economic spiral. They feel resentful about their position and take refuge in a fundamentalist attitude, be it Islam, Christianity, or nationalism and then feel justified in taking the lives of others, however collective. Terrorism often tends to arise in states that are on their way out of poverty. Bin Laden was a wealthy man. Alderdice (2005) notes that things become vulnerable to violent breakdown, rather like when the depressed persons get better or begin to improve, they are often more likely to kill themselves.

The tragic victims of terrorism are not the real targets; the victims are a way of getting at an authority, usually a government. In suicide bombing where the victim is, in part, the terrorist's own body, it also gets at the authority via the fear it generates.

Second, there is the need to understand the immense impact of the past, with all its emotion and meaning. Such emotions and meanings cannot simply be set aside. Alderdice (2005) writes, "The set of thoughts and feelings that has impressed me as most significant in generating violence has to do with experiences of disrespect and humiliation." The desire to be treated with respect is "insatiable", as in the Hackney kids with guns and knives, joking when they have been "dissed", what Donald Campbell (2009) calls the reassertion of phallic dominance.

Psychoanalysis shows that, contrary to the popular view, time is often no healer. Grievances replace accumulated grief and it is here that terrorism can feed on identifications with past or historic victims and/or inner conflicts that the individual carries from the past. They feed a justification of righteous violence. "The sense that the very existence of a community and all that it holds dear has been threatened, provokes deep fears and creates a capacity for responses at least as violent as those which it has experienced" (Alderdice, 2015).

An ex-terrorist I saw said, "Joining a terrorist organisation was consciously seen both as a way of protecting their community and satisfying the wish for revenge for the death or injury or marginalisation of their loved ones."

Terrorists may also be following rules that pertain more to the unconscious than conscious world; a dream world "driven by basic feelings of hatred and rage or pleasure and elation; by uncomplicated associations that lack nuance and deploy sweeping symbolisms; by wish fulfilments; by a false sense of freedom from the strictures of waking reality, space and time" (Vernon, 2015).

Alderdice suggests that describing terrorists as fundamentalists can be misguiding here. He prefers the word "primitive" meant in the psychoanalytic sense, "like that of a child who refuses to be comforted and screams out of sheer rage. More complicated still, the child may grow to enjoy its rage because it delivers a secondary gain; being able to control or even kill in fantasy the parent." In this way he suggests the terrorist derives a secondary gain where he (usually) can overcome feelings of impotence by being able to reverse these feelings through violent acts that command a great deal of attention. It reminds me of the arsonist who with a very small match can create such mayhem.

Further again, like parents who must contain the screams of their child and resist being drawn into his primitive world, governments and societies faced with terrorism must resist cultivating primitive feelings and actions in response. This begs the question what form containment can take other than suffering and hoping our intelligence agencies are able to prevent the worst atrocities (Vernon, 2015).

Some violent responses are of course necessary. Alderdice (2015) states:

> that whilst there may be the need at times to contain the terrorism with violence, violence that is presented as punishment or vengeance will not work. To put it another way, shoot-to-kill will not in itself deter. This is because of the need in terrorism to avenge perceived humiliations. So such action by a strong government feeds the rage of the self-perceived weak, and further, makes the actions of the weak seem all the more honourable in the minds of those who share the humiliation.

He does say optimistically that "a stage will arrive when it's possible to think more clearly and act constructively, and then everything must be on the table; be capable of being talked about. There must be no no-go areas." This radical honesty and openness is said to lie behind the successes of the truth and reconciliation activities in South Africa and Northern Island, and is lacking he says in the Middle East.

Although, I would argue, this is more complex, as I think our involvement in economic expansionism and exploitation of raw materials, specifically oil, in the Middle East has been utterly thoughtless and mendacious. The neglect of Palestinians by all Western powers and the support for Zionist encroachment into disputed territories is an ongoing horror. The identification with the aggressor within some of Israel's foreign policy seems unarguable as is the building of ghettos.

Appealing to long-term solutions is usually of limited help because emotion is the real issue.

> People who propose peace plans in such circumstances seem to be living with the unstated assumption that if the "right plan" could be invented, everyone would suddenly grasp it with relief and implement it. Of course this is an illusion. It is not the content of a solution that is critical but the process of achieving it. So the diagnosis of the problem is of limited use; it is the working through which is transformational. To put it another way, we must learn to tolerate the long, painful game and be prepared to invest accordingly when an opening, if it occurs, happens. (Alderdice, 2005)

Unfortunately, we have not learned from Vernon, Alderdice, and Northern Ireland. Instead of listening to the grievances arising from the Middle East, we in the West employ professional soldiers to perform what might seem acts of state sanctioned terrorism in the name of foreign policy, such as the invasion of Iraq, a peculiar response to the 9/11 attacks.

In these situations, aren't those attracted to the armed forces, usually working class and relatively uneducated, whilst appearing to do their job to keep us safe from the extremists, aggrieved at their perceived treatment by Western policy makers, willing to also lay down their lives to enforce dubious policies of their countries (see US involvement in Vietnam, Soviet involvement in Afghanistan)? These young men volunteering to put themselves in a firing line are also arguably the victims of manipulation of distant senior political figures, driven more by economics than humanitarian concerns. Are they that different to the religiously motivated zealots of fundamentalist Islam? How many of us for instance would think it was worthwhile for anyone's sons or daughters to die in the service of keeping the Falklands Islands British or during the invasion of Iraq, whether this action is seen as an atrocity or "liberation"? Even the relatively safe drone controller must suffer somewhere for his "clean" and illegal tactical killings (Mayer, 2009).

Western colonialism

The greatest acts of terrorism in the last century have in fact been perpetrated by Western colonialism and economic expansionism. We are now arguably reaping the backlash of those policies. As Noam Chomsky (2017) in "How to Create a Terrorist" and Abby Martin (2017) in her recent work "Empire Files" state, if you want to create a terrorist with legitimate grievances, look no further than US and UK foreign policy; they have been long-time supporters of brutal dictators in the Arab world and still are.

We in the West have a long ignoble history of actually supporting extreme radical jihadist Islamist states, as a barrier to foil Arab secular nationalism, which is what has been really feared. When these West-sanctioned dictatorships fall, due to Western invasion as in Iraq or the hopeful but ultimately sad Arab Spring, there is nothing substantial on the left to take their place, as social democracy in these countries has not been encouraged by Western foreign policy.

We have not been encouraging of democratic nationalism in these states because it has not been in the interest of Western economic and strategic policy to do so (Newman, 2006). When these puppet dictator regimes inevitably fall, there is no opposition to take their place except the fundamentalists with their return to ancient regimes and religious Sharia law.

This example of aggression by the West is very familiar to us throughout the twentieth century. It was the same in Chile, with the repression and overthrow of the legitimate Allende government and the support of the brutal dictator Pinochet, and in many other theatres of foreign policy like Vietnam and South Africa where local interests were repressed for the long-term economic or strategic interests of the West.

What was surprising in these coups and US-sanctioned atrocities is that there weren't more freedom fighters (or terrorists) from these countries to fight back. The treatment of Victor Jara, a singer and political activist in Chile, killed and tortured by the Pinochet regime, and the many, many more who disappeared, demonstrates the effectiveness of US-sanctioned terrorism on the part of the Pinochet government forces and their expertise with CIA assistance at eradicating any justified dissent.

This question of why isn't there more resistance against US hegemony is reminiscent of the same question asked of resistance to the Nazi regime. The answer is similar, in that the regime was brutal and all opposition crushed and destroyed as with the student protest of Sophie Scholl and the White Cross. There were similar actions by US and UK governments in South Africa, in support of the apartheid government against the ANC, the same in Pakistan where the most fundamentalist regime was supported, while the most relevant in the current jihadist problem is the really shameful support of a truly hideous regime in Saudi Arabia that is known to finance virulent Islamic fundamentalism.

If you want to create a terrorist, ignore the effects of these policies on indigenous peoples and you create a legitimate grievance that can lead to acts of violence on Western targets, effectively reversing the sense of helplessness, by evacuating it back into the perceived aggressor.

For instance, Nelson Mandela was deemed a terrorist. He remained on the US terrorism list most of his life. Reagan and Thatcher both viewed Mandela as a threat. Indeed he was at first involved in violent guerrilla actions against the apartheid state, although he was later openly regretful about this; and Mandela is an interesting example of a "terrorist", as he was able to change the way history thought about him and thus change his legacy, as was in some ways, Martin McGuinness.

A terrorist in these situations is created, not born. We have to accept that no one has the right to take another's life, never mind how justified their grievances. However, it is true that some people can feel that their own identity, country, and belief system is so under threat that the annihilation of the other, to preserve their own belief systems, is sometimes justified. In others, these same grievances can seem quite mad, as in the Unabomber in USA, but all, even the mad, are driven by a hostility to attacks on their beliefs, whether based on accurate perceptions of cruel regimes or imagined ones. This allows for a murderous response to the real or perceived attack as a threat to cherished beliefs, sometimes involving a regression to the ancient regime and old cherished ideas, as in religious fundamentalism, perhaps in the face of confusion and uncertainty caused by the growing threat of secularism or loss of identity.

There can be an entrenchment in concrete thinking at these times because it provides a certainty that economic disadvantage or loss of power cannot. Poverty of various sorts can be alleviated by standing under a flag or proselytising a strict religion. The way to alleviate the seduction of these fundamentalist states of mind is to alleviate poverty and ignorance, to encourage an evolution to more symbolic forms, as a way out of dogma and flags, but this can only occur in situations that are conducive to thought or, as we might see it, towards a capacity to bear uncertainty and improvisation and flexibility. These usually occur in environments that have relative wealth and security.

How to create a terrorist

Therefore, to create a terrorist, this is what you do: first, ignore the underlying factors of poverty, inequality, and Western exploitation as well as the severe effects of climate change and global warming, arguably caused by unscrupulous Western economic policies. This occurred in Syria where the effects of climate change pushed the rich farmers into cities after a four-year drought. The rich class of farmers then created flash points and unrest in Aleppo, conditions where middle-class kids fall foul of police and then conflict ensues.

Second, ignore the creation of Western-influenced and financed dictators such as in the Middle East in countries set up by Sykes and Picot after they secretly carved up the Middle East in 1916 along lines that don't take into account tribal loyalties. In these circumstances, brutal systems arose such as those of Saddam, Gaddafi, and others. The USA recently, as we know for various reasons, moved in to kick open doors in Iraq in a post 9/11 action, so that allegedly democracy would flourish. They de-Baathised Iraq, and the Baathist army who have war skills were then interned with Islamic fundamentalists, and these old army types, disenfranchised Baathist military in prison, then created an alliance with the fundamentalists.

So we are reaping the rewards of years of mismanagement or deliberate undermining of national democracy to maintain the status quo. This reminds us of the West's involvement in South Africa and the maintenance and support of the apartheid regime. In the case of Nelson Mandela, much of his terrorist identity came from his association with the African National Congress. The organisation remained a militant group long after Mandela had chosen a different path. It was in 2008 that the US delisted the ANC. So we have to understand that all terrorism may stem from a perceived justifiable cause for grievance, and that however difficult it may be getting to this grievance and understanding it, it might be the beginning of some change. Nelson Mandela is an extraordinary example of a man who was able to do this at an individual level despite years of imprisonment and abuse. Martin McGuinness must have also achieved this to some extent.

This insight is hard to imagine with the like of ISIS and their ilk. The attacks that they encourage probably do show that there has been a serious degeneration in the type of terror attacks that are no longer motivated by any ideological warfare but are now more the result of psychopathic rage. The lone terrorist, as at Westminster Bridge, will probably turn out to be a very ill man. The attacker in Russell Square in August 2016 was later admitted to Broadmoor Hospital with a diagnosis of paranoid schizophrenia. In previous histories of terrorism, the aim has usually been specifically a political one and as with the PLO and the IRA, the attacks were rational, however awful they might have been.

These current random attacks do seem to be carried out in the main by unstable young men for personal reasons and have nothing to do with politics or religion; except the idea of having a great enemy does allow an externalisation of disturbing aspects of themselves into the other, thus providing temporary relief from these disturbances. We have had other examples of this from other young men, who are not from an Islamic background, doing similar randomised acts, for example in America, in the form of James Jackson against black people; Dylan Roof on Afro-American Christians;

Ali Sonboly on the American general public and gay people; and in the UK, Thomas Mair on an MP. I think these people are basically looking to evacuate parts of themselves that they find disturbing; the causes that they become wedded to, or are encouraged by, just provide them with the vehicle that they need to turn murderous thought into action.

In an unfair world

We must understand that in a world where there are disadvantages, neglect, and unfairness, there will always be collective and individual activity to reverse the inferior position by finding other bodies and minds to carry it. One way of doing this is for the unstable individual, through terrorist attacks, to project personal impotence into the other. One aspect of this is to understand how feelings of impotence in the face of life's cruelties can lead to such retributive acts.

Maybe we can put into words the inchoate suffering that often remains unnoticed in pockets of the world that are unsung. To try to reach individuals who perpetrate the attacks, and also whole cultures that feel aggrieved by the perception that their lives, experience, and belief systems are marginalised, we might yet save ourselves from the ever-present threat of war and the evacuation into others that it perpetually offers. Instead of expansionism and the need for more growth to get bigger, maybe we just need to get better?

I would like to finish with a poem by a friend, J. J. Bola who is a Congolese poet and writes about state terrorism and the inhumanity of the effects of war on those that one knows or loves. This poem is set in Congo, but speaks to a suffering that is often unspoken and unknown and can lead to powerful pockets of resentment and rage over perceived aggression and loss. This is happening in many scenarios and they represent transgenerational time bombs of cruelty that can explode in some form at some time in the future. For instance, we create refugees by our economic policies and then we blame them for wanting a better life by coming to our country.

> Tell them (they have names)
> and when they turn the bodies over
> to count the number of closed eyes.
> And they tell you 800,000: you say no. That was my uncle.
> He wore bright coloured shirts and pointy shoes.

2 million: you say no. That was my aunty.
Her laughter could sweep you up like
the wind to leaves on the ground.
6 million: you say no. That was my mother.
Her arms. The only place I have ever
not known fear.
3 million: you say no. That was my love.
We used to dance. Oh, how we used to dance.
Or 147: you say no. That was our hope. Our future. The brains of
the family.
And when they tell you that you come from war: you say no. I come
from hands held in prayer before we eat together.
When they tell you that you come from conflict: you say no. I come
from sweat.
On skin. Glistening. From shining sun.
When they tell you that you come from genocide: you say no. I come
from the first smile of a new born child. Tiny hands.
When they tell you that you come from rape: you say no. And you tell
them about every time you have ever loved.
Tell them that you are from mother carrying you on her back. Until
you could walk.
Until you could run. Until you could fly.
Tell them that you are from father holding you up to the night sky.
Full of stars. And saying look, child. This is what you are made of.
From long summers. Full moons. Flowing rivers. Sand dunes.
You tell them that you are an ocean that no cup could ever hold.

(J. J. Bola, poet)

References

Alderdice, J. L. (2005). Understanding terrorism: the inner world and the wider world. *British Journal of Psychotherapy, 21:* 577–587.

Alderdice, J. L. (2015). Devoted actors: the psychology of fundamentalism. Public lecture, Political Mind Seminars. British Psychoanalytical Society. London.

Bola, J. J. (2015). *Refuge.* Senegal: African Renaissance.

Campbell, D. (2009). Gangs, guns and the absent father. For the Multilingual Psychotherapy Centre lecture, Freud Museum, London.

Chomsky, N. (2017). How to create a terrorist. YouTube. www.youtube.com/watch?v=708pvp0E9dI

Martin, A. (2017). Empire files. YouTube. www.youtube.com/watch?v=0w9OA0FK_w0

Mayer, J. (2009, October 26). The Predator war. *The New Yorker*, pp. 24–32.

Newman, R. (2006). YouTube. www.youtube.com/watch?v=GIpm_8v80hw

Rylance, M. (2001). Q&A: Mark Rylance discusses Richard III and his long interest in mental health issues. www.psychoanalysis-bpa.org/docs/JT_Mark_Rylance%20Jan%2013.pdf

Vernon, M. (2015, November 17). Paris, terrorism, and psychoanalysis. Blog post. www.Markvernon.com/paris-terrorism-and-psychoanalysis

CHAPTER EIGHT

Psychoanalysis and Palestine–Israel: a personal angle

M. Fakhry Davids

As I sit down to write, news comes in that an Arab citizen of Jerusalem has rammed a car into a group of his Jewish compatriots, killing six. My heart sinks. A violent response to this is inevitable—the Israeli authorities, whose no-tolerance attitude to attacks on "its" citizens is well known, have already promised to hit back hard. And then there will no doubt be a violent backlash. With this battle going on in the background, how is it possible to find a space for quiet reflection and thought on Israel–Palestine?

It has been like this for months now. I had originally intended to write this chapter in the summer, but the kidnap and subsequent killing of three yeshiva students in the West Bank effectively put paid to that. In no time an Arab youth was kidnapped and murdered in East Jerusalem in an act of reprisal from the other side. More ominously, when Israel publicly held Hamas responsible, one knew that it would be only a matter of time before "we", the Israelis, would get "them", "the Hamas"—where else but in Hamas-land, Gaza? As the airwaves filled with sounds and images of that brutal war (Rothchild, 2014)—of bombings and buildings being reduced to dust, of streets filled with the blood of the dead and wounded and the agony, pain, distress, grief, and rage of the survivors—and of politicians fighting a propaganda war, it became just about impossible to think. At a time like that how could one turn off the news in order to write about Palestine–Israel? Yet, how can one have the news on and think?

Polarisation and identification

A clear psychoanalytic inference can be drawn from the above dilemma: for one to be so powerfully immobilised by external events implies that one must, in some way, be emotionally implicated in them. One is identified with one or more elements in that situation of conflict. I think this emotional involvement is far more pervasive in the psychoanalytic world than is immediately apparent, and accounts in part for our profession's relative silence on matters pertaining to the Israel–Palestine situation. Our natural inclination is then to leave it to the politicians.

At a recent talk at the Tavistock Clinic on "The survival and well-being of the Palestinian people", arranged as part of the Clinic's Thinking Space programme (Lowe, 2013) and delivered by a Palestinian psychiatrist, the first questioner from the audience launched into a spirited objection to what he saw as political bias and a lack of even-handedness on the part of the presenter. However, the questioner was not content simply to make this observation—an opinion to which he had every right—but launched into a lengthy exposition of his own, designed to put right the matter of the perceived bias in a concrete way. Interventions from the chair, to the effect that the speaker's point had been made and noted, were ignored and, after several further minutes and attempts by the chair to move things on, the speaker was eventually cut short only when another audience member literally took the microphone from him. However, he—and a number of others he appeared to be speaking for—clearly felt aggrieved and victimised on account of being unfairly silenced.

The presence of a Palestinian speaker seemed in itself to have been the stimulus for bringing into the room the war between Israel and the Palestinians, something commented on by later speakers. In this atmosphere, there was very limited possibility of a proper discussion that might bring together a meeting of minds, let alone minds that acknowledged their differences. Instead the atmosphere was one of opposition and battle, of taking sides: one was either for Israel or for the Palestinians. The prospect of a thinking space where two sides in a debate might be properly aired, away from the heat of the front line, had been successfully subverted.

A second example of the polarised mindset as far as Israel–Palestine is concerned occurred when, some years ago, the editors of the major psychoanalytic journals jointly condemned, in a special editorial, a decision by two (non-psychoanalytic) UK-based journals to dismiss Israeli academics from their editorial boards. The special editorial sought to uphold academic freedom and deplored the fact that the academics were excluded purely on the grounds of their "nationality". What was surprising was that no mention was made of the fact that the dismissals were part of an academic boycott of Israel—this was receiving some publicity in the popular press at the time—and thus the merit, or otherwise, of this case was not considered at all. Instead the action of the journals concerned was portrayed as blatantly racist (anti-Semitic): the academics had been dismissed quite simply because they were Israeli.

The complex question of the academic boycott—the central matter in the original action to which exception was being taken—was indeed raised by two respondents to the editorial (Chiesa, 2002; Kemp, 2005), but a third (Poland, 2005) rounded on Kemp's view that "Zionism is a racist ideology", branding it as "vilely destructive … passionate prejudice" (p. 903). This prompted the editors, who had hitherto maintained a silence on the issues raised, to express regret at publishing Kemp's letter on account of its "partisan hatefulness", and promptly to draw the discussion to an end. For Poland, the view that Zionism is racist reflects an anti-Israel/Semitic prejudice, and he condemns Kemp's "intemperate partisanship" and "incendiary provocativeness" on account of it. Though he notes the latter's acknowledgement that a brief letter responding to an editorial is but a "condensed response", a poor "substitute for a reasoned analysis of the original editorial", he gives him no leeway on account of it. To him there is no possibility that Kemp may indeed have a reasoned view—the rest of us may or may not agree with it—as to why he sees Zionism in this way. Instead, Kemp is dismissed as quite simply prejudiced. It is not difficult to see that, were the discussion not closed, Kemp may in turn have pointed out that Poland's letter itself reveals a powerful, if not intemperate, emotional reaction; he may have gone on to question whether this reflects an identification with Israel, the counterpart to his perceived identification against Israel and with the Palestinians.

These brief examples show how difficult it is to engage psychoanalytically with matters pertaining to Israel–Palestine (here, on the psychological condition of Palestinians—as "second class" citizens within Israel, or "under occupation"[1] in the West Bank and Gaza—or a proposed academic boycott of Israel). Instead, a polarised us-and-them mindset is mobilised, which in turn places proper dialogue beyond reach. Indeed, Poland, who blames Kemp for bringing a partisan mindset into the proceedings, states explicitly that an engagement with the us-and-them dynamic is beyond our proper "academic concern", belonging instead to the "polemics of international events". This seems to mean, "Let the politicians fight it out—we are above such ugly hostility." The fact that we are powerfully drawn in, however, demonstrates the opposite, namely that we are not above the hostilities involved in this situation.

Nor are these difficulties restricted to psychoanalysts, or confined to events related exclusively to Israel–Palestine. Schonfeld (2016) reports on two interdisciplinary conferences addressing the Holocaust where similar polarised dynamics were mobilised, interfering with the process of trying to engage creatively and critically with the task of locating an understanding of that atrocity within a wider historical context relevant to the present. He focuses on powerful forces of compliance and political correctness that held sway, and notes his own silence on these matters, up to the time of giving voice to his observations by writing the paper some twenty years later. The elements he describes—polarisation and powerful forces of political correctness, including pressure not to step out of line and, if one does, finding oneself in a psychological minefield—are similar to those I described above, and raise the question of whether the Holocaust itself may be implicated in the difficulty with bringing proper thoughtfulness to the Israel–Palestine situation. Or, whether it is the fact that the Holocaust is now inevitably embedded in the latter context that makes it so difficult to find an optimal distance from which to permit objective reflection.

Either way, we may conclude that the battle between the two sides pulls us in, the supposedly neutral parties, in a way that is unexpected. Does the Palestine–Israel situation serve as a magnet for feelings of such intensity that they lead inevitably to polarisation? Martin Kemp (2011) has suggested that guilt over the Holocaust is a powerful factor, operating unconsciously at a societal level in the West, that plays a part in a polarisation of this sort. This leads to overcompensation in the form of a reluctance to criticise Israel openly, insofar as doing so risks attracting the accusation of anti-Semitism; hence, any thinking that might lead in that direction is avoided. (One might add that the same could well apply to non-Westerners, but the other way around.) For those from Third World (including the Arab and Muslim world) backgrounds, the alliance—perceived or real—between Israel and the West may also attract to Israel powerful feelings that belong to the reality of having been colonised and oppressed by Western powers.[2] This, in turn, draws the accusation of racism on the part of those from the Third World (e.g. the view that Zionism is a form of racism). Such emotional factors may account for why the situation becomes so polarised that dialogue and discussion are out of the question, and we end up in different and opposing camps.

Enmity and war

There is a further psychoanalytic element that may also be playing a part in the problem of engaging properly with the Palestine–Israel situation. It may be that in our ordinary discourse about Israel–Palestine anxieties are generated that touch on an unconscious conviction that war, including its incarnation as a polarised mindset, is inevitable. Why should this be so?

The state of Israel was established in 1948 in the midst of a territorial war. However, war after war has failed to resolve a situation that has today reached a stalemate widely regarded as one of the most deep-seated and intractable that our world has known. Seemingly unending cycles of violence and destructiveness produce ever more suffering, fuelling further hatred and enmity, time after time reigniting the fires of revenge. To a neutral observer, it is inexplicable that a peaceful accommodation, involving compromise on both sides, should prove so elusive. The protagonists, however, remain locked into a cycle of violence and to them such a step remains out of reach as each seems content to settle for blaming the other and justifying its own position. Meaningful dialogue seems impossible and the sense of hopelessness is palpable as attempt after attempt to address the situation is derailed, almost inevitably, by a violent backlash. The state of war between Israel and the Palestinians seems here to stay.

Why does war have such a hold over us? Freud (1933b) suggested that it provides an opportunity for aggression—for him a primary inner drive—to be directed outwards, as violence against an enemy. This solves our problem of living with a death instinct that is opposed to the life instincts and that strives constantly and silently against them, in pursuit of a quiescent, inanimate state. Paradoxically, war's destructiveness in the outside world is therefore life-enhancing at the level of individual psychology.

Freud (1912–13, 1921c) draws on his metapsychological account of the primal horde—a mythic prehistoric event in which sons unite to kill

a tyrannical father, guilt over which results in the father being symboli-
cally installed in the mind as a superego that creates inner pressure against
such violent excesses—to account for the pull within each of us towards war
and violent conflict. In this narrative the murderous primal horde battle
predates guilt, upon which the building of a more civilised world depends.
These are, therefore, later and more tenuously established developments
that, in the warring mindset, give way almost inevitably to mankind's
earlier and more innate nature: ontogeny repeats phylogeny. War thus has
a regressive pull on us. Avoiding war, on the other hand, requires something more—we must resist open aggression and engage the other in nego-
tiation and dialogue, both of which are later achievements that depend on
the superego. The regressive pull tugs at our more primitive nature, hence
is more powerful.

Subsequent generations of clinicians have supplemented Freud's picture
with more detail from the consulting room. We now have a fuller account
of the earliest pre-oedipal stages of development, which tends to supplement how we see the regressive pull within the mind. For example, drawing
on different frames of reference, Volkan's (1988) discussion of our need for
enemies emphasises the primitive roots of the warring mindset and stresses
especially the ways in which primitive (narcissistic) vulnerability is externalised in group conflicts, mobilising in the process large group dynamics
that sweep us in. In the Kleinian tradition, we think of the enemy as a current version of the bad object first encountered in infancy when paranoid–
schizoid functioning prevailed (e.g. Rustin, 1991); that the mechanisms of
splitting and projective identification are central; and that psychotic level
defences such as omnipotence and mania are mobilised to protect us from
a warring situation that is feared as catastrophic.

Despite our increasing clinical and theoretical sophistication, however,
Freud's idea that there is a primitive pull towards war continues to colour
our thinking, translating today into a regressive pull attributed to the paranoid mindset. In my view we should think of that mindset as the psychological concomitant of being at war rather than causing war, and note that
this renders the depressive position and secondary process functioning
practically inaccessible—as I have illustrated above, it is difficult to think
under fire. However, what primary aggression did for Freud, a primitive
need for enemies—primitive developmentally rather than because ontogeny repeats phylogeny as it did for Freud—now does for us (see Grotstein,
1982). Our overall attitude to the inevitability of war and, by extension, the

polarised mindset that prevails with respect to the conflict between Israel and Palestine remains very much in line with the Freud of 1933.

However, I think this approach is overly reductive and obscures another more hopeful aspect of the psychoanalytic project, in which Freud places psychoanalysis firmly on the side of more "civilised" and progressive ways of dealing with primitive aspects of our inner life—the very aspects that are subject to the pull of regression. Psychoanalysis does so by engaging, rather than avoiding, these aspects of the mind, but its aim is certainly not a hedonistic surrender to the instincts or, as we might say today, the primitive aspects of our nature. On the contrary, the act of bringing them into the light of awareness is seen as a superior and more adaptive way of living with our inherent animal nature, a direction of travel captured well by the Freudian dictum, "Where id is let ego be." When we give ourselves over to a polarised mindset as far as Israel–Palestine is concerned, I think we sell our discipline short. Moreover, when we leave it to the politicians, for whom the lure of operating in a polarised world holds out the prospect of cheap political gain, we may be complicit in encouraging the mindset of conflict and war—the most primitive aspects of our psychological make-up—to hold sway.

It does not have to be like this. Today our discipline has evolved sufficiently for us to consider that even the most primitive aspects of our minds are not so fearful and intense as to place them beyond the reach of psychoanalysis. However, to reach these levels, the clinician must abandon the stance of the neutral observer, who comments on the analytic process from above the fray, as it were, and accept instead that, contrary to Freud's original assertion, the profoundly disturbed patient does indeed have a transference, but one that is quite different from the more familiar neurotic version of it (Bion, 1957). While the latter's transference is symbolic and can be inferred from verbal material, dreams, associations, and so on, the disturbed patient's transference consists of intense and concrete projections forced into the analyst. This alters profoundly how the analyst is perceived and experienced. Such projections are concrete—for the patient, the analyst is literally the way she or he is shaped by the (unconscious) projection, and the transference lacks the as-if quality characteristic of neurotics. To be caught up in this state of affairs is deeply disturbing, but the analyst's ability to tolerate the process allows the most primitive aspects of the patient's mind to come to life in the room, and through these enactments to become known. This lived experience deepens the patient's contact with the most feared contents of the mind (see Rosenfeld, 1965, 1987; Segal, 1964; Stewart, 1991), thereby containing them. Negative capability—the willingness to allow the deepest and most frightening aspects of a patient's inner world to emerge, without prejudice (Bion, 1967)—plays a key role, and the process aims, simply, to deepen the engagement with whatever is in the patient's mind.

Returning to the theme of our identification with warring parties, the "Nazareth conferences"—a series of group relations events devised originally to address the psychological aftermath of the Holocaust—have applied these principles directly to this problem. Taking as a starting point the fact that descendants of victims and perpetrators of the Holocaust are powerfully identified with the enmity of the previous generation, the organisers aimed not at talks and reconciliation, but set out instead to create a setting that would deepen the engagement with whatever each carried within in relation to the other. Identification with warring parties thus lay at the core of this work.

The Nazareth project

When invited to join the staff of these events several years ago I had two interests. First, to gain first-hand exposure to the complex field of the transgenerational transmission of trauma (of the Holocaust) (e.g. Kestenberg, 1993; Kogan & Chasseguet-Smirgel, 1995). Second, I was aware of an assertion often made publicly, namely that Palestinian suffering at the hands of Israel is, in some way, a consequence of the persecution suffered by Jews at the hands of the Nazis. At root, there is an aspect to this formulation that we might expect psychoanalytic inquiry to illuminate, namely, was the trauma inflicted on Jews collectively so powerful that it could not be processed, and was its violence therefore destined to be repeated (Freud, 1914g; Schonfeld, 2016)?

When this assertion is made, usually in the public domain, it suffers the same fate that I described earlier in relation to all matters pertaining to Israel–Palestine. It becomes a signal for polarisation and a digging in of heels—one is either on one side or the other, and the possibility of engaging meaningfully with the question is placed beyond reach. Would a more containing setting such as the Nazareth one, with its specific focus on the aftermath of that atrocity, be able to facilitate a proper psychoanalytic engagement with this question?

The Nazareth project—named after the venue of the first event in what has become a series—began in 1984 when a group of German and Israeli psychoanalysts recognised that they carried within themselves a legacy of the Holocaust that marred their relationship. Working with other colleagues, they sought a means whereby this problem might be investigated psychoanalytically, and settled on the group relations approach, adapting it to work with the psychological aftermath of the Holocaust (Erlich, 2009; Miller, 2009).

The group relations model was developed originally at the Tavistock Institute in the UK to address issues of authority and leadership in the work setting (see Hayden and Molenkamp, 2002). It is built on Bion's (1961) conceptualisation of the group as an entity in its own right, rather than as the sum of its individual members. A group has a primary task—its *raison d'être*—and an emotional life centred upon grappling with it. When a group succeeds in working at this task the group ego dominates and it is in "work group" mode, but when defences against doing so predominate, it is in the grip of "basic assumptions" that protect it from anxieties generated by the task. As in analysis, interpreting these anxieties and defences appropriately can help the group to recover its capacity to face what might otherwise be avoided altogether, and the process as a whole can yield important insights into unconscious forces involved in the task.

A group relations "conference" is usually residential and takes place over several (five to fourteen) days, making it an intensive emotional experience. There are several settings—large and small study groups, review groups, and system event—each of which involves a different level of dependency and intimacy, which enables them to generate differing levels of anxiety in relation to the task. In each setting, what unfolds is observed and made available for reflection and study and, from across the system as a whole, a nuanced and variegated understanding of different dimensions of the problem at hand emerges, deepening our appreciation of the issues involved. Members are not addressed individually. Instead, their contributions are seen as giving voice to the group mind, where interventions are also addressed. Nevertheless, their active engagement means that they are powerfully identified with the work, and this deepens their individual emotional experience and learning.

The adapted form of the group relations approach proved helpful in bringing to the fore anxieties and defences, together with the projections that lay behind these, which allowed a deeper engagement with the problematic German–Israeli relationship and made these dynamics available for work (Erlich, Erlich-Ginor, & Beland, 2009). Participants in that series felt that the depth of involvement achieved bore testimony to the fact that the inner German–Israeli relationship had indeed been accessed in a real way. The physical presence of the other had brought issues powerfully to the fore, which enabled this setting to do work that could not otherwise be properly accessed (e.g. in individual analyses).

Across the Nazareth series as a whole the need to involve groups affected by the Holocaust other than Germans and Israelis had gradually emerged. By the time I joined (the fourth conference) these "affected others" were included in the working title of the conference. Consciously, this made room for those who were neither German nor Israeli/Jewish, yet who were profoundly impacted by the events of the Holocaust (e.g. children evacuated on the *Kindertransporten* and raised as Gentiles, children of mixed Jewish and "native" European heritage, etc.). However, the designation "affected others" also opened the way for exploring the question I raised above regarding a possible connection between the Holocaust and the situation vis-à-vis the Palestinians, as the opening sequence I report below shows.

Before proceeding I want to emphasise that in this chapter I shall be presenting selected observations that are relevant to my theme of the Israel–Palestine situation. As I have indicated, this is a strand of work that drew me personally to that project. Likewise, every conference participant comes to do his or her own work, encompassed within the primary task, and the conference aims to deepen participants' engagement with the issues they bring as they emerge. Each person could therefore write a personal narrative like mine, and each would be different. In addition to these personal journeys, work takes place at the group level that reveals preoccupations in the group unconscious relevant to the task, together with group-level defences against them. This creates a complex, interweaving web of personal and group dynamics, to which no one narrative can do justice. The narrative that follows should be viewed in this light.

Bringing in the third

Where are the Palestinians?

At the outset I was aware that, unlike the colleagues I was joining, I had no personal connection with the Holocaust. I shared this with my colleagues, saying that I was raised in a Muslim community in South Africa, which was part of the larger black[3] population targeted by the apartheid system. The apartheid doctrine shared a racist core with the Nazi doctrine of Aryan supremacy, and it was often said that, were it not for blacks, Jews would probably have been the targets of apartheid. Moreover, a number of Jews were prominent in the struggle against that system. Relations with Jews were, therefore, on the whole cordial, helped by the fact that Jews have a special status in Islam as earlier recipients of the message of monotheism. However, when the injustices against the Palestinians came to the fore, a schism opened up between Muslim and Jew. I was interested in whether a psychoanalytic light could be shone on this phenomenon.

From the outset, bringing a third party into the established equilibrium of working at the German–Jew/Israeli interface proved difficult. In the opening plenary of my first conference (the fourth in the series), a member asked directly why, given that the conference was to address "others" affected by the Holocaust, there was no Palestinian on the staff. I suggested that we now knew that Palestinians were indeed present—not as participants in the flesh, but in the mind. As it does in plenaries, the discussion moved on to other matters, but across the conference as a whole there was no return to the question of how the Palestinians may be present in the mind.

In that conference I was a consultant to a small group (SG), where there was some initial interest in how my first name—readily recognised by Israeli members as Arabic—came to coexist with an apparently Jewish surname. At the time I interpreted this interest as a resistance to real work on their part: as a transference object I was to contain two opposing polarities within my own person, relieving them of responsibility for identifying and working with the polarised, oppositional identities—Arab and Jew respectively—present in their inner worlds and thus in the group. This incident shows how I used a perfectly good here-and-now interpretation to steer the group away from a deeper exploration of the meaning of the Arab/Muslim–Israeli/Jew dimension as it was present in the group at that moment, that is, between myself and them, a group of Jews/Israelis and Germans.

Later there was a flashpoint, on this same theme, that occurred within the staff system. In one discussion (during the system event) when the entire staff team was present, the point was made that genocide is usually secondary to some other aim (such as the conquest of land), but the Holocaust was different in that it was Hitler's explicit aim to exterminate the Jews as a people. The staff group had been working together for three days by now and this was not the first time the Holocaust had been discussed among us. On earlier occasions my colleagues responded to my self-confessed ignorance of the Holocaust by letting me, gradually and in a three-dimensional way, into the meaning of this event and its impact on both Germans and Jews. It is one thing to learn about the Holocaust from written materials, where it is embedded in historical and political discourses; to hear directly from descendants of the parties involved is a very different emotional experience that permits a new kind of reflection. I think, for example, of an aged Jewish woman in my small group who, in understated tones, recounted how her liberal parents had resisted fleeing from Europe—on account of their identification as citizens of a plural, secular Europe—until it was too late, and only she, their teenage daughter, could escape to Palestine. Her entire family were to perish in the concentration camps. This was the culmination of a long history of experiencing anti-Semitism in Europe, which her father resisted in the name of a common humanity, only for that aspiration to be crushed in the cruellest way possible.

Vignettes like these, which also emerged in the staff team, bring depth to one's appreciation of what is involved; they make one reflect, think, and learn. Thus, for example, I came to see the inadequacy of a Muslim/Arab response that states baldly, "We did not do this to you—Hitler did." That would be quite simply a failure to engage fully, on a human level, with the dimensions of an atrocity that is now part of the history of our shared world. One could see how such a response would re-traumatise the traumatised, and this learning was important for me.

On this occasion, however, there was a new element—the distinction between the Holocaust and genocide secondary to territorial conquest. Was this an attempt to bring in the emerging accounts of the "new historians" who spoke of ethnic cleansing involved in the creation of the state of Israel (e.g. Pappe, 2006; Shlaim, 2009)? I thought it might be helpful to bring in an idea that enjoyed wide currency within the Arab/Muslim world, and suggested that a case could be made that Golda Meir's much-publicised assertion that Israel was a land without a people for a people without a land contained an explicitly genocidal idea in that it necessarily obliterated the existing Palestinian population of the land.[4] At that moment our conversation was interrupted by a knock on the door requesting a colleague and myself to consult to an inter-group meeting.

We returned with time for only a brief report back on our consultation, but later, in passing along a corridor, I was told that my remark had sparked a heated furore where I was accused of minimising the Holocaust by equating it with events involved in the creation of the state of Israel. This was a serious accusation associated with Holocaust denial—a crime in much of Europe. However, we did not return to this emergence of a nascent conflict between a Muslim/Palestinian and a Jewish/Israeli perspective. It underwent repression, together with awareness of the aspect of my identity involved in it.

Return of the repressed

In the dying moments of the closing plenary of that conference, an Israeli colleague noted that there had been no comment on the fact that a staff member had an Arabic name (it had been raised in the relatively "private" setting of my own small study group). Did this silence have a meaning? This was the first public mention of this part of my identity, which had not been worked on in the staff group, and it left me completely paralysed. As the gaze of the entire membership settled on me, an Israeli voice asked, "What has it been like for you to be here?" My numbness eventually gave way to a shrug and the words, "What can I say?"

I felt disowned as a colleague and instead held up like a specimen—someone from another world. That single act left me feeling that all my work at the conference had been completely rubbished. I experienced my colleague as telling me that for him I was, after all, "only a Muslim"—not an ordinary colleague but present solely as a representative from the Palestinian–Muslim world. That identity and how it relates to being German or Israeli had not been properly explored at all within the staff group, so that its appearance in this way, at the eleventh hour, felt hollow and token rather than real. I felt that the staff member wanted to be given credit for taking the courageous step of letting in a third, but without having done the emotional work involved in this by engaging with the meaning of that difference. This would have brought depth to his statement. Instead, in that final plenary, I was placed in an impossible position: on the one hand I could hardly deny my difference as described; on the other, if I accepted his statement at face value, I was colluding with a lie—I had not been properly let in to the staff group as a Muslim. Words on a page cannot convey the depth of emotion that I felt at this attempt to make of me an "other". I resolved not to do any further work with this group. We were in effect at war and this was one battle in which I had no investment.

With hindsight it is possible to see that my stance at the time was partly defensive: quite early on I had taken refuge in my identity as a professional in order to avoid the powerful emotions involved in being present as a very particular other—Muslim, felt to be in sympathy with the Palestinians, and unwanted. Several years later, when we had long moved on from this difficult struggle, my colleagues acknowledged the reality of what I represented at that first conference.

A moment of transition

Some time before this conference I had signed up to a visit to Auschwitz organised by a group of colleagues in London. Although we were fully aware of what we were letting ourselves in for, trudging through the death camp with its macabre exhibits nonetheless completely overwhelmed our minds. Six decades had failed to extinguish the emotional impact of the terrible atrocities committed on that soil—their incomprehensibility, the complete triumph of the death instinct, and the industrial scale of an undertaking that made the notion of a "final solution" sound banal and inadequate: how could it possibly capture the inconceivable cruelty that single-mindedly and systematically stripped its victims of every ounce of dignity before finally killing them in the most degrading way possible? One could glimpse why the atrocity was described as a crime against humanity itself, and the sheer horror of exposure to it left us completely numbed.

That night, as I was dropping off to sleep, I had a "dream" where I saw, beside my bed, row upon row of people stretching out as far as the eye could see. I knew instantly that they were the people of the death camp. They did not threaten, but looked at me directly and expectantly, without saying a single word. A chill went down my spine. What could they possibly want? As the realisation hit me I reached instinctively for the light switch and, in an instant, they were all gone.

In the shadow of the death camp it was impossible to find a meaning beyond the manifest content of the dream: Hitler's victims, silenced by death, needed us, the living, to speak for them. In the fullness of time, however, I came to see its latent content. The dream used day residues from our visit to the camp to address a very personal connection of mine with the aftermath of the Holocaust, namely the Nazareth work. By walking out, I had silenced the many viewpoints I might bring to the proceedings; this was one meaning of the many silent voices. Another related to the location of the dream—it was the scene of a crime against humanity. This stood for an accusation that walking out was a crime against the human attempt to bring a meeting of minds where otherwise only polarisation and enmity would prevail. Walking out was a final solution. A third meaning related to the chill that woke me. It was disapproval from a superego, which had to be fragmented into many little figures in an attempt to dilute the power of its rebuke. Seemingly non-threatening, the collective presence of these superego figures was nonetheless so spine-chilling as to disrupt my sleep. This meaning of the dream helped me to understand that I should revisit my decision to leave. I did, and resolved to continue with the work, of which I will now give a brief account.

Nazareth: containment

The comment that had such a violent impact on me could be considered as a symptom of a larger systemic difficulty. In the Nazareth model, detailed work among the staff group, on issues relevant to the conference theme, is essential in order to prepare emotionally for what lies ahead: Israelis and Germans had done this over several years in preparation for the first series. By comparison our work on issues relevant to bringing in a third, especially in the form of a Muslim with its link to the Palestinians, had been at most perfunctory. We agreed therefore to make substantial time available prior to the start of the next members' conference, as well as after its end, for this purpose. From a psychoanalytic point of view this can be understood as the work of containment.

That was a fortuitous decision, for the next conference took place just after Israel's invasion of Lebanon in 2006. The staff group's work began with the unfinished business from the last conference, two aspects of which I will discuss here: first, the perceived relevance of the Palestinian problem, and second, the intense feeling generated by my Golda Meir comment. We also considered in some detail the meaning of the Lebanon invasion from our differing perspectives.

Palestinians

It turned out that the idea that the Palestinians were included among the others affected by the Holocaust, and thus relevant to the work of the previous conference (and the current one, which worked under the same general title, "Germans, Jews and Affected Others"), was not shared across the staff group. The need to include groups other than Germans and Israelis had grown organically through the presence of individuals (such as Norwegian Jews) with clear Holocaust-related emotional work to do, but whose presence was not properly incorporated in the conference title. The decision to include these groupings was not an a priori, "political" one. My view, stated above, that the Palestinians were indeed present in phantasy was but one possible explanation of why that grouping was mentioned in the opening plenary. They could have been invoked as a way of avoiding real work with the "affected others" present in that conference. On its own, the reference to Palestinians in the opening plenary could not therefore be taken as evidence that the Palestinians were indeed, in the unconscious, among the "others" affected by the Holocaust. By this time, therefore, the Nazareth process had not established any link between the Holocaust and the Palestinian situation.

Specificity of the Holocaust

My comment on the statement attributed to Golda Meir now received a good deal of heated discussion. Two interlinked issues were raised. First, the idea that the establishment of a state defined as Jewish involves an obliteration of Palestinians, as a people who are legitimate inhabitants of that land, was unacceptable. There was considerable discussion of this, with traditional historical accounts brought as evidence of a free choice allegedly made by Arabs to abandon their lands, and so on, which was contrasted with the different narrative described by the so-called new Israeli historians who appear to validate Palestinian accounts of their displacement. These accounts, of course, remain controversial within Israeli society. The two views of the situation were aired, with no attempt to resolve the differences between them.

Second, my Israeli colleagues found the equation I implied between the Holocaust and the "genocide in phantasy" against the Palestinians completely unacceptable. Detailed arguments were advanced as to why the Holocaust was an event unique and unlike any other in history. I myself thought that one could concede the uniqueness of the Holocaust without precluding the possibility of it having aspects in common with other genocides, especially in the psychological realm. However, I came to appreciate that Israelis felt there was something unique in the Jews' experience of the Holocaust to which I, an outsider to that experience, did not have access. This was of course entirely possible. Privately, I wondered whether, whatever the basis of the Israeli position, their stance might also be defensive—against guilt, say, for cruelty perpetrated against Palestinians.

Work on this matter was incomplete, and in the conference following this one (i.e. my third) it emerged that an Israeli colleague considered the Holocaust to be part of his very identity. There was considerable discussion of this issue. Accepting it made it possible for Israelis, when the time came, to consider that for Palestinians the experience of the Nakba[5] might equally be constitutive of their identity, without this implying equivalence between the two atrocities. The latter turned out to be a vexed issue with considerable power to divide.

The war in Lebanon

The war in Lebanon provided the staff group with an opportunity to bring in the very different ways in which that event was viewed in Israel and the West on the one hand, and in the Muslim world on the other. Israeli colleagues were convinced that there was an international Islamist conspiracy, with the Hamas–Hizbullah–Iran axis at its core, that threatened not only Israel, but was part of a global strategy that threatened the West itself. In this scenario Israel faced the prospect of a Holocaust all over again—indeed the Iranian president, Mahmoud Ahmadinejad, explicitly denied the Holocaust, all the while openly vowing to wipe Israel off the map. Should Israel not defend herself—and, by extension, Western civilisation—by whatever means possible, with questions of proportionality an academic luxury?

I myself put the view that a powerful current of Islamophobia coloured Western perceptions of the Middle East (Akhtar, 2010), which reduces a complex social-political reality into a simplified us-and-them, either-or duality. Thus deployed, we are drawn powerfully into stereotypes that make objective observation—let alone critical thinking—very difficult, as each side tends to justify its position and to demonise the other. This matters because it shapes how we perceive reality, so that a selective view is mistaken for the totality. For instance, when an Iranian politician makes an intolerant and racist statement, such as the one cited above, it is seen as reflecting an objective truth about what "Iran, or the Muslim world wants", whilst a similarly intolerant and racist statement from a right-wing Israeli politician may more easily be contextualised and recognised for what it is—a means of appealing to a particular political constituency by playing the race card.

I do not want to give the impression that we came to an agreement with one another on these matters—we did not. However, we made space to hear the other's views, to try to understand them as far as possible, and to be aware of our emotional responses, doing our best to put things into words. From an emotional point of view this work was extremely difficult. Think, for example, of a Jew whose relatives had perished in the Holocaust and who had resolved never again to run the risk of another one, having to listen to me suggest that he was wrong to take literally that very threat, especially when voiced against Israel by an Iranian president who, at that moment, had proxies on Israel's borders. Or, of someone in my position— with a personal empathy with victims of injustice and oppression, and who has heard, first hand, distressing accounts of the deep damage inflicted on Palestinians at the hands of Zionist militia in the past and the Israeli military in the present—having to witness Israelis' refusal to entertain the idea that their state had brought cruel suffering on another people. It was our willingness to bear these very powerful emotions, to avoid political correctness, and to speak as truthfully as possible that created a containing setting. This is work that cannot be done but in the presence of the other, which brings feelings to life in a very real way, and is a central aspect of the Nazareth approach.

Conclusion

Towards the end of the above conference (my second), a significant development took place. In the system event, where participants themselves decide the groups relevant to the task they will form and work in, a "group" of two emerged who could not find any existing group willing to accept them as members. In the end they asked to sit in on the work of the management (staff) group, where their role in the system event became clear—they were the homeless group, the people without a territory, enacting a role that, in external reality, belonged to the Palestinians. This interpretation had the ring of an emotional truth: the Palestinians had arrived. In the unconscious they are indeed a group of "others" affected by the Holocaust.

The Palestinian presence had emerged organically within the process, and they were therefore formally included in the next conference. Their presence is a necessary first step that will enable us to study psychoanalytically the question I posed earlier: is the suffering of Palestinians today connected with the suffering of Jews in the Holocaust? If so, how?

These matters usually produce division, polarisation, and stalemate. However, we found that it was indeed possible to move things on by acknowledging explicitly our identifications within this polarised world, facing the powerful conflicts stirred up within, and deepening our engagement with them, partly through addressing them directly in the presence of the other. While counter-intuitive—usually we give up and speak only to the like-minded about such delicate and divisive matters—the approach I have described is entirely in line with established psychoanalytic principles.

Notes

1. I use the quotation marks to indicate that this is how the Palestinians concerned would describe their own condition.
2. By some analyses Western hegemony continues unabated in the post-colonial era.
3. I am using the designation "black" for groups sometimes collectively referred to as "non-white", a description that became unacceptable to them during the apartheid years.
4. I have since learnt that there is no record of Meir using this emotive phrase, which does, however, have a long and controversial history (Muir, 2008). It may have become associated with her on account of an assertion (in 1969) that, when she arrived in Palestine in the 1920s, the "Palestinian people" as a national entity did not exist (Erlich-Ginor, personal communication). However, whatever its factual basis, in the popular Arab/Muslim imagination the phrase remains powerfully associated with Meir, and it was this usage that I intended to bring in to our proceedings.
5. The Palestinian term for their displacement from the land in 1948, which remains hotly contested in Israel.

References

Akhtar, S. (2010). Editor's introduction: An alternative to the current literary sport of Muslim bashing. *International Journal of Applied Psychoanalytic Studies*, 7(3): 231–234.

Bion, W. R. (1957). Differentiation of the psychotic from the non-psychotic personalities. *International Journal of Psychoanalysis*, 38(3–4): 266–275.

Bion, W. R. (1961). *Experiences in Groups and Other Papers*. New York: Basic Books.

Bion, W. R. (1967). Notes on memory and desire. *Psychoanalytic Forum*, 2: 272–280.

Chiesa, M. (2002). Response to special editorial. *International Journal of Psychoanalysis, 83*(5): 1437–1438.

Erlich, H. S. (2009). Supplementary comments on design and structure. In: H. S. Erlich, M. Erlich-Ginor, & H. Beland (Eds.), *Fed with Tears—Poisoned with Milk: The "Nazareth" Group-Relations-Conferences. Germans and Israelis: The Past in the Present* (pp. 43–47). Giessen, Germany: Psychosozial-Verlag.

Erlich, H. S., Erlich-Ginor, M., & Beland, H. (2009). *Fed with Tears—Poisoned with Milk: The "Nazareth" Group-Relations-Conferences. Germans and Israelis: The Past in the Present*. Giessen, Germany: Psychosozial-Verlag.

Freud, S. (1912 –13). Some points of agreement between the mental lives of savages and neurotics. In: *Totem and Taboo. S. E., 13*: 1–161. London: Hogarth.

Freud, S. (1914g). Remembering, repeating and working-through. *S. E., 12*: 147–156. London: Hogarth.

Freud, S. (1921c). *Group Psychology and the Analysis of the Ego. S. E., 18*: 69–143. London: Hogarth.

Freud, S. (1933b). *Why War? S. E., 22*: 199–215. London: Hogarth.

Grotstein, J. S. (1982). The spectrum of aggression. *Psychoanalytic Inquiry, 2*(2): 193–211.

Hayden, C., & Molenkamp, R. J. (2002). Tavistock Primer II. Portland, OR: The A. K. Rice Institute for the Study of Social Systems. http://static1.squarespace.com/static/538bb8e0e4b0723fe429f5f3/t/543eae47e4b0d6a781053631/1413393991912/AKRI+Tavistock+Primer+II.pdf, accessed 10 April 2015.

Kemp, M. (2005). On: A boycott by passport. [Editorial.] *International Journal of Psychoanalysis, 86*(2): 551–553.

Kemp, M. (2011). Dehumanization, guilt and large group dynamics with reference to the West, Israel and the Palestinians. *British Journal of Psychotherapy, 27*(4): 383–405.

Kestenberg, J. S. (1993). What a psychoanalyst learned from the Holocaust and genocide. *International Journal of Psychoanalysis, 74*(6): 1117–1129.

Kogan, I., & Chasseguet-Smirgel, J. (1995). *The Cry of Mute Children: A Psychoanalytic Perspective of the Second Generation of the Holocaust*. London: Free Association.

Lowe, F. (Ed.) (2013). *Thinking Space: Promoting Thinking about Race, Culture, and Diversity in Psychotherapy and Beyond*. London: Karnac.

Miller, E. (2009). The process of conference design. In: H. S. Erlich, M. Erlich-Ginor, & H. Beland (Eds.), *Fed with Tears—Poisoned with Milk: The "Nazareth" Group-Relations-Conferences. Germans and Israelis: The Past in the Present*. Giessen, Germany: Psychosozial-Verlag.

Muir, D. (2008). A land without a people for a people without a land. *Middle East Quarterly*, *15*(2): 55–62.

Pappe, I. (2006). *The Ethnic Cleansing of Palestine*. Oxford: Oneworld.

Poland, W. S. (2005). On: A boycott by passport. [Letter.] *International Journal of PsychoAnalysis*, *86*(3): 903.

Rosenfeld, H. A. (1965). *Psychotic States: A Psycho-Analytical Approach*. London: Hogarth and the Institute of Psychoanalysis.

Rosenfeld, H. A. (1987). *Impasse and Interpretation: Therapeutic and Anti-Therapeutic Factors in the Psychoanalytic Treatment of Psychotic, Borderline, and Neurotic Patients*. London: Tavistock.

Rothchild, A. (2014). *On the Brink: Israel and Palestine on the Eve of the 2014 Gaza Invasion*. Charlottesville, VA: Just World.

Rustin, M. (1991). Psychoanalysis, racism and anti-racism. In: *The Good Society and the Inner World: Psychoanalysis, Politics and Culture* (pp. 57–84). London: Verso.

Schonfeld, J. (2016). A totem and a taboo: Germans and Jews re-enacting aspects of the Holocaust. *European Judaism*, *49*(2): 87–106.

Segal, H. (1964). *Introduction to the Work of Melanie Klein*. London: Heinemann Medical.

Shlaim, A. (2009). *Israel and Palestine: Reappraisals, Revisions, Refutations*. London: Verso.

Stewart, H. (1991). *Psychic Experience and Problems of Technique*. London: Routledge.

Volkan, V. (1988). *The Need to Have Enemies and Allies: From Clinical Practice to International Relationships*. Northvale, NJ: Jason Aronson.

CHAPTER NINE

Psychoanalysis and feminism: a modern perspective

Ruth McCall

I've been involved with psychoanalytic ideas for twenty-five years and with feminist ideas for about forty, so it's probably easy to understand why I'm interested at applying ideas from each discipline to the other. Both disciplines have something striking in common. In the 1970s, being a feminist or a psychoanalyst was voguish and represented being in the vanguard. Today, both terms—feminist and psychoanalyst—seem to have acquired a patina of something unpleasant and unwanted. It's usual now to hear women refuse to describe themselves as feminists; feminism continues to be savagely ridiculed, and the same can be said for psychoanalysis, now considered by many to be a slow, old-hat treatment practised by elitist pedants.

So, I find myself with a foot in two unpopular camps but I continue to believe that both arenas are important for society and young people as much today as when I was a student forty years ago.

When I decided to change from my previous career in the media and business management to psychoanalysis, my feminist friend and company investor told me she just could not understand my move. She said all she could think of was Freud's theory of penis envy and female sexuality and she wondered how I could join such a discredited profession, one that undermines and devalues women.

Undeterred I made my move and I wonder how many feminists still feel suspicious of psychoanalysis. Equally I wonder how many psychoanalysts are suspicious of feminism and what some might see as the monstrous regimen of women that courses through modern psychoanalytic thinking.

At this point, forty-five plus years on from Juliet Mitchell's groundbreaking work on *Psychoanalysis and Feminism* (1974), breadth is as interesting as depth and I believe that feminist positions and preoccupations vis-à-vis psychoanalysis have altered. Freudian truisms that led my second-generation feminist colleague to be so disturbed twenty-five years ago have, I think, diminished in their power but new positions require elaboration and comprehension. And so, I will be asking you to consider Freudian theory, but also that of Melanie Klein, Donald Winnicott, and more contemporary psychoanalysts. Let's look at the myriad objections some women and feminists both male and female have expressed at the tenets and practice of classical psychoanalysis and let's see where we are now.

I will look at the position of women in the profession itself. Do feminist principles prevail? Or are we the second sex in our institutes and consulting rooms? How do we think of psychoanalysts? Male and old? White and upper class? Authoritarian? Or young, female, non-white? A few minutes with psychoanalysts in literature will help us see where the clichés and assumptions take root and then in turn promote a not entirely true vision of what I believe is still today a revolutionary and life-changing set of ideas.

Some of us argue that even the very nature of how mental disturbance is construed is filled with cultural and gender prejudices. Black males are so much more likely to be diagnosed as paranoid schizophrenics, and white women once as hysterics and now as borderline personality disordered. These tropes emerge from Western psychiatry but find some place in psychoanalytic thinking. All of us in the profession have to acknowledge and know something about our own unconscious, our own normalising tendencies and developmental history in culturally specific domains.

I am Ruth McCall, I have been in the field of psychoanalysis for twenty-five years or so, as analysand, postgraduate student, member of the British Psychoanalytical Society, academic at University College London, and I am now in full-time private practice in London. Prior to my analytic training, I worked in television in the UK and founded the production company I left for psychoanalysis. My working life has been in the United Kingdom. I have always been a feminist. I took for granted the achievements of the suffragettes and the feminists who were paving the way for huge social change as

I was growing up. My generation knew nothing much of a world without effective contraception, abortion, and relative equality in the workplace, though all these incredible and society-changing innovations arrived only during my lifetime.

Juliet Mitchell's publication of *Psychoanalysis and Feminism* (1974) arrived just four years after Barbara Castle (a female Labour cabinet minister) pushed through the Equal Pay Act in Britain. But let's note that research reveals that women across the Western world continue to earn between 10% and 25% less than equivalent male workers and the Wikipedia article I consulted to confirm the date of the Equal Pay Act does not even refer to Barbara Castle herself. Her name as a woman has been lost. Something I will return to later, briefly, is a glance at whether psychoanalysis can help us understand why the Conservative Party has managed to field two women prime ministers and party leaders while the Labour Party has managed none, and the first iteration of Jeremy Corbyn's shadow cabinet aroused disapproval and disappointment because it was notably short of women.

I entered university in 1976 when women's groups in Britain were fashionable. Every student male and female that I knew belonged to one and we read the work of feminist authors Kate Millett, Shulamith Firestone, Eva Figes, and Germaine Greer. I discovered during my researches that in the same year, a Spanish psychoanalyst, one Marina Prado, wrote an article published in the *American Journal of Psychoanalysis* about "Feminism and women analysts" (1976). Casually, she informs the reader that, at that time, women in Spain were compelled to live with their parents until the age of twenty-three, they could own property but not sell it without their husband's consent, and single incidences of female sexual infidelity were punished while men's considerable infidelity went unnoticed. Prado tells us that "Until recently, women devoted most of their energies to the cycle of conception, pregnancy and nursing. Today however, internal and external circumstances have made it possible for them to aspire to something else" (1976, p. 82). But apparently at that time it was accepted practice in Spain that an individual would have two psychoanalysts, one male and one female. Each could then manage different parts of the patient and the weakness of the woman analyst could be countered by the ego strength of the male. Leaving aside the logistical and expense considerations of this unusual arrangement, the article tells us something about the traditionalist sense of masculine and feminine identity deep within psychoanalysis in a patriarchal society in Spain in the 1970s.

While I am interested to be reminded that feminists and women in the 1970s seem to have taken access to straightforward conception, pregnancy, and nursing for granted, and hoped that women's experiences would be extended and developed out of the home with corresponding access to contraception, abortion, and career development, the same is not true in my contemporary milieu and it is in the realm of anxieties around partnering, conceiving, assisted or not, birthing, feeding, and mothering that the women in my practice often seem to be exercised, in what seems to be a reversal of feminine and feminist concerns. But then, to be fair, these are often now male concerns too as we all wrestle with the consequences of huge social shifts. Indeed, some of what I argue should be a fruitful relationship between feminism and psychoanalysis stems from recent developments in the psychoanalysis of women as females with diverse but specific experiences. Contemporary female psychoanalysts have developed understanding of the conscious and unconscious significance of menstruation, pregnancy, birth, infant feeding, and menopause. But then that can bring us into conflict with those feminists who wish to repudiate the conventional role of woman and the feminine as being defined through specific female biological experiences, including the maternal. Both feminism and psychoanalysis contain different groups: those who emphasise anatomical and biologically determined difference between males and females and those who argue for socially and environmentally constructed gender difference.

So, let's turn to psychoanalytic theory and theorists and sketch some of the concepts and preconceptions on both sides that have caused problems for feminists, and also some of the developments that I believe take psychoanalysis and feminism into greater harmony.

When Juliet Mitchell was writing about psychoanalysis and feminism a couple of generations ago, she was writing to redress the view that psychoanalysis is inherently anti-female, with Freud, the founder, a proven misogynist. To refresh your memory let me take you through some of Freud's propositions that led to these responses.

Freud's earliest cases were bourgeois women from his home city of Vienna. They were characterised as hysterics and as Freud developed his working ideas about psychoanalysis through the treatment of hysteria, then epidemic in the Western world, they provided the live clinical material around which Freud commenced his psychoanalytic theorising. Famously, Freud firstly believed that the florid organic symptoms of hysteria, the paralyses and fits, being struck dumb and bedridden and so on, told stories from an unconscious dominated by sexual wishes, often incestuous, made unconscious through repression. He notably didn't think of the effects of male-dominated social structure.

Patients told Freud of childhood sexual experiences that led him to theorise that childhood seduction (really rape and molestation—seduction sounds so misleadingly gentle) were the root causes of hysteria. But he reversed this fundamentally sociological idea of the origins of hysterical pathology into ideas that looked at phantasies of sex and love with parents and elders through the development of his ideas about the Oedipus conflict as the source for unconscious conflict. So from the start Freud seemed to step away from the idea that children, especially girl children, might be the actual victims of incestuous and other child abuse that was causative of pathology. Freud apologists remind us that Freud did not deny that children were sexually abused in reality, instead he added the concept of infantile and child sexuality and crucially added the desire and fantasy of the child to the conception of psychosexual development. But this issue perhaps began the characterisation of Freud as being blind to the social oppression of his female patients, preferring instead to endow them with sexual desire and turning a blind eye to actual assault.

Forty years later the Hungarian psychoanalyst and theoretician Sandor Ferenczi turned this position around and restated his belief in the widespread sexual molestation of children, girls and boys, placing these childhood assaults at the heart of pathological later development. In modern times I have never come across a psychoanalyst, however traditionalist, who flat out denies the frequency of sexual assault and violence to children and adults, but Freud's somewhat contradictory and complex positions on the actuality of rape and molestation and his depictions of the ubiquity of unconscious phantasy and oedipal desire have made him the target for both feminist and scholarly condemnation.

As Freud began developing his methods of free association—in essence encouraging his patients to speak freely about any ideas and images that come to mind—he became fascinated with the other world of the unconscious part of the mind that revealed itself to him through free talking, the interpretation of dreams, and the famous Freudian slips and mistakes that when examined show that the unconscious is timeless, infantile, and contains instinct-initiated fantasy and repressed experiences, some from earliest infancy. He thought that the power of the sexual drive, libido, could be discerned from the earliest months and as he worked to put together a theory of psychosexual development he began to set out thoughts about the sexual differentiation between male and female. Freud's writing is complex and his theories not always consistent (a truth which continues into psychoanalysis today). He appeared to set out an unavoidable biological destiny for men and women based on innate sexual differentiation while simultaneously, and with striking modernity, maintaining that we are not born male and female but are inherently bisexual and bi-gendered, acquiring characteristics of masculinity and femininity only over time. From my perspective there is a clear duality in Freud's theorising and it is very easy to slip into either camp but it is striking that it is a duality which continues to divide both feminism and psychoanalysis. Both have their adherents to the view that "biology is destiny" and both have practitioners and theorists whose view of gender is less anatomical, more psychological and sociological.

But to return to the feminist charge sheet we see that Freud's position is hard to comprehend from a modern perspective. Freud asserted that the penis was the only organ known to both boys and girls because it is visually present from birth. According to his theorising both sexes are aware of the penis but not any female sexual organs and this recognition involves inculcating in males the terror of castration, which could render them into wounded, lesser humans like the penis-less girls they see, and invokes in girls a resentment towards their mothers for endowing them so cruelly with nothing. And from this castration complex, with Freud's addition of an Oedipus complex that involves the father threatening the male child with castration for desiring the mother, springs the idea of that most disliked Freudian concept of all, "penis envy". Penis envy was made part of the female destiny, and ideas about envying the penis, or the phallus, feeling less than the male and producing hatred towards the mother and an unconscious quest for possession of the penis understandably brings forward now, and brought forward then, the resentment of female psychoanalysts and women generally. Freud came to the idea that the longing for a baby is the inheritor and solution for penis envy and how the little girl comes to find compensation in her female state. Freud essentially believed the little girl was a diminished little boy until recognition of the fact of her castration propels her to the father and leads to a passive longing for penis and baby through penis envy. Freud compounded these assertions by toying with the idea that activity is intrinsically masculine and passivity feminine, beginning a trend in psychoanalysis towards explanations for masochism in women that was taken up by first-wave female psychoanalyst followers such as Helene Deutsch and Jeanne Lampl-de Groot.

Famously Freud suggested that the little girl endowed her clitoris with phallic grandeur and as part of a move to mature feminine sexuality had to transfer clitoral sensuality to vaginal receptivity and sensitivity, a move that he felt was hard to make and which mirrored a move from what he called the girl's homosexual attachment to her mother (female) to the love and desire for her father (male). Freud thought the boy's journey was easier since in heterosexuality the boy remains attached to a female love and sex object and, of course, although he may fear castration he is in safe possession of a penis. Finally, Freud believed that women through their relative lack of castration anxiety had a weaker superego than men and so a poorer moral conscience. We are now of course amply aware that many people, considerably more than was once assumed, are neither clearly adherent to male or female gender certainty or heterosexuality and as I will be discussing later, perhaps surprisingly, other lines of Freud's theories can help us grasp and see these as ordinary developments.

Freud's dualism of thought, his anatomical elaborations and symbolic considerations about the elusivity of masculinity and femininity found different homes. In the pragmatic English-speaking world, it seems psychoanalysts took a more literal biological and sociological perspective, particularly in America, home of ego psychology. There, tackling penis envy in women's psychoanalytic treatments and ensuring a move from clitoral to vaginal climax was seen explicitly as part of the aim of the treatment and conforming to the role of the submissive, maternal female, an important development.

In 1970 Sue Kaufman published the novel *Diary of a Mad Housewife*, later made into a successful movie, based on her own experience of being a wife in the 1960s and being in psychoanalytic treatment. Bettina, the protagonist, is unhappy with her housewifely lot and struggles in her marriage with her domineering husband, Jonathan. Jonathan forces her into treatment with the Freudian psychoanalyst Dr Popkin to bring her to rights, just as the famous young hysteric Dora's father did with her in 1899 when he took her to Freud to be brought to order. But unlike the Freud who did actually listen to Dora and refused to conceal her father's extramarital affair, Dr Popkin fulfils the expectation of the day. As Bettina says, "He'll be thrilled by the brilliant simplicity of it all. You know—the Forceful Dominant Male, the Submissive Woman? The Breadwinner who has every right to expect the Obedient Wife to carry out all his orders? He'll lap it up." But by the end of the novel Bettina has been apparently successfully treated by Dr Popkin, though the putative female reader is probably supposed to see through her "enlightenment". "I know at last what I'm going to settle for and who I'm going to be. Who? Who is that? Why, Tabitha-Twitchit-Danvers, of course. The lady with the apron. And check-lists. And keys. It's me. Oh, it's very me, and I can't for the life of me see why I didn't realize that before." This illustration from popular culture shows perhaps why Betty Friedan, writing at exactly the same time in America could say, "Over and over women heard in voices of tradition and of Freudian sophistication that they could desire no greater destiny than to glory in their femininity" (1963, p. 5).

But it was also in America in 1966 that Mary Jane Sherfey, a New York psychoanalyst, dropped a bomb on the contemporary psychoanalytic profession. Based on Masters and Johnson's research into human sexuality, Mary Jane informed psychoanalysts that there was only one form of unified female orgasm and that a main tenet of American psychoanalytical treatment of women was unfounded in science. She also drew attention to an obscure finding from 1950s embryology that the human foetus is female until hormonally masculinised and is in fact the default human model. So Freud's myth of the girl child as a little damaged man was dramatically reversed. The irony for me is that while Mary Jane Sherfey's prophetic and lucid findings were absorbed, accepted, and changed practice, her name is not known to contemporary psychoanalysis. Like Barbara Cartland, another female presence lost.

While psychoanalysis in America took to normalisation and adaption to market forces, in Europe things looked a bit different. Ernest Jones, founder of psychoanalysis in Britain, was a champion for a psychoanalytic view of female development that expounded primary femininity and did not regard the little girl as a little castrated man. Karen Horney and Melanie Klein both provided early in the twentieth century developments in psychoanalytic theory that brought new perspectives. Horney and Jones began to put forward the idea that both little boys and girls knew of female anatomy. Psychoanalysts began to play with the idea that perhaps males too might experience body envy, above all of the experience of conception and childbirth, alongside a female's envy of the penis.

Freud came to look to women psychoanalysts to elaborate the significance of early attachment to mother. He acknowledged in *The Question of Lay Analysis* (1926e) that for him "the sexual life of adult women is a 'dark continent' for psychology". By and large Freud's final words and works still seem to contain the germ of misogyny. I quote from "Analysis Terminable and Interminable": "We often have the impression that with a wish for a penis [in women] and the masculine protest [in men] we have penetrated through all the psychological strata and have reached bedrock, and that thus our activities are at an end. This is probably true, since, for the psychical field, the biological field does in fact play the part of the underlying bedrock. The repudiation of femininity can be nothing else than a biological fact, a part of the great riddle of sex" (1937c, p. 17).

In the UK during the 1930s, the popularisation of Freud's work began to mutate into another familiar psychoanalytic trope—that is the idea that murky happenings in early childhood will ruin a person's character for life. Alongside this came the beginnings of an understanding of some basic psychoanalytic ideas that were percolating through to the intelligentsia of the day, which also included an idea of a particular propensity for women to form obedient transferential bonds to their authoritarian male psychoanalyst. In *Cold Comfort Farm*, a comic classic from 1932 authored by Stella Gibbons, we find the unfortunate Judith Starkadder fixated on her male child, Seth, sexually drawn to him and enacting an uncomfortable oedipal scenario within her family. The Mary Poppins-like protagonist, Flora, wastes no time in calling in Dr Mudel, an émigré Viennese psychoanalyst. In a short lunch break Dr Mudel effects a transference to himself of Judith Starkadder's fixated sexuality.

"Judith began to glow darkly and do the slumbering volcano act in Dr Mudel's direction. Flora could not help admiring the practiced skill with which he had effected the transference in the course of the commonplace conversation during lunch ... Dr Mudel said, "I shall take her to the nursing home and let her talk to me ... I make her interested in old churches, there are hundreds in Europe, she has money yes? Do not distress yourself she will be quite happy without the sexual neurosis."

This comic vignette shows us the financially grasping male psychoanalyst in charge of the naive but neurotic woman, the percolation into literary life of basic Freudian truisms, and the presence of the émigré psychoanalyst, that Mitteleuropean male character who exemplified psychoanalysis in the popular media then and probably now.

While the Americans and the Brits held to Freud's most biological views about women's sexuality and character formation, French psychoanalysis even pre-Lacan was never drawn to such a literal and medicalised path.

Always more allied with philosophy, it was Jacques Lacan with his famous return to Freud who took Freudian thinking in another direction. Telling us that the unconscious is structured like a language, Lacan took on Freud's understanding of castration and made it central to his thinking. He converted an everyday anatomical organ, the penis, into a phallus. In depicting the effect on both anatomical sexes of the desire of the mother and the symbolic and unattainable nature of the phallus, Lacan provided a system of thought that could be used to equalise between the sexes the sense of inadequacy brought about through lack. Many of us women continue to note drily that it remains suspiciously male triumphalist to make the key signifier of lack, male, and the penis the supposedly abstract phallus. It was though to Lacan that Juliet Mitchell turned in 1974 when she wrote *Psychoanalysis and Feminism* as she embarked on the rehabilitation of Freudian views of women. It is her contention that the biological and literal accounts of Freud miss the centrality of the unconscious.

It was that European émigrée to Britain, Melanie Klein, who gradually turned phallocentric, father-focused Freudian psychoanalytic theory on its head. Over the course of a working life in which she too claimed a return to Freud with her strong adherence to his concept of life and death instincts, Klein simultaneously provided a striking turn to what is now called object relations theory and finally ushered in mother. Mrs Klein worked with little children and saw their play as the counterpart to adult free talking and through her observation of the fundamental human scenarios children enacted, and through her work analytically with adults, Klein came to feel that a child's early relation to the breast, and subsequently the whole object, mother, was critical in forming an internal sense of goodness for every individual. But for Klein too there have been dualist misunderstandings. How biological and real is her breast? Or is the breast only a symbol of nurturance that can be provided by male or female carer? Klein made the acquisition of an internal good breast object an important development towards health for all people and she took very seriously the experiences of both male and female infants in their earliest weeks and months at mother's breast.

Klein was aware of Karen Horney's assumption of primary innate femininity and her idea that masculine narcissism contributed to denial of knowledge of the vagina in male psychoanalysts as well as in children, because she was part of the intense debates about female sexuality that took place in the 1920s and 1930s between London and Berlin and Vienna.

Klein reworked Freud's masculist Oedipus complex and shifted it back into babyhood. She thought that both male and female children experience a femininity phase wherein like mother they want to produce babies and milk and contain father's penis. The Kleinian mother is the big cat who got all the cream and the kittens want to be the same. But Klein thought the child's wish to be the same could easily turn to envious appropriation and with theft in mind the children came to fear that mother would retaliate. So, mother was at once the nurturer and the condemner and taking the essence of her in produced the beginning of the superego. Klein was not averse to biologism herself and seems also to have assumed that anatomy was destiny in her theory that as little children pass into a depressive position in which they realise mother is both good and bad object, they will respectively identify with father or mother depending on their biological sex. But Klein had succeeded in bringing mother and her breast to the psychoanalytic table to join father and she has never left.

I won't go into fine theoretical details of the list of all the women psychoanalytic theorists who have repudiated Freud's repudiation of femininity. In America, Karen Horney who emigrated from Berlin was a striking early doyenne of feminist psychoanalysis, alongside home-nurtured Clara Thompson. Both founded their own training institutes. In more recent times Nancy Chodorow and Jessica Benjamin have refashioned elements of psychoanalytic theory to produce object relations-based theory that looks to the role of mother and explores understanding of discriminatory practices in society. The French of course do it their own way and Hélène Cixous, Luce Irigaray, and Julia Kristeva have all richly developed Freudian thinking from a feminist perspective.

But pure theory is one thing and what it might lead to can be quite another.

Take D. W. Winnicott, a British paediatrician and psychoanalyst who began in the Melanie Klein fold but who developed his own distinctive theory of human development. Winnicott came to the attention of the British public through radio talks he began giving in the late 1940s, just after the Second World War, on baby care aimed at "ordinary devoted mothers", a phrase he intended as respectful but one that women now can find condescending. Dr Winnicott gave importance to the impact of the actual non-fantasised mother–baby relationship and made it central to his thinking of human development. He wrote about a baby's early emotional development and how it depended on the presence of a mother who could meet her infant's needs for a period absolutely, through identifying with baby in a stage he called primary maternal preoccupation. Only gradually could absolute 100% baby sensitivity and care give way to what he came to call the love and occasional benign neglect of the famous "good enough" mother. Father's role was to look after mother and society's role to look after the family. All this produced a boy or a girl who could attain a sense of true self. These are theories I like and work with a lot, but feminists have been as distressed by the implications of Winnicottian theory as they were by Freud's. Is it really the case that babies need such individual, maternal care? Can father or nanny or granny not suffice? Because if modern psychoanalytic object relations theory tells us that babies need mother and need her for years, how can mother be writing, working, thinking, creating, and developing? And, more to the point, be economically viable? Psychoanalysis does not know the answer to these questions.

The psychoanalyst John Bowlby opened another door with his research work on attachment. At the heart of this is the attachment between mother and baby. That research led to what we now call attachment theory. This recognises that humans form attachment patterns, templates of relating in our minds, based on our early experiences of care with, guess who, mother. The ideal is that of secure attachment. Currently there is a fashion for attachment parenting, a mode of looking after babies with maximal psychological empathy and long-term physical closeness. The American paediatrician William Sears and his wife Martha explicitly developed attachment parenting in response to Bowlby's research findings and advocate that there is no higher purpose for a woman than as mother, which takes us back in a circle to where women have always been. Some academic feminists are aghast at this turn. Harvard gynaecologist Amy Tuteur has stated that "Attachment parenting amounts to a new subjection of the woman's body under social control," and a recent book by Élisabeth Badinter, *The Conflict: How Modern Motherhood Undermines the Status of Women*, specifically attacks attachment parenting for its retrogressive effects on women's lives.

More privately, in the consulting room, the confusion about how to be a good enough mother is powerfully felt. The terrible feelings of failure and regret that are experienced by women who have difficult births or who cannot or do not choose to breastfeed are very significant. Attachment parenting, designed to be a liberal alternative to nineteenth-century regimens of controlled feeding and crying can also produce anguish.

Implicitly much modern psychoanalysis continues to echo the idea that there is no higher calling for a woman than through motherhood. A common practice in many psychoanalytic trainings is the period of time psychoanalytic trainees observe a baby, from birth on for a year or more. The baby is observed for an hour weekly, the trainee writes a detailed description of what he or she observes, and small groups of trainees meet weekly with an experienced psychoanalyst to discuss the observations. The aim is to help trainees manage the role of observer in highly charged emotional situations whilst also providing direct experience of the beginnings of life. In my experience, too often these seminars turn into mother observation rather than baby observation, and as a profession we can turn our theory and no doubt our own unconscious mother grievance to the task of holding these mothers to account for the pathologisation of their babies. Father is most often at work so escapes the denigration and implication in non-optimal parenting.

But it is actually in the process of becoming a mother that many women find themselves looking for psychoanalytic help. Some dread postnatal breakdown perhaps because their own mother suffered this. Some find the process of pregnancy tormenting and the prospect of being a mother horrifying, and some women believe that helping themselves will help their babies.

I believe that modern psychoanalysis, drawing on threads of theory from Freud onwards, has much to offer in the realm of supporting men and women through life-changing transitions, including many of the classically female dilemmas around relationships, fertility, birthing, and mothering. Over the last twenty or more years there has been a development of psychoanalysis to apply to mothers and infants simultaneously, helping mothers to find ways to imaginatively relate to their babies.

But how, you might ask, is psychoanalysis as a profession? How is life in our psychoanalytic institutes, clinics, and trainings? Freud's own record in this direction was surprisingly solid. Despite the prejudices of his time which perhaps marked some, but not all of his theorising, Freud was a relatively equal opportunity psychoanalyst. He famously promoted lay psychoanalysis and did not think that only medically qualified professionals should hold the field. This was particularly important for women because up until the 1970s in the Western world, medical schools admitted fewer than 15% of women on a deliberate quota basis. Freud actively encouraged the early women psychoanalytic thinkers, Lou Andreas Salome, Marie Bonaparte,

Sabina Spielrein, Helene Deutsch, and his own daughter Anna. His male disciples were also relatively welcoming to women analysts and, as we saw, president of the British Psychoanalytical Society, Ernest Jones, eagerly invited Mrs Melanie Klein to England to enlighten and develop British psychoanalysis. So far so good. But in practice psychoanalysis as an institution seems to be prey to some of the same difficulties that pervade society—as Ms Prado's article from Spain in the 1970s graphically illustrates. Whilst I think all psychoanalytic societies in modern times have at least equal representations of men and women and quite often more female practitioners, and while many women psychoanalytic thinkers are published and much respected, it is striking how in their self-administration our institutes mimic standard power structures. In my home British Psychoanalytical Society, there have been thirty member presidents. Six have been women. I was until recently honorary treasurer for our society and was unsurprised to discover that I am only the second woman in this role.

As so often in committee life, psychoanalysed or not, men and women fall easily into gendered divisions of labour. And men still seem just that bit more prepared to put themselves forward as seniors, as training analysts, supervisors, and speakers.

A question that our profession has found difficult to know about is whether it matters if you have your psychoanalysis with a man or a woman. Freud began to think that maybe women could tease out traces of earliest pre-oedipal preverbal experience in ways that were less accessible for him. In treating the American poet H. D., he famously bemoaned how hard it was to endure being mother in the transference when he felt himself so very masculine. Conventionally nowadays I think we mostly hear an idea that the anatomical gender of the analyst does not matter. In the transference we will contain both maternal and paternal projections and our capacities for imaginative intuition should mean that our bodies should not limit our understanding. But I think these sentiments may mask unknown complexities. How much can I know at a gut level about erectile dysfunction or my male colleague of premenstrual tension? Some women psychoanalysts have argued that since the female body is subject to particular experiences of body change over a lifetime, mirrored by psychical complexity, it can be helpful for some women to be in analysis with women. Or should we just do the best we can, recognising that every psychoanalyst–analysand match is but one of myriad possible pairings and we each of us have inside us an unconscious kaleidoscope of male and female identifications and experiences? Some of us see the analytic enterprise as analogous in part to re-parenting. Do we need to be re-mothered or re-fathered? Some choose their psychoanalyst with this consideration somewhat in mind and this can then be thought about in the consulting room.

I would like to make a few brief comments about factors informed by psychoanalytic principles that may play some part in considering both antipathy towards women in positions of authority and, conversely, enthusiasm. Many commentators have speculated that misogyny played its part in the refusal of the American public to elect its first woman president, although there were clearly many other factors, including, in my view, Mr Trump's presentation of masculist triumph, a man whose building erections bear his name and whose whole family presents an idealised view of white, reality-television-style, tribal success. Perhaps more relevant here in Europe is the part women play in right-wing movements. Angela Merkel, perhaps the most politically powerful woman in the world, is from the right; Marine Le Pen, who achieved a big vote for the far right in France is female, and we have our own Mrs Thatcher and Mrs May. Sociologically, I would make the point that in wealthier sections of society, women have been freed to write, to be involved with politics, and to work generally, because they can afford to hire help. Whereas in working-class societies there has traditionally been a stronger emphasis on more stereotypical male and female roles. Until very recently the trades unions fought for the working man and indeed some opposed the introduction of equal pay for women. The polarity in the battle of the sexes can seem more acute where the fundamental battle is for more resource all round and changing an entire system.

It is in the realm of transference to nanny or mother and family conservatism that I believe the link of female leaders and the right wing resides.

Most people have been cared for by females in early life. By mothers, or nannies, or grannies. And this relationship forms a particular transference to women which includes love and hate. Women will have been experienced very frequently as the guardians of home and hearth, sometimes as arbiters of nurturance and frequently as the dispensers of discipline and the law. These early seeds provide a tendency in later life to look to women to uphold and defend conservative structures, a role played notably by the Virgin Mary in religion. And with reference to family, it is not surprising that so very many women leaders are the daughters and widows and wives of admired male leaders, including of course Hillary Clinton herself. It seems that the tendency to regress to family structure and certainty is deep in many cultures. Finally, only 7.5% of the world's leaders are indeed female.

It is only relatively recently that it has been acceptable to challenge some of the theoretical conventions in our field, and psychoanalytic feminists have work that remains to be completed. But as a profession and professionals who are of our time and our own cultural milieus it seems to me that change will always be yoked to what we mirror from outside. Every era has its challenges and its limitations. What seemed revolutionary in Freud's day still seems revolutionary in some respects but restricted in others. Like Freud, we cannot see our own blind spots, we can only hope to bring our truthful and passionate belief in the power of the unconscious to what lies before us now.

References

Badinter, E. (2012). *The Conflict: How Modern Motherhood Undermines the Status of Women*. A. Hunter (Trans.). New York: Metropolitan.

Freud, S. (1926e). *The Question of Lay Analysis. S. E., 20.* London: Hogarth.

Freud, S. (1937c). Analysis terminable and interminable. *S. E., 23.* London: Hogarth.

Friedan, B. (1963). The problem that has no name. In: *The Feminist Mystique* (pp. 5–20). London: Penguin Classics, 2010.

Gibbons, S. (1932). *Cold Comfort Farm*. London: Longman.

Kaufman, S. (1970). *Diary of a Mad Housewife*. New York: Thunder's Mouth Press.

Mitchell, J. (1974). *Psychoanalysis and Feminism: A Radical Reassessment of Freudian Psychoanalysis*. London: Allen Lane. [Republished London: Penguin, 1990.]

Prado, M. (1976). Feminism and women analysts. *American Journal of Psychoanalysis, 36*(1): 79–84.

Sherfey, M. J. (1966). The evolution and nature of female sexuality in relation to psychoanalytic theory. *Journal of the American Psychoanalytic Association, 14*(1): 28–128.

CHAPTER TEN

Reflection or action: and never the twain shall meet

R. D. Hinshelwood

There is a major problem in using psychoanalysis in political activity. The ways the individual is influenced by unconscious forces and by external social influences are essentially different, and these categories can be bridged conceptually only with some difficulty. I have been struck for some time by the conceptual divergence.

If economic activity and bodily experiences create separate theories, they also generate separate superstructures—the world of social relations and the world of object relations respectively. The upshot (of this argument) is to show that the two superstructures converge. They lean together (Hinshelwood, 1996, p. 100).

In this chapter, I shall reflect on the issues involved in this leaning together stance.

Group dynamics and the Labour Party

Back in the 1990s, I was part of a group that worked out some ideas which we might take to the Labour Party. In the dying regime of the Conservatives at the time, Margaret Thatcher and John Major were hanging on until the election in 1997. The Labour Party was desperate to convince the electorate of its better policies. The idea was whether we could give an account of group dynamics which might be helpful to Labour to understand the way to create a more democratic society. At the time Labour were talking about "the third way"; somewhat vague, but it appeared that it might promote more measured attitudes in society suggestive of depressive position thinking— ambivalence, considerateness towards everyone, and generally a reluctance to accept the unrealistic perfectionism of ideologies. It seemed there could be a match between the political rhetoric and the study of unconscious group processes. In the event when we met a couple of people at Millbank (Labour headquarters), it was clear they were politely indifferent to what we were trying to present. Their interest was whether we had the secret of how to influence the electorate to vote for Labour. They wanted advice on their marketing. There seemed a radical disconnection between our earnest views about a more mature society, and their wish for effective marketing.

I have thought, over the years, about our naivety. Obviously, there is a potential for psychology to be used as a social and public instrument for manipulation. In this context I came across the writing of one of the founders of marketing and public relations, in the US back in the 1920s. He wrote, "If we understand the mechanism and motives of the group mind, is it not possible to control and regiment the masses according to our will without their knowing about it?" (Bernays 1928, p, 71). In the same work, *Propaganda*, he wrote, "The conscious and intelligent manipulation of the organized habits and opinions of the masses is an important element in democratic society. Those who manipulate this unseen mechanism of society constitute an invisible government which is the true ruling power of our country" (p. 10).

I find this unpalatable. Shamefully, this author, a founder of this "invisible government" as he called it, was Edward Bernays, Freud's nephew. He, like Freud, was interested in the "unseen mechanisms" at work in individuals— but for different purposes.

Political change and psychoanalytic change

The aim of psychoanalysis is to change things. That is what patients want help with. The aim of politics is *also* to change things. But the changes, and how they are brought about, are completely different. Is that difference bridgeable? Influencing a patient towards some healthy state, and doing the same for society, shouldn't be impossibly different. After all, a society is made of people. So what really is the difference, and how can one inform the other?

Practising psychoanalysts address the internal unconscious factors that determine an individual's personality—and how the individual is captured and controlled by them. On the other hand, political attitudes and actions are *socially* generated, arising, many would say, from the economic system of production. The individual is located at the junction of these two sets of influences, one from inside and one from outside. If someone has a phobia for spiders, he is driven by internal factors (his unconscious imagining, say, that the web-like embrace is a controlling mother). If someone drives his car on the left-hand side of the road, it is from social forces—the Highway Code, police patrol cars, and so on.

These are inherently different kinds of influences. How do social and unconscious determinism fit together? Edward Bernays decided it is simple, the external social category is used to manipulate the individuals' interior unconscious choices. Well ... for me that is not good enough, and I am interested in whether there are other ways by which these two categories of influences can be combined in our understanding (Hinshelwood, 1996).

Interpreting society!

I claim we need to find models of interaction between social relations and psychodynamics. It is, otherwise, so easy for us psychoanalysts to approach society or social institutions *as if they were individuals*. To equate a social organisation with the individual mind risks leaving out the very valid social, historical, and political forces that act on organisations and create cultures.

I am thinking of the campaign started by psychoanalysts in the 1980s, Psychoanalytic Psychotherapists against Nuclear War (PPANW). Led by Hanna Segal's especial interest, expressed in her paper "Silence Is the Real Crime" (1987), the individual defence mechanisms she suggested seemed to be simply aggregated, and she talked of regression during wartime from depressive position to paranoid–schizoid functioning. The campaign remained largely ineffective, so it seemed there were serious limitations to this kind of individualistic political approach. The political problem only disappeared with a political solution—the collapse of the Cold War in 1990. I would suggest that attributing individual dynamics to social and political issues risks psychoanalysis becoming irrelevant to social scientists and politicians.

Freud (1912–13) did something similar in *Totem and Taboo*, interpreting whole societies in terms of the psychodynamics of the Oedipus complex. He had relied on outdated texts such as Frazer's *Golden Bough* so that anthropologists contemporary with him, such as W. H. R. Rivers, Elliott Smith, or Malinowski, dismissed Freud easily as a positive danger! In fact, Malinowski described psychoanalysis as "an infection … of the neighbouring fields of science—notably that of anthropology, folklore and sociology" (1923, p. 650).

The need is to understand how the general social attitudes and policies resonate with unconscious processes, notably anxiety and defence, deep within individuals. This is easier said than done, and there is a place for some persistent thinking about these reverberating social–psychological dynamics.

Words as action

Psychoanalysis, the talking cure, is confined to using words to create meaning and conviction. Political action uses a very different resource, the power of numbers/crowds. Is the use of words and meanings adaptable to political campaigning?

Words are active things, they achieve more than transferring information. The Oxford philosopher J. L. Austin (1962) wrote a book entitled *How to Do Things with Words*. Words have impact. Can we do political things with words?

Some elements of what used to be called Western Marxism would have it that we can campaign by verbal argument or confrontation. These are the critical theorists. Critical theory is a body of social and philosophical debates which aim to go beyond just knowing things—not just to know how and why things are. Critical theorists aim to change things, particularly to emancipate human beings from dominance and slavery—as announced by Horkheimer (1931).

Closely associated is the concept used by Lukács (1971), "false consciousness". This very pregnant idea considers that much of the proletariat is sold an illusion about their value and place in society, and that this is false. But it is in the interests of the dominant class to cultivate the false notion. The working class for instance is there merely to sell their working time to commercial interests, without question. And so a political *act* would be to inform the proletariat of their rightful place as part owners of the products of their labour, for instance. This activity is sometimes called "consciousness raising".

The important point, however, is that listening in to these corrective arguments does not necessarily have impact. Instead, people under an ideological domination often have such a profound identification with a false consciousness, that a truer insight even to their own benefit is prevented. So the question is, how does that inhibition take over the consciousness of the proletariat?

In fact reflective insight is very difficult to sustain. The action of psychoanalysis is to stimulate a reflective practice in patients and the way they manage relationships. It has been possible to extend that sort of practice to group settings, and attempts to develop reflective practice for health workers and professional carers is now quite widespread. If we were really to follow the line of Lukács and Horkheimer and the critical theorists known as the Frankfurt School, we would need to extend reflective practice still further—beyond small groups of those who work with people, out to society at large. That is a tall order. But it is even more difficult because beyond the size problem there are the particular forces which jeopardise the fate of reflective practice in whole cultures.

"Social resistance"

Words are action, but they can be used in the opposite direction—against insight. In psychoanalysis this is called rationalisation. In political life it is called propaganda. How else could the hegemony of a social false consciousness come about except through words? There are a number of factors, and they are not all verbal, and their non-verbal quality makes them difficult to influence.

First is the Marxist theory of the social relations that develop in the course of production. The factory mode of production involving high levels of initial investment and capitalisation, structures a society into those who have or have not. The possession is money but not just money; it is also power. And it goes together. The factory owner has the power to give jobs (and take them away), he also owns the physical power of the factory, the power used in the manufacturing. The owner of power in the production process is the owner of power in social relations.

A *second factor* is the unconscious, and the psychologically internal one that sustains the construction of social relations, often long after they have ceased to be useful. This important idea about the persistence of social relations came from one of the Frankfurt school, Herbert Marcuse (1955), with his idea of surplus repression. Marcuse took up a remark of Freud's that the developing person does not take on the parents' value system, but the parents' superego, and that had been taken on from the grandparent generation, and so on. There is inevitably a considerable lag in any change. The end result for instance is that a superego embodying a Protestant work ethic from say the eighteenth century may have changed little by the twentieth century. Hence the repression of energy and its direction into work for industrial production is now far in excess of what is actually needed for contemporary production methods.

This is not necessarily the only form of mistaken self-consciousness due to a time lag in the development of the internal world. Consider the observations of Michael Šebek (1996, 1998), a Czech psychoanalyst. He found in ordinary relations outside the consulting room, that people in the Czech Republic hung on to ideas of totalitarian authority long after 1990, when the totalitarian Soviet regime disappeared.

Why is this internalisation of inappropriate value systems so difficult to shake? Perhaps only psychoanalysts can say much about the intricacies and problems of internalisation since it is so far outside conscious knowledge and control. Something can be done, and has been, using various practical steps for consciousness raising. This means the development of new ways of thinking, using debates, courses, and so on—and it has had some impact on feminist issues, racism, and so on. But it cannot really be said to have a broad impact, and people involved in it are usually already interested in changing their attitudes anyway.

And a *third factor* that sustains false consciousness is the deliberate manipulation of consciousness, often unconsciously. For instance, *Sun* newspaper headlines blast certainty in the form of paranoid outrage at millions and millions of people every day. How can people stop and reflect, when so many are struggling with contemporary capitalist austerity? This takes us back to the methods evolved by Bernays in his "invisible government".

Labour process

Something which troubles people when they think about it, though they don't think about it much because it is not so easy to grasp, is what is called "labour process" (Braverman, 1974). To explain this, consider a worker in a factory. The worker has necessary costs that go into sustaining his life.

This can be quantified in terms of money, and he is paid what he needs to survive and live. Each day he is paid that wage, and in exchange he provides a day's work. The factory has other expenses, the raw materials, tools and machines, the cost of the factory itself, some administration, banking costs, and so on. Altogether these are the manufacturing costs.

If the man is making, shall we say, nails in the factory, then a certain number of nails, at the market price, will roughly equate with the manufacturing costs, in other words the worker's wage plus the correct proportion of the other costs.

Then if the factory is a successful one, the worker will be making his quantity of nails in *less* than a full day. And so, for the rest of his working day, he will be making more nails than he costs. Now, under the system of hired labour, the extra nails will belong not to him, the worker, but to the factory—and its owner, who is a person or an enterprise, who have bought the whole day's work from him. Much of labour relations turns on the ownership of the extra number of nails, which the worker has made, over and above the manufacturing costs.

This is a system which does not apply just to factory work, but to a slave society, or any society where the ownership of the product is not vested in the worker who supplied the hours of work. This system of overproducing as it seems, with the accumulation of products, is especially characteristic of the capitalist mode of production. In contrast is a society based on self-employed land workers, craftsmen, or professionals. They own what they produce. These activities often tend to be those without manufactured products, but instead the provision of services. Of course, today by one means or another there is a move to commodify services in the same way as manufactured products, even using the same term "product" for a unit of service.

Incidentally, the concentrated effort in the Western economies to maximise the accumulation of products that *appear to be independent* of their makers, may have made an impact on other cultures. The anthropologist C. A. Gregory (1982), has attributed the strange phenomenon known as the potlatch to the arrival of Western explorers and merchants in New Guinea. The potlatch is a ritual requiring a seemingly bizarre accumulation of goods that are circulated apparently aimlessly around tribal communities. Of course there are other explanations, but it is possible that these tribes mirror for us the illogical nature of our system of production as it appeared to other cultures. The drastic division of production and ownership may seem odd to those cultures onto which the system has been slowly foisted as a model of mature civilisation.

Alienation

The reason for the unease in us about labour process and the ownership of manufactured products needs some understanding. In our society, there appears to have been an historical development of a particular bond between the producer and the products which emerge from his work. For instance, since the humanistic age of the Renaissance, painters sign their own pictures. That tells a story of how the bond between the individual producer and his opus has become a peculiarly significant feature of Western cultures. And it also shows the notable need to stamp one's ownership on what one produces.

So it is of interest that this division of the worker from the product of his work is also paradoxically so characteristic of our modern age. This culturally enforced division is especially significant in manual work. The factory worker's labour is physical, and he has therefore a particular bodily closeness to his product. There is an intimate connection between the worker and his product. So, the sale of his working hours removes the ownership of what is felt to be connected to him, and is in his experience a part of him. It is not too fanciful to accept that what we physically create—indeed what we intellectually create, like the chapter I am writing—is closely identified with me, and vice versa. I know that I am seen to a considerable extent as the person who has written certain things. Or, an artist, say Francis Bacon, is identified with the paintings he produced. In fact a painting of his may be referred to as "a Francis Bacon", meaning one of his pictures.

Marx seemed especially angry about this labour process which rips the product from the worker, like a new baby from its mother. Long before his classic book, *Das Kapital*, in 1856, we can read his humane ranting about this. In 1844 he was writing his notebooks which were published as *Economic and Philosophic Manuscripts* (1975). There he dealt with the unfairness of this separation of the producer from his product. As he put it,

> ... the object that labour produces, its product, stands opposed to it as something alien, as a power independent of the producer. The product of labour is labour embodied and made material in an object

... this realisation of labour appears as loss of reality for the worker, objectification as loss of and bondage to the object, and appropriation as estrangement, as alienation. (p. 324)

If the work product is disconnected, then the producer is disconnected to some degree from what is felt—by him, and by others—to be him. He becomes a lesser person as these aspects of himself are removed from him, or, as Marx said, "The worker becomes poorer the more wealth he produces" (p. 323). He becomes poorer in a psychological sense. This is a psychological understanding, not something that we would normally go to Karl Marx for.

Many years ago (Hinshelwood, 1983), I was struck by a parallel kind of description to be found in the psychoanalytic literature. For example, "In such fantasies products of the body and parts of the self are felt to be split off, projected into mother, and to be continuing their existence there" (Klein, 1955, p. 142).

No surprise that that comes from Melanie Klein, describing the mechanism of splitting of the ego, or self, and subsequent projective identification of a part of that divided self into some other person with harming effects: "I have referred to the weakening and impoverishment of the ego resulting from excessive splitting and projective identification" (Klein, 1946, p. 104).

For the idea of alienation, it would seem splitting is central, because the object that is the product of the worker "stands opposed" to him, and it is projected, *alien* and *independent*, yet it retains an identity with the worker, it *is labour embodied*. In other words, products of the person's (worker's) body are felt to have become separated off, alienated as if someone else.

In that paper of mine, I looked carefully at the way Marx described what he called "alienation", and I made a comparison with the psychoanalytic phenomena of splitting and projection. The similar descriptions of the way alienation is experienced, and the way splitting and projective identification are experienced is striking.

Implicit in this comparison is a particular view of the relations between social influences from the wider culture, and the individual level of the psychodynamics of personal experience and unconscious mechanisms. We know that alienation is conceptualised as having its origins in the mode of production, whilst its counterpart, splitting and projective identification, have their origins in the unconscious need to deal with an anxiety—the fear of annihilation, or a fear for survival. The alienation from the ownership of the product and the psychological mechanisms of splitting and projective identification, converge in this case—the outside social influences and the inner mechanisms coincide.

Self-perpetuating systems

So, it seems, alienation is an interesting instance where political processes play on already existing psychological mechanisms. With that convergence, politics may succeed handsomely. We know that psychological mechanisms are defences aimed at managing anxiety by avoiding it, and like all defence mechanisms, as Freud showed, they are usually imperfect and cause further effects known as symptoms. And this is the case, no less, with the mechanisms of splitting and projective identification. They are aimed at avoiding fears about annihilation, and achieving personal survival. However, splitting enhances the feeling of going to pieces, and projective identification "impoverishes the ego". The conscious anxiety may be avoided but it is unconsciously enhanced. And then the defence mechanisms are driven even harder—that is, splitting and projective identification are sustained. A vicious circle is set up.

Thus alienation fits into and enhances the survival anxiety, and turns the vicious circle that reverberates between psychological and social forces. In effect the mechanisms of splitting and projective identification *allow* the social process of alienation. And the redistribution of ownership of the products of labour becomes stabilised as a self-perpetuating system, resting on the vicious circle of anxiety and defence just described.

Another vicious circle also occurs. The operation of projective identification has another aim. It is a means of denying separation. Projective identification establishes a merging with the person into whom some part of the self is projected. So, projecting some part of the self into the factory or its owner inevitably promotes a sense of solidarity in the worker *towards the owners* into whom the worker has projected his products. Moreover, the reality situation in which the product is actually removed in a concrete way, separated and sold on from the factory, must enhance the painful feelings of separation which the projective identification was intended to deny. Thus the anxiety of separation is enhanced, which then drives the projective identification to deny the separation.

Both these are enduring social–psychological dynamics which underpin the alienation, allow it to endure, and significantly impoverish the egos of the producers. The political alienation and solidarity are stabilised by resting on these enduring psychodynamic cycles. The result is an enduring resistance to change despite the hardship to so many of the more exploited people.

One aspect of the success of the neoliberal emphasis on monetary value is that survival of the individual is increasingly felt as financial survival. The aim is in part to motivate people through a fear for their survival. It is a motivating strategy which raises the survival anxiety for the individual and for working organisations. Thus it plays on the fears of the worker who already feels impoverished in himself, and has sought solidarity through merging with the organisation.

Indeed today a large proportion of personal identity is constructed through consumer activity—that is, what you buy is what you are, and therefore if you can't buy you can't exist. Such culturally promoted attitudes provide, and stabilise, the inner psychodynamic cycles just described. Financial survival plays into the anxieties about ego survival to harmonise with them and add to the needs for the characteristic defences. The elevation of monetary value and financial survival to trump ordinary human values, in the work and commercial aspects of social life, is a spin-off from the conjunction of external and internal influences that are realised in the two vicious circles. Then human values are left to exist only within the much restricted field of the family. We are allowed to be generous and grateful, and honest, and concerned, and so on, within the family. But outside that, only monetary value counts, and there financial survival is almost equated with personal survival.

Conclusions

One contribution we can make to political understanding is the necessary condition that a social process, embodied in a political policy, needs to have an important unconscious dimension within individuals in order to be successful—that is, the policy must access some personality dynamic in individuals. So, as psychoanalysts, we could give to political debate an awareness of those anxieties that are played upon, and the resulting defences that establish vicious circles within individuals on which political action is grounded.

It is not enough to take a high-minded position about this. We need to help the understanding of why people might go along thoughtlessly with quite disastrous policies. In such a case described here—the occurrence of alienation at work—there is the operation of both social influence and psychological mechanisms. Both influences converge in the vicious circles and work together. The anxiety–defence system resides unconsciously and is the bedrock of false consciousness.

But policies do not always find a suitable internal dynamic. Social policies are not all powerful, and from what has been said, they can be successful only insofar as they can play upon possible unconscious mechanisms which they are able to activate. Psychology is then a limiting condition for political economy. *Only* when there is a positive interaction between the social forces, and the unconscious cycling of anxiety and defence, can a stable political economy arise.

I have tried to create a sketchy model for understanding some aspects of doing politics psychoanalytically. It is not necessarily easy to apply. Politics needs to be done by decisions and actions on policies. But it needs to be done with some understanding of the hidden psychodynamics that resonate between individuals and the social. There are two specific principles. Political action needs to be guided by some psychoanalytic insights. We will never eradicate the primitive mechanisms from society. Though psychoanalysis is perhaps the only discipline which can really supply an understanding of unconscious processes, one might hope that, and investigate whether, the unconscious dimensions could possibly be conducted publicly without too sophisticated a knowledge of the human unconscious.

We will all have our favourite parties and policies, with perfectly valid *conscious* reasons for supporting them. Our contribution needs to draw attention to the underlying unconscious issues, the vicious circles, the level of understanding, amongst others, that affect not just policies but the political process itself; which of them are, or are not, being mobilised by conscious policies and debates. In all this I have tried go beyond the particular politics I might support. The attempt has been to reflect on politics as an ethical activity in terms of promoting opportunities for individuals to be less alienated and to achieve a degree of greater maturity (at least in terms of the psychoanalytic unconscious).

References

Austin, J. L. (1962). *How to Do Things with Words*. Oxford: Oxford University Press.

Bernays, E. (1928). *Propaganda*. New York: Liveright.

Braverman, F. (1974). *Labor and Monopoly Capital: The Degradation of Work in the Twentieth Century*. New York: Monthly Review Press.

Freud, S. (1912–13). *Totem and Taboo. S. E., 13*: 1–161. London: Hogarth.

Gregory, C. A. (1982). *Gifts and Commodities*, London: Academic Press.

Hinshelwood, R. D. (1983). Projective identification and Marx's concept of man. *International Review of Psycho-Analysis, 10*: 221–226.

Hinshelwood, R. D. (1996). Convergences with psycho-analysis. In: I. Parker & R. Spiers (Eds.), *Psychology and Marxism* (pp. 93–104). London: Pluto Press.

Horkheimer, M. (1931). The present situation of social philosophy and the tasks of an institute for social research. In: *Between Philosophy and Social Science: Selected Early Writings* (pp. 1–14). Cambridge, MA: MIT Press, 1993.

Klein, M. (1946). Notes on some schizoid mechanisms, *International Journal of Psychoanalysis, 27*: 99–110. Republished in M. Klein, P. Heimann, S. Isaacs, & J. Riviere (Eds.), *Developments in Psycho-Analysis* (pp. 292–320). London: Hogarth, 1952.

Klein, M. (1955). On identification. In: *The Writings of Melanie Klein Vol. 3: Envy and Gratitude and Other Works, 1946–1963* (pp. 141–175). London: Karnac, 1993.

Lukács, G. (1971). *History and Class Consciousness*. R. Livingstone (Trans.). London: Merlin.

Malinowski, B. (1923). Psycho-analysis and anthropology. *Nature, 112*: 650–651.

Marcuse, H. (1955). *Eros and Civilization: A Philosophical Inquiry into Freud*. Boston, MA: Beacon.

Marx, K. (1844). Economic and Philosophic Manuscripts. In: *Early Writings* (pp. 279–400). London: Penguin, 1975.

Marx, K. (1867). *Capital*. London: Penguin, 1976.

Šebek, M. (1996). The fate of the totalitarian object. *International Forum of Psycho-analysis, 5*: 289–294.

Šebek, M. (1998). Post-totalitarian personality—old internal objects in a new situation. *Journal of the American Academy of Psychoanalysis, 26*: 295.

Segal, H. (1987). Silence is the real crime. *International Review of Psycho-Analysis, 14*: 3–12.

CHAPTER ELEVEN

"We're all in it together": austerity's myth*

Renée Danziger

Introduction

In 2010, a large section of the British population voted for a party which was committed to a radical programme of austerity. In this chapter I want to look at some of the ways that psychoanalytic thinking can help understand how and why the Conservative Party's austerity policies were endorsed by many of the people who stood to suffer most from them, not only in 2010 but again in the general election of 2015. Although my focus here is on the experience of Britain, I hope that at least some of my analysis will have a wider applicability.

Broadly speaking, austerity policies aim to reduce government deficit through the scaling back of state-funded services. In some cases they may be accompanied by increases in taxation, but experience shows us that conservative and neoliberal parties generally favour reducing government debt through reductions in public sector spending rather than by raising money through tax increases.

*With thanks to Neil Mitchell, Steven Groarke, and Michael Rustin for their helpful comments on an earlier draft.

Background

In Britain, austerity came to be seen by all the major political parties in the late 2000s as essential for addressing the Treasury's growing deficit which had risen considerably in recent years, particularly following the Labour government's use of £141 billion of public funds in order to rescue the banks after the 2007–2008 financial crisis (National Audit Office, 2013). However, while parties of the Left favoured a more gradual introduction of limited austerity, the Conservative Party proposed swift and far-reaching measures to deal with what was described as the debt crisis. This approach, they said, was vital if the country was to be pulled back from the brink of what they regarded as financial disaster.

The idea of government austerity is, of course, nothing new. Mark Blyth points out that, in terms of its underlying ideology, austerity has its roots in the seventeenth-century economic liberalism of John Locke whose philosophy explicitly "pits the individual against the state" (2013, p. 105). During the eighteenth and nineteenth centuries the state became increasingly involved in raising money through taxation in order to provide public services. Not surprisingly, perhaps, debate has flourished between those who consider it the state's duty to provide welfare and other essential services to those in need, and others who argue that the increase in taxation required by a "welfare state" constitutes an infringement of the rights and freedoms of the individual. Alongside these ideological, or moral, arguments are debates about the economic merits of different fiscal policies. While some believe that government should raise taxes and borrow significantly in order to invest in infrastructure, industry, and other areas so as to build a strong economic future for the country, others are equally convinced that high taxes act as a disincentive to entrepreneurs, workers, and investors; and that borrowing leads to economic weakness and collapse.

In the 1980s a different approach was taken: instead of using fiscal measures (i.e. control over tax and government spending), monetary measures were used to try to manage the economy. Policies were introduced to control the amount of money circulating in the economy through high interest rates, lower borrowing, and low taxes; the aim of these measures was ostensibly to keep inflation low, because it was believed that this would stimulate economic growth. Monetarism clearly risked significant increases in unemployment and poverty, but proponents—such as Margaret Thatcher—argued that the gains which would accrue to the well-off and high earners would "trickle down" so that all levels of society would ultimately benefit.

The promises implied by trickle-down theory were something of a sweetener to make rising unemployment and declining public services palatable. By contrast, recent austerity policies have had no such sweetener. Whether these policies have been pursued for ideological or pragmatic reasons (or a combination of the two), they call above all for swingeing cuts in public spending in areas such as social welfare, health, education, and publicly funded housing. The *sine qua non* of austerity is therefore that it disproportionately hurts the people who depend most heavily on public services—and yet many of these very same people voted in governments that were openly committed to radical austerity policies. There are of course a number of sociological and political factors that help to explain this paradox (see for example Clarke et al., 2016), but I'd like to look at whether psychoanalytic insights can also help us to understand it.

Some psychoanalytic reflections

In his 1921 paper on *Group Psychology* Freud asks what happens to an individual's mind when he or she becomes part of a group. Whereas "groups", "mobs", and "the masses" had previously been associated with destructive and dangerous "herd instincts", Freud's starting point was altogether different. Drawing on the concept of *libido*, he suggested that it was "love relationships (or, to use a more neutral expression, emotional ties) … [which] constitute the essence of the group mind" (1921c, p. 91).

Acknowledging that the libidinal ties that bind together the members of a group are not an expression of a mature form of sexual love, Freud suggested they arose out of a more archaic form of love which, inhibited in its sexual aims, is expressed instead through *identification*.

The concept of identification is complex and meets many of the criteria for what Gallie in 1956 had referred to as "essentially contested" concepts (Collier, Hidalgo, & Maciuceanu, 2006). In 1985 the focus of the IPA Congress was on "identification and its vicissitudes", and not surprisingly a wide range of conceptualisations were developed and discussed. It is beyond the scope of this paper to consider the different ways identification can be understood; for the purposes of this discussion I will draw on Freud's earlier and more straightforward use of the concept, where he refers to it in terms of "a psychic connection based on a perceived or imagined quality of sameness" (Abend & Porder, 1995).

In other words, members of a given group share a sense of being a group thanks to their identification with one another, based on a perceived common quality or shared set of values. The more important this shared quality is seen to be, the more successful the identification. As a helpful description of the world around us, this sounds logical and convincing. It applies as much to the members of a political party, as to the fans of a football club, as to the supporters of a clean air campaign. And it takes account of cross-cutting identifications that most of us have. But Freud goes further than this. He is interested in the change that goes on in the individual's mental activity when the individual identifies him- or herself as a member of the group. As Freud says, "His liability to affect becomes extraordinarily intensified, while his intellectual ability is markedly reduced, both processes being evidently in the direction of an approximation to the other individuals in the group" (1921c, p. 88).

How can this be accounted for? Freud attributes the tendency towards group identification—and its consequences for the individual's mind—to something he calls suggestion, or suggestibility. Why, he asks, can we resist a particular emotion but when we find ourselves in a group which seems to experience that emotion, we succumb to it? His answer is that "what compels us to obey this tendency is imitation, and what induces the emotion in us is the group's suggestive influence". Suggestion and its corollary, suggestibility, are as puzzling as they are pervasive, says Freud, who describes suggestion as "an irreducible, primitive phenomenon, a fundamental fact in the mental life of man" (1921c, p. 89).

So we are left with the notion of the group being formed out of libidinally driven identification and held together at least partly by our suggestibility and the primitive urge to imitate the group. There are two other key elements in the formation and cohesion of groups. The first is the in-group's relationship to the out-group. Among members of the in-group, feelings of love, or affinity, are such that individual members of the group will tolerate each other's otherwise unattractive traits. Feelings of hostility are directed instead outwards, toward non-members (or the out-group). I will return to the importance of the out-group as a binding force in a moment.

The second element relates to the role of the group leader, which Freud examines in fine detail. Group members identify not only with one another but, as Freud says, also with their leader. This is partly a narcissistic identification, but is also based on an idealisation of the leader, which accounts for the individual's loss of a sense of ego in favour of identifying with the *ego ideal* as embodied by the group leader.

Freud's work on group psychology has been used to explain the rise and compelling hold of authoritarian leaders and totalitarian regimes. Theodor Adorno for instance comments that "Freud's psychological construction of the leader imagery is corroborated by its striking coincidence with the fascist leader type," and he goes even further by suggesting that Freud's applied group psychology is "*peculiar* to fascism rather than to most other movements that seek mass support" (1991, p. 149). Although the fascist or totalitarian model may be paradigmatic of Freud's depiction of group psychology, his work in this area can also help to explain why, despite the absence of a fascist leader or totalitarian state apparatus, a large number of people in Britain voted for radical austerity despite it not being in their personal interests to do so.

"We're all in it together": propaganda and the myth of austerity

Britain's Conservative Party lacked a strong, charismatic leader but I would suggest that its highly sophisticated propaganda campaign was sufficiently suggestive to foster what Bion called "basic assumptions", in other words, deep-seated and primitive emotional impulses and fantasies of omnipotence. For Bion, a basic assumption group is one which shares these emotions and fantasies, many of which are and remain unconscious. As Bion notes, although basic assumption groups include the existence of a leader, "the leader need not be identified with any individual in the group; it need not be a person at all but may be identified with an idea or an inanimate object" (1989, p. 155). Austerity propaganda succeeded in stirring up and directing primitive emotions of hate and anger, as well as fantasies of omnipotence and of being saved, which resulted in what we might call a basic assumption group of fight or flight.

In his 1928 study of propaganda, Edward Bernays (who was Freud's nephew) wrote that "the conscious and intelligent manipulation of the organised habits and opinions of the masses is an important element in democratic society" (p. 37). One might question Bernays' apparently unshakeable belief in the "salutary influence [of propaganda] on mass society" (Miller, 2005, p. 18), but it seems unarguable that—for better or worse—information and misinformation, news and fake news, all play their part in shaping our understandings of the social world as well as our affective responses to it.

To the extent that voters took on board the assertions and identified with the affective qualities of Conservative propaganda, they became a basic assumption group of fight-or-flight, one which shared a fantasy that by collective sacrifice "the people" could defeat the external bad object as embodied by "the deficit".[1] It may be helpful here to quote from the 2010 election manifesto of the Conservative Party to give a flavour of the propaganda that is being referred to. In the opening statement, the then party leader, who was soon to become prime minister, David Cameron addressed the country with these words:

> Today the challenges facing Britain are immense. Our economy is overwhelmed by debt, our social fabric is frayed and our political system has betrayed the people. But these problems can be overcome if we pull together and work together. If we remember that we are all in this together …
>
> How will we deal with the debt crisis unless we understand that we are all in this together? How will we raise responsible children unless every adult plays their part?
>
> Only together can we get rid of this [Labour] government and, eventually, its debt. Only together can we get the economy moving … Together we can even make politics and politicians work better. And if we can do that, we can do anything. Yes, together we can do anything. (Conservative Party, 2010)

The message was that the country was facing a major crisis caused by an irresponsible Labour government's excessive public spending. Little if any attention was given to the Labour government's extensive use of public funds to prevent the collapse of private banks, leaving the impression that there was an overspend on welfare. Nor was there reference to the inherent instability of the advanced capitalist economy, with regular cycles of boom and bust—what the New Economics Foundation refers to as the "casino economy" (2013). Instead, the message was that the country faced an anomalous and terrible debt crisis which could only be addressed by a radical reduction in public spending as promised by the Conservatives. The simplicity of the message was misleading but effective, not least because many of us could apply it to our own lives: too much spending and too much debt would cause a crisis in our households. The only solution would be to stop spending and tighten one's belt. When the government suggested that the only way to reduce the debt was to stop spending on public services, this seemed not only logical, but essential.

The Conservatives' rallying cry—that "we're all in it together" was crucial for developing a sense of group identity and loyalty. This slogan, repeated often by the Conservative Party leader and other top party officials, was highly suggestive, harking back as it does to World War II, when Winston Churchill exhorted fellow Britons to join him in waging war against "a monstrous tyranny", saying "I feel entitled to claim the aid of all, and I say, 'Come then, let us go forward together with our united strength.'" (1940). The associations with the Blitz in London, and the widely believed myth that all social groups and classes joined together in stoic and triumphant solidarity against the terrible enemy, made it difficult to oppose the austerity programme (Calder, 1992). To do so would be unpatriotic. There was an allure to joining the heroic in-group which was prepared to make the necessary sacrifices in order to bring the country back from the brink of disaster. The affect was one of togetherness, heroism and—crucially—collective sacrifice.

Once elected as the dominant party in a coalition government, the Conservatives implemented a wide range of cuts. It did not take long for evidence to appear showing that the sacrifices demanded by austerity were distributed disproportionately among the poorer and more vulnerable sections of society. When all austerity measures were taken into account, including cuts to public services and tax changes, the poorest tenth of the population saw a 38% decrease in their net income between 2010 and 2015, the richest tenth lost just 5%, and the richest 1000 people in Britain saw their wealth actually increase by £138 billion between 2009 and 2013 (Oxfam, 2013). There were studies too of the ill effects of austerity on public health (particularly among the less well off) (Stuckler et al., 2017), and reports on the exponential increase in the use of food banks in order to feed hungry families (Butler, 2015). Yet despite this and other evidence, austerity continued to hold sway, and the Conservatives were re-elected to lead the government in 2015 (this time not in a coalition).

The role of the out-group

The out-group was crucial for this continuing support for the party of austerity. Through the period 2010–2015 there was a subtle but decisive shift in emphasis in the implementation of the public spending cuts, whereby they became increasingly focused on the very poorest and most vulnerable sections of society. By 2014, people classified as living in poverty who formed 20% of the total population were suffering 36% of the cuts; disabled people living in poverty (4% of the population) had to bear 13% of the cuts; and people dependent on social care (3% of the population) were targets of 13% of the cuts (Duffy, 2014). These statistics suggest that, while austerity was clearly affecting the country as a whole in areas such as health, education, culture, and housing, the onus of the policy was shifting ever more onto those who were most vulnerable, most marginal, and least able to bear it—and also perhaps least able to protest against it. Looking at the impact of austerity on British society, the Archbishop of Canterbury, Justin Welby, was recently moved to write: "Austerity is not merely an economic term. It ... almost invariably conceals the crushing of the weak, the unlucky, the ill, and a million of others. Austerity is a theory for the rich and a reality of suffering for the poor" (Harries, 2018).

When David Cameron resigned as prime minister in June 2016, he was replaced by Theresa May. In her first speech as prime minister she declared her priority to be helping the "just about managing" (known as the "JAMs"). This may at first sound relatively benign, but in fact it reveals a lack of concern for those who were perhaps not managing at all. This latter group had effectively been consigned to the margins of society and the political agenda.

This was a key development, not least because this marginalised group formed the core of an important out-group. Supporters of austerity, many of whom were suffering from public sector cuts and job insecurity, were able to project feelings of anxiety, guilt, shame, and anger onto this marginalised out-group. The unemployed were particularly disparaged, as anxieties rose about job insecurity and were projected onto those who had already lost their jobs (O'Hara, 2015). Society became divided in the minds of many between "workers vs shirkers", and "strivers vs skivers". Even as late as 2016, although austerity had begun slowly to fall out of favour and opinion polls indicated growing support for increased public spending, the unemployed remained a despised out-group. The National Centre for Social Research in its 33rd annual report on *British Social Attitudes* found for instance that public support for higher taxes and increased public spending was at its highest level (45%) for a decade, and yet 45% of the 4,000 respondents also backed further cuts in unemployment benefits; 60% said there should be a limit to how long people were entitled to these benefits; and more than 80% said that people should take a job that is unsuitable in order to come off of unemployment benefits (NatCen Social Research, 2016). Along with the unemployed, others were also lumped into this hated out-group, most notably immigrants, who were targeted in some of the most egregious hate campaigning that accompanied the 2016 Brexit referendum (Meleady, Seger, & Vermue, 2017).

Perhaps as important as the projection of difficult feelings aroused by austerity was the disavowal of its consequences. Freud explores the concept of disavowal in his paper on "Fetishism" (1927e) and again later in "Splitting of the Ego in the Process of Defence" (1940e), but even before writing these papers, Freud had used the concept of "disavowal" in relation to children's reactions to observing the anatomical differences between the sexes (Strachey, 1961). Unlike denial which is a turning away from a piece of reality, disavowal involves an intellectual awareness of that reality, but a complete repudiation of all that it may mean. Hanna Segal, when writing of the nuclear threat in 1987, depicted the attitudes of governments as one of disavowal in that they "both envisage a nuclear war and deny the reality of what it would entail". A similar process of defending against reality through disavowal has occurred in popular perceptions of austerity in Britain. A poll carried out by YouGov in 2015 found that as many as 55% of respondents reported not feeling affected personally by austerity measures—and this despite living among hugely growing hospital waiting lists, overstretched GPs, overcrowded classrooms, closed libraries, reduced social welfare benefits, rising numbers of homeless people and food banks, and increasing burnout among public sector workers. This stunning statistic of 55% not feeling affected by austerity while living in Austerity Britain can only be made sense of when understood as an instance of disavowal, which, as Hall and Pick (2017) write, "can be linked to the notion of a 'blind eye' or the rejection or rebuttal of something in plain sight, so carrying the implication of knowing and not knowing all at once".

Conclusion

Austerity was introduced in Britain as a response to the financial crisis. Although there were other ways of responding to the Treasury's deficit, austerity was presented as the only option, and support for it was driven by effective propaganda which built on the notion that "we're all in this together". As evidence grew that in fact austerity had had its worst impact on those least able to withstand it—the poor, the unemployed, the disabled, and the homeless—the basic assumption group supporting austerity found ways to defend themselves against this reality, through splitting off and projecting their feelings of anxiety, anger, and hatred, and through disavowal of the consequences of austerity.

Slowly but surely, it is becoming more and more difficult to disavow reality, and so there is less and less support for austerity, and more people calling for increased public spending. However, the last eight years have taken a toll on society, with old splits having deepened and new ones having been created. The challenge now is to replace austerity with an efficient fiscal policy which heals rather than deepens society's splits.

Note

1. Interestingly, economic deficit has not always been considered to be unconditionally harmful. John Maynard Keynes, for instance, argued that at times of deep deflation, government deficit is in fact imperative because its inflationary effect will help to stimulate the economy.

References

Abend, S. M., & Porder, M. S. (1995). Identification. In: E. M. Burness & B. D. Dine (Eds.), *Psychoanalysis: The Major Concepts*. New Haven, CT: Yale University Press.

Adorno, T. W. (1991). *The Culture Industry: Selected Essays On Mass Culture*. New York: Routledge.

Bernays, E. (1928). *Propaganda*. New York: Ig Publishing, 2005.

Bion, W. R. (1961). *Experiences in Groups and Other Papers*. Hove, UK: Routledge, 1989.

Blyth, M. (2013). *Austerity: The History of a Dangerous Idea*. New York: Oxford University Press.

Butler, P. (2015, April 22). Food bank use tops million mark over the past year. *The Guardian*.

Calder, A. (1992). *The Myth of the Blitz*. London: Pimlico.

Churchill, W. S. (1940). Winston Churchill's "Blood, toil, tears and sweat" speech, May 13, quoted on Historyplace.com website. http://www.historyplace.com

Clarke, H. D., Kellner, P., Stewart, M. C., Twyman, J., & Whiteley, P. (2016). *Austerity and Political Choice in Britain*. Basingstoke, UK: Palgrave Macmillan.

Collier, D., Hidalgo, F. D., & Maciuceanu, A. O. (2006). Essentially contested concepts: debates and applications. *Journal of Political Ideologies, 11*(3): 211–246.

Conservative Party (2010). Invitation to Join the Government of Britain. [Manifesto.] London: Conservative Research Department.

Duffy, S. (2014). *Counting the Cuts.* Sheffield, UK: Centre for Welfare Reform.

Freud, S. (1921c). *Group Psychology and the Analysis of the Ego. S. E., 18.* London: Hogarth.

Freud, S. (1927e). Fetishism. *S. E., 21.* London: Hogarth.

Freud, S. (1940e). Splitting of the ego in the process of defence. *S. E., 23.* London: Hogarth.

Hall, C., & Pick, D. (2017). Thinking about denial. *History Workshop Journal, 84.*

Harries, R. (2018, February 26). Book Review: *Reimagining Britain* by Justin Welby. *The Guardian.*

Meleady, R., Seger, C. R., & Vermue, M. (2017). Examining the role of positive and negative intergroup contact and anti-immigrant prejudice in Brexit. *British Journal of Social Psychology, 56*: 799–808.

Miller, M. C. (2005). Introduction to E. Bernays' *Propaganda.* New York: Ig Publishing.

NatCen Social Research (2016). *British Social Attitudes 33.* J. Curtice, M. Phillips, & L. Clery (Eds.). London: NatCen Social Research.

National Audit Office (2013). HM Treasury Resource Accounts 2012–2013: The Comptroller and Auditor General's Report to the House of Commons, quoted in *The True Cost of Austerity and Inequality: UK Case Study. Oxfam Case Study September 2013.* London: National Audit Office.

New Economics Foundation (2013). *Framing the Economy.* http://neweconomics.org

O'Hara, M. (2015). Work maketh the person: The demonization of the jobless: austerity and the myth of the skiver. Chapter 4 in: *Austerity Bites: A Journey to the Sharp End of Cuts in the UK.* Bristol, UK: Policy Press, University of Bristol.

Oxfam (2013). *The True Cost of Austerity and Inequality: UK Case Study. Oxfam Case Study September 2013.* Oxford: Oxfam.

Segal, H. (1987). Silence is the real crime. *International Review of Psycho-Analysis, 14*: 3–12.

Strachey, J. (1961). Editor's note. Introduction to S. Freud's paper on Fetishism (1927e). *S. E., 21.* London: Hogarth.

Stuckler, D., Reeves, A., Loopstra, A., Karanikolos, M., & McKee, M. (2017). Austerity and health: The impact in the UK and Europe. *European Journal of Public Health, 27*(S4): 18–21.

YouGov (2015, October 1). Majority support winding down austerity. https://yougov.co.uk/news/2015/10/01/majority-support-winding-down-austerity/

CHAPTER TWELVE

A psychopolitics of the slacker

Josh Cohen

In the mid-1980s, I made much-anticipated termly trips to Carnaby Street to stare furtively at punks and sift through the records and memorabilia of my favourite bands. It was during one of these trips that I was stopped in my tracks by a poster: a woman, lying on her back, tilted languidly to the left. Peeking out of the black swamp of bedding, bleached shoulders hinted at nakedness. But she was as oblivious as Sleeping Beauty to the desire she might be arousing. Her body was a cancelled erotic promise radiating indifference. Stare long enough at the dense shock of hair and it became the dark void of night, swallowing everything but sleep itself.

The poster was tacked to the wall, bordered above and below by spiky letters, spelling out a confession, an injunction, a seduction of sorts: "I DIDN'T GO TO WORK TODAY ..." and "... I DON'T THINK I'LL GO TOMORROW/LET'S TAKE CONTROL OF OUR LIVES AND LIVE FOR PLEASURE NOT PAIN".

The picture plunged me into sadness and panic, as though an invisible missile had been launched into the heart of my adolescent life, polluting my sense of meaning and purpose. The pleasure of a long lie-in, suggested the girl, might conceal a wish for the renunciation of the world beyond my bed.

Heading home, my gloom began to dissipate. The words I'd read as a rejection of life now sang with a strange hope: you do not have to live under the tyranny of the world's, or your own, expectations. You are not obliged to comply with the daily agenda set by your parents or your school or your boss or you own head. If you don't like the day that's been doled out to you, erase it and choose another one, one you like better.

The girl was suspended at the threshold of sleep and wakefulness, where solid reality quivers like projected images on a shaken screen. Perhaps her preference for sleep over the regimented consciousness of the working day wasn't nihilism but an affirmation of human possibility. To think of my daily routine as optional dissipated its suffocating givenness, loosened the real world's constrictive grip on my young body and mind.

Seven years after seeing the poster of the dozing girl, I was finding myself more attuned than ever to her state of mind. I was beginning a PhD, and a research council award meant I could pursue it free from the sordid obligation to earn an income, a privilege more ambiguous than I could have anticipated. Even as an English Lit undergrad, I needed to be at the odd lecture and seminar. Now I was stranded in a zone off any institutional or personal radar, where no one seemed to expect me to do anything or be anywhere. I could have gone days, weeks, perhaps even months without my absence being noticed by a soul.

During those first autumnal weeks, I would wake up to the unbidden thought, at once glorious and tormenting, that if I didn't read or write a single word, it would make no difference to anyone. Even as anxiety clawed at the front of my head and the pit of my stomach, I was aware of a quietly voluptuous, outlaw pleasure in being bound to nothing and nobody. Like the dozing girl, I could absent myself from the overbearing congestion of the world beyond my bed merely by closing my eyes.

But as weeks went by, the pleasure of inaction, precarious from the first, was diminished by anxiety. With much of the morning slept off, I would sit immobile on a straight-backed living room chair, staring groggily into the shadows until jolted into awareness by a train rattling past my kitchen window. I showered, ate, and drifted aimlessly around the grey Neasden streets, my inner voice churning out a fog of nonsense to obscure my one clear thought: I have no idea what I'm doing.

The cinema handed me an unexpected lifeline. Richard Linklater's *Slacker* was one of those handful of films that, like the first breathless sight of a lover's face, you know immediately will never leave you. I paid £2.50, roughly £10 less than admission to the same cinema today, albeit to sit on a tattered seat, soles lightly soldered to the sticky floor. For this film, a run-down fleapit felt like a carefully designed immersive environment.

It didn't take me long to see the aimlessness of my own life reflected in the funhouse mirror of Linklater's film, comprised of weird, randomly connected episodes from the makeshift subcultures of Austin, Texas, teeming with amateur metaphysicians and madmen, conspiracy theorists and street entrepreneurs, tinkerers and petty criminals, anarchists and poseurs, linked only by their uncompromising renunciation of "the kind of work you have to do to earn a living".

I slouched in my seat, staring in enraptured lassitude from the opening shot of the amiable-looking young guy, the director himself I later found out, arriving at a bus station and sauntering over to a cab with his backpack. Within seconds he was delivering a monologue in an unbroken shot trained through the windscreen on both occupants of the cab, the guy's drawling fantasia in cahoots with the silent blankness of the driver, as though total disconnection were a form of connection. Sharing the same tight space, they occupy different universes.

The young guy spoke of dreams and fantasies and the daily forking paths of life. Just now, he might have stuck around at the bus station and been picked up and taken home by a beautiful stranger, a version of events which at this very moment might be unfolding in some alternative reality. The camera leaves him as he exits the cab, arriving at the next scenario before strolling casually minutes later to the next, each scene in a relation of random disconnection from and intricate connection to the last. Stories begin, break off, begin again, over and over, but this breathless sequence of abortive stories seems to be a way of telling one and the same story.

Rambling through the grass and concrete landscape of Austin, the camera runs up against its own forking paths, each scene implicitly forsaking a different one, so that the film I was watching seemed haunted by any number of films I didn't get to watch. Not that this was a privative experience; on the contrary, the spectral presence of other scenes gave me a delirious sense that each moment is pregnant with other moments. For someone so abjectly empty of purpose, so "unpregnant of my cause" (in the words of Hamlet), there was something crazily enlivening about such a thought, which the film's drawling, listless bodies and voices paradoxically enhanced.

It wasn't that I identified with the fleeting characters, or aspired to their comically aimless lives. I wasn't going to play in a band called The Ultimate Losers or write a book called *Conspiracy-a-Go-Go*, and I wasn't the type to berate his girlfriend with a line like, "Every single commodity you produce is a piece of your own death."

It was more the spirit of the camera that inspired me, in its radiation of laziness, distraction, curiosity, and freedom. I was entranced by its movement between the loosely connected scenes, its hesitant, sluggish drift from the departing back of one character to the indifferent person of the next, as though it only just bothered to keep going. The film's title seemed to allude less to its characters than to itself, its own slack relationship to its subjects, at once fascinated and distracted, alive and lackadaisical.

The term "slacker" was coined to disparage draft dodgers during the Second World War, gradually evolving to encompass all forms of apathy and indifference towards life and work. The slacker would seem to be the exemplary naysayer, a connoisseur of all forms of refusal—work, activity, emotional agitation, choice, and belief swallowed into the black hole of his indifference. So how could these vignettes in lassitude and stagnation feel so intensely affirmative?

Watching *Slacker* opened up a different way of relating to my own life, one that wasn't measured and valued by the externally imposed targets and achievements. It offered a glimpse of what Roland Barthes termed "idiorrhythmy", "where each subject lives according to his own rhythm" (2012, p. 6). To live life in this way means to refuse the regimentation of your time and space by the impersonal forces of work and leisure, giving yourself over to the pace and style of the impulses, curiosities, and desires unique to you. But it is equally a social ideal, whereby the rhythms of all our individual lives coexist without encroaching on each other.

The landscape of *Slacker* was no Utopia if by that we mean a community in which all work in concert to achieve the same moral, social, and economic ideals. But it gave a sense of what our lives might look like when lived at once singularly and together, without the demand to comply with a single, overarching physical and psychic rhythm or ethos. It encouraged me to find my own idiorrhythm, the discovery of which it turned out I'd been in real need.

Pyrrho, the ancient Greek forebear of philosophical scepticism, would go to ridiculous lengths to evade the lure of commitments and the seductions of belief. Straying to the edges of cliffs, in sight of dangerous animals, he defied the law of nature and risked his life rather than acknowledge its reality. Pyrrho's scepticism is radically debilitating, as it doggedly evades all decisive action, consigning the self to ataraxia, or unconcern, towards its own fate.

The key premise of Pyrrhonism is that experience tells us there is no reliable measure for natural or moral truth: the air a young person finds mild will make an old person feel cold, the act one individual considers wicked another considers virtuous. Pyrrho had extrapolated from this condition of cosmic undecidability that we may as well allow ourselves to be blown willy-nilly by the winds of chance, as no positive action or state of being is preferable to any other, including existence itself.

For most people, this is hardly a viable way to live. Around 500 years later, when the medic and philosopher Sextus Empiricus codified scepticism as a body of thought, he adapted Pyrrhonic thinking to the ordinary demands of daily life. While still oriented towards the ataraxia achieved by suspending all judgements and rejecting all definitive claims to truth, Sextus recognised the pragmatic requirement to act in accordance with "guidance by nature, necessitation by feelings, handing down of laws and customs, and teaching all kinds of expertise" (*Outlines of Scepticism*, p. 9). In other words, if we cannot know which truth to live by, we can at least have rules.

The true and the good may not be knowable to us, but custom and feeling allow us to live as though they were. There is no way of determining if it really is cold, but I can certainly tell if I feel cold, and this is sufficient motive for putting on a coat. Thus, without contesting Pyrrho's radically sceptic stance, Sextus found a way to moderate its extreme implications for how we live. Like the good medic he was, he pointed out that "we are not able to be utterly inactive" (p. 12); by extension, we cannot let ourselves sink into total indifference towards ourselves.

As with the wild speculations and schemes of Linklater's slackers, so uncannily evocative of sceptic thought in their feeling for undecidability as a basic condition of life, the appeal isn't the content of the argument, which seems absurd from our smug retrospective vantage point (which affords us, for example, scientific methods and instruments to measure air temperature). Scepticism's appeal today, especially in a culture that encourages the narcissistic drip feed of preferences and opinions, lies in its stance of reticence, its wariness of mouthing off. In our social media landscape, opinion has become the currency and substance of our selfhood. The positions we publicise have become a way of affirming the reality of our existence to the world. We pontificate therefore we are.

Sextus tells a story that illustrates the sceptics' more modest relationship to truth and rightness. The painter Apelles was painting a horse and wanted to render accurately the lather on his mouth. In frustration at his failure to get it right, he flung his wet sponge at the picture; "and when it hit ... it produced a representation of the horse's lather" (p. 10).

As long as we actively seek the state of ataraxia, by trying to decide or resolve a given problem we only exacerbate our feelings of tension and frustration. But let go of the zeal to be right and ataraxia will come to us "as it were fortuitously, as a shadow follows a body" (p. 10). There is an unmistakable psychoanalytic resonance to the story in its suggestion that what we most want to say or do slips out of us in spite of our conscious intention. But it hints by the same token at a link between scepticism and ethics. Sextus shows us that the most desirable orientation to life, the one least likely to tie us in knots of irritable dissatisfaction, is one that renounces the illusion that we are master of the truth.

It was this aspect of scepticism that spoke to Roland Barthes, who found in it an expression of what he called the "Neutral" state: "the Neutral ... is good for nothing, and certainly not for advocating a position, an identity". This neutrality is not some bland mean point between political or ethical extremes. It is a state of being, an orientation to life, implying the existence in us of what the aphoristic Romanian philosopher E. M. Cioran (1949, p. 3) calls a "*faculty of indifference*" (the emphasis is his).

Deadly ideologies and movements take root, argued Cioran, when ideas are animated with the same impassioned zeal human beings once invested in gods: "Once man loses his *faculty of indifference* he becomes a potential murderer." Indifference is not simply an attitude we assume, but a fundamental dimension of our being, which struggles to avoid becoming submerged by the violence of dogma and ideology.

For Cioran, there are no virtues nobler than the so-called vices of "doubt and sloth", for these preserve us from the terrors of fanaticism and the exclusive claim to truth. "Only the sceptics (or idlers or aesthetes) escape" the contagion of fanaticism, "because they *propose* nothing, because they— humanity's true benefactors—undermine fanaticism's purposes ... I feel *safer* with a Pyrrho than with a Saint Paul, for a jesting wisdom is gentler than an unbridled sanctity" (p. 4).

The sceptic stance, at least as Cioran interprets it, is a quiet resistance to the conception of the human as a propositional animal, a being defined by his proclaimed beliefs and public actions. To recognise a faculty of indifference or neutrality is to insist on the human being as irreducible to these badges of identity. Doubt and sloth, the twinned moods of the slacker, protect us from the terrors of unbridled sanctity.

The slacker challenges the unquestioned privilege of action and purpose in our culture of relentless accumulation and competition. She confronts the fundamental question of what makes a life worth living. For example, in the name of what, do we protest neoliberalism's creation and exacerbation of social division, economic inequality, inhumanity, and chaos? We can respond to such evils with a raft of worthy progressive aims and policies: protecting the welfare safety net, redistributive taxation, living wages, and so on. Such policies may rightly seek to improve the conditions under which we live; but they do not address what we might want to live for. Social policy propositions address the needs of the human being as a creature of action, as a product of particular affiliations and identities. The quiet virtue of "proposing nothing" is that it encourages us to think about and experience ourselves as irreducible to the sum of what we do and opine, as creatures who, beyond any action or achievement, simply *are*.

From this perspective, the slacker's life of sloth and doubt is a protest not in the name of this or that cause, but for the very right to be, to exist in what philosopher Frédéric Gros calls a "suspensive freedom" (2014, p, 3), outside the confines of personal, professional, or any other identities. In the modern age, this right is under threat. The manic productivity of capitalism, the demands and aspirations of social status, and the mechanical rhythms of industrialism all corral the individual into a perpetual state of anxious and compliant activity.

The so-called "countercultures" that have sprung into being at every stage of modern history are models of living forged in opposition to these alien mechanical rhythms. The Romantics of the latter part of the eighteenth century, the aestheticists and decadents of the nineteenth, the beatniks and hippies and punks of the twentieth, all conceived new modes of social, creative, and sexual life, encompassing what we might call idiorrhythmic experiments in communal living, opiate consumption, artistic forms, and everyday fashion.

The Romantics were the first in this long chain, protesting against the coercive demand to do and comply with industrial society and its regime of permanent productivity. In Romantic poetry and prose, such protest often takes the form of episodes of reverie in which the writer, transported by a sublime landscape into the depths of the self, floats free of the external world and its encumbrances. In such moments, the nervous agitations of reality dissolve, leaving him in a bubble of perfect, though necessarily transient, tranquillity.

While there are many such episodes in Romantic literature, few are more definitive or more transfixing than the "Fifth Walk" of Rousseau's last, unfinished masterpiece of 1776, *Reveries of the Solitary Walker*. Now in his final years, Rousseau meditates in these "walks" on his state of solitary exile, the ideal remedy for the traumatic blows of intrigue and treachery he has endured through his life.

The Fifth Walk sees Rousseau taking refuge on the tiny Île de Saint-Pierre, set in the middle of the Swiss Lac de Bienne, following the stoning of his house by a mob in the nearby village of Môtiers. The quiet and solitude of the island prove the ideal balm for his state of persecuted agitation. Dedicating himself to "precious *far niente* [doing nothing]" (p. 11), he embraces a daily life of inactivity—idly gathering botanical specimens, sitting on the banks of the lake, or drifting in a little boat into the middle of it. This mode of minimal activity induces a perfect inner state:

> But if there is a state where the soul can find a position solid enough to allow it to remain there entirely and gather together its whole being, without needing to recall the past or encroach upon the future, where time is nothing to it, where the present lasts for ever, albeit imperceptibly and giving no sign of its passing, with no other feeling of deprivation or enjoyment, pleasure or pain, desire or fear than simply that of our existence, a feeling that completely fills the soul; as long as this state lasts, the person who is in it can call himself happy, not with an imperfect, poor and relative happiness, such as one finds in the pleasures of life, but with a sufficient, perfect and full happiness, which leaves in the soul no void needing to be filled. (p. 51)

There is a painful paradox about this moment of happiness: perfect and eternal it may be, but it cannot last. The sensation of nirvanic bliss, of permanent liberation from the ups and downs of daily life, is an effect of the moment's transience. This bubble of pure selfhood retains its timeless perfection only for as long as one is sealed inside it, immobile and indifferent to the world outside. But as Sextus had already noted more than 1,500 years earlier, "We are not able to be utterly inactive." As soon as the sun starts to set, as soon as the breeze on the lake blows us awake and reminds us that the boat needs taking ashore, we are back in the workaday world of passing time and its frustrations.

Still, the fact that this moment must pass is no reason to dismiss it as trivial. Something profoundly significant happens in that boat; the drifting Rousseau discovers a radically free region of the self, defined, in the words of contemporary German philosopher Peter Sloterdijk, by "its ecstatic unusability for any purpose" (2015, p. 23). From the perspective of an instrumental world bent on exhausting the physical and creative resources of individuals in being useful, this region of the self is very dangerous. The Rousseau "of the Fifth Walk", writes Sloterdijk, "is like a nuclear reactor that suddenly radiates pure anarchic subjectivity into the environment" (p. 33).

Useless, shiftless, good-for-nothing—the contemptuous words and phrases we use to denigrate the slacker attest to the secret fear he induces in us. No sooner does his "anarchic subjectivity" appear, whether in the form of Romantic reverie, Bohemian intoxication, hippy freak-out, or punk nihilism, than it's attacked for its brazen parasitism, irresponsibility, and delinquency. So invested is our manically productive culture in the image of us as active and purposeful beings that we seek to erase or destroy all evidence to the contrary—the slacker must put on a suit, get a job, lose his benefits, and make himself useful. Harmlessly ineffective as he may be, we hate and fear him for showing us the useless dimension of our own selfhood, for voicing our own impulse not to go to work today, or tomorrow.

That impulse to recover the personal rhythms of our own being from the imposed rhythms of the modern world continues to haunt us. For those of us caught up in this world's twin demands of permanent activity and distraction, all the basic elements of everyday being—sleep, eating, sex, movement, thought—survive in a state of chronic deprivation. Disturbed, accelerated, truncated, and confused, our bodily and mental lives seem barely to belong to us. The consulting room is only one of many spaces in which I'm made aware of this predicament; every Tube carriage or social gathering or office seems to hum with declarations of exhaustion and time poverty—of sleep interrupted, of electronic devices intruding themselves between couples and family members at the dinner table or in bed, of evenings and weekends swallowed up in work.

Into this enervated culture steps the so-called "slow movement", a loose affiliation of practical advocates for slowing the pace of daily activities from cooking and gardening to design and medicine. As crystallised in its informal bible, Carl Honoré's *In Praise of Slow* (2005), the aim of the movement is not to promote slowness for its own sake, but to allow the activity itself, rather than some imposed schedule, to set the speed at which we perform it. A slow-braised stew, a yoga pose, a kiss, or a chat will tell us, if we allow them to, the time for which they should be cooked, assumed, and enjoyed.

Taken in this way, the ordinary pleasures of the world are felt rather than consumed, giving us the joy of an actual experience rather than the grim satisfaction of the next task executed. It isn't hard to see the appeal of slowness, the promise it offers of recovering the fullness and depth of real life from the manically accelerated impersonation of life dictated by consumer capitalism.

But there is another strain of argument audible in the proliferation of books, TED talks, and blogs promoting the ethos of slow: the assurance that slowness will make us not only happier but more productive. To do things slowly is to do them properly rather than in the mode of resentful carelessness fostered by the rage for speed. Honoré cites the IBM manager who encourages employees "to make the most of email (and life) by using email less" (*The Independent*, 2010). More haste, less speed; the quality of email use as well as its efficacy is maximised by placing limits on it.

With such counsel, the imperatives of purpose and productivity, which slowness seemed at first to subvert, are returned to the driving seat. Slowness ceases to be its own justification and instead becomes a means to the end of a healthy work–life balance. And what's wrong with that? Surely to remedy the pervasive malaise of exhaustion and agitation by resetting priorities and recovering a measure of control over the pace of daily life can only be sensible and humane?

It also keeps intact, and indeed bolsters, a conception of us as essentially instrumental, task-driven creatures. Slowness, no longer a brake on productive efficiency, is instead put in its service, cultivating the healthier bodies and clearer minds we need to become better workers, parents, lovers, cooks. Like most self-help movements, the argument for slowness is liable to get pulled between a fundamental challenge to the status quo and cosmetic amelioration of it.

Rousseau's mid-lake reverie, after all, doesn't end with his declaring himself newly invigorated for his return to work and society. It isn't an early version of the yoga retreat or mindfulness course that recharges the batteries for those twelve-hour days at the office, but a plunge into "pure anarchic subjectivity"—a dangerous energy that resembles the defiant dozing of the girl on the poster, corroding the will to serve as a good worker and citizen. It is slowness as the enemy rather than ally of social responsibility and cohesion.

In today's overworked executive culture, there is a striking contemporary analogue for Rousseau's drifting boat: the flotation tank. In their 2012 book *Dead Man Working*, Carl Cederström and Peter Fleming observe the increasing popularity of this elaborate device among "over-worked, hyper-stressed employees of London who simply cannot turn off" (2012, p. 51). They describe the experience of entering the tank and floating in the warm salt water. In the darkness, the contours of the body seem to dissolve, so that "you can no longer distinguish between your different body parts. As you lie there, in the dark, hearing the ambient music slowly fading out, your brain activity slows down and you willingly surrender to a dream-like state. Then, finally, you have become no one."

As in Rousseau's reverie, the self here feels neither surfeit nor deficit of pleasure, dissolving instead into a state of pure anonymity, a nirvanic emptiness more perfect than any worldly happiness. But the differences are at least as instructive as the resemblances. Where for Rousseau the state of blissful self-sufficiency cannot be reconciled with the workaday world lurking at its edges, the flotation centre sells itself on its positive effect on our dynamism and productivity. "A float session", says Floatworks' PR, "is guaranteed to eliminate stress, leaving you with a clear mind to concentrate 100% on the matter in hand. It increases creativity, the ability to solve problems, concentration span, personal motivation and energy levels" (Cederström & Fleming, 2012, p. 52).

Corporate workplaces have become increasingly invested in pressing such fleeting experiences of pure being, including mindfulness meditation and yoga as well as flotation, into their service. If the worker is to be made maximally productive, then the slacker in him must become subservient. The corporate strategy isn't to dismiss the slacker as some loser wandering the streets outside its shiny glass towers but to recognise him as a dimension in all of us. In encouraging the employee to cultivate inner peace, it acknowledges an inertial tendency, an anarchic refusal of the demand to be useful, or, in today's dehumanising parlance, a "net contributor". The clever ruse of sending the employee to a flotation tank during the lunch hour marshals this outlaw region of selfhood for the corporation's own uses.

In Slow TV we are faced with a strand of the slow movement that isn't so easily co-opted. Slow TV is a style of broadcast inspired by Andy Warhol's experiments in long-form cinema recording a continuous static or near-static entity—his sleeping lover, the Empire State Building. Its earliest experiment was contemporaneous with Warhol's films. At Christmas 1966, WPIX showed the famous *Yule Log*, a looped film of a burning fire set against a festive music soundtrack and broadcast without commercial interruption. But it wasn't until 2009 that a series of programmes produced by the Norwegian Broadcasting Corporation turned Slow TV into a fully fledged television subgenre.

The NRK's first foray into Slow TV was a real-time record of the seven-hour train journey between Oslo and Bergen, using four alternating cameras fixed on both exterior and interior viewpoints. Its popular success, which saw 1.25 million viewers tune in to some portion of the programme, has since led to the commissioning of similar broadcast events, among them further train as well as boat rides, a salmon fishing expedition, a compilation of three months of recorded bird life, a night of chopping and burning firewood, and a knitting marathon.

Ever since television insinuated itself into our homes and lives, it has been the object of bitter polemic from cultural critics lamenting its stupefying effects on our moral, intellectual, and political faculties. TV, we are told, renders us docile, pliable, credulous. It drip-feeds the new opiate of the masses, a pappy diet of vapid entertainment and pseudo-information. Fictional or factual, its flow of programming is tacitly directed towards entrenching and normalising moral depravity (for its conservative critics) and political subservience (for its revolutionary enemies).

These critics point to TV's capacity to induce a collapse of the erect and alert bodily and mental stance we're supposed to maintain during the working day, striding down corridors or seated at desks. In this state of exhaustion, our weary bodies are massaged and our drained minds filled with stories, opinions, and information. TV, in other words, exploits the inertial region of our selfhood. For us on the sofa as for Rousseau on the lake, the sorrows of the day past and the anxieties of the day to come seem to dissolve. But where the beautiful vista before Rousseau wants nothing from him, and so leaves him to sink into his blissful oblivion, the vista on our screens seduces our attention, pleasure, and interest.

Slow TV is different in this regard, closer to a Fifth Walk for our times. It lets us experience the stupor induced by the medium of TV, without the stimulus aroused by the message. Instead of filling up empty time with content, it encourages us to keep it empty, without past or future, to let ourselves waste time watching next to nothing.

The pioneering NRK Slow TV producer Thomas Hellum tells of a man of eighty-two who sat enraptured for a full five days in front of a real-time fjord cruise. What was he looking at? Was he, as Hellum jocosely suggests, not wanting to leave his chair in case he missed something? Or was the catatonic fascination more an effect of the absence of anything to miss, the increasing loss of any sense of differentiation between moments, places, images?

Watch the Oslo–Bergen train journey for long enough, staring into the endless yards of track rolling towards the horizon, bathed in the shadow of the driver's car, and the contents of the scenery—the fitfully illuminated pitch black of rail tunnels, the grey mountain rock bathed in the resplendent glare of the sun, the towering pylons and hulking shipping containers dotting the station yards, the flat stretches of sea and sand, the blindingly white snow and lush grasses and glassy lakes nestled under the same expanse of cloudless blue sky—will eventually dissolve into a single, endless flow of colour and sound.

It isn't the landscape so much as your own mind that you're immersed in by this point. The things looked at become secondary to the act of looking. The effect of real slowness is to pull us away from our everyday view of the world as a series of discrete objects and events, and recall to us an experience of the world as the undifferentiated stream of sensory effects it once was when we first arrived in it.

From Rousseau to Slow TV, reverie has served as a kind of silent protest, a yearning to live within the indifferent region of ourselves that can't be used or put to work. The obvious objection to reverie is that it's profoundly antisocial. It models happiness on narcissistic withdrawal, in which the basic conditions of the external world—time, space, the presence of others—have melted away. This is probably why slacker types are so often accused of "living on another planet", the indignant contempt provoked by their apparent unconcern for the rules and norms that govern this planet.

Like scepticism, Epicurus' doctrine of hedonism promoted ataraxia, or tranquil unconcern, as the highest good of life. Its route to this goal was not, as the term hedonism now connotes, endless pleasurable indulgence, but the avoidance of the physical and psychic pressures that induce tension and pain. In Rousseau's boat or the Slow TV viewer's armchair is experienced "no other feeling of ... pleasure or pain ... than simply that of our existence". It's hard to imagine a fuller realisation of Epicurus' counsel: "Live in hiding and do not care about the world." (For a good selection of Epicurus' thought, see *The Art of Happiness*, 2013).

Perhaps anticipating the strange pleasures of Slow TV, David Foster Wallace's epic 1996 novel *Infinite Jest* centres on the clandestine circulation of a film so captivating it causes its viewer, unable to wrench himself away from it, to expire in a state of stupefied bliss. This is the logical outcome of surrendering oneself to a state of pure ataraxia. If you stay in the boat or chair long enough, you'll die; perfect tranquillity must at some point give way to biological necessity. But is the slacker tendency in us so thoroughly incompatible with the reality of existence in a world of others? Why is it so difficult to imagine a world in which my own personal rhythms can exist peaceably alongside yours?

A good part of this difficulty can be chalked up to the need to procure and sustain the means of our survival, an imperative which imposes on us the obligation to adapt ourselves to rhythms that are not our own—those of the field, the street, the factory, the office. Our survival requires work, or more precisely labour. Hannah Arendt argues that what we call work gives rise to a tangible product. Labouring, in contrast, is an endless process, a matter of surviving rather than making. We labour for the means to feed, clothe, and shelter ourselves and our dependants, meaning the cycle must begin again the next day and the next. When it comes to labour, writes Arendt, "what makes the effort painful is not danger but its relentless repetition" (1959, p. 101).

Relentless repetition is painful because it means submitting to a rhythm imposed on us from without. It means sitting in stationary traffic or waiting for overdue trains on overcrowded platforms; adapting mind and body to the rhythms of keyboards, power drills, conveyor belts, cash registers; executing tasks to tight deadlines that override any urge to, say, have a nap or go for a stroll. We dislike labour because it makes us experience the day on terms that are not our own.

For more than two centuries, anarchists and socialists have sought to imagine forms of work that would put an end to the drab tyranny of labour, among them Charles Fourier, the utopian socialist who inspired a string of communitarian experiments across the nineteenth century; Paul Lafargue, son-in-law of Karl Marx and author of an inspired polemical defence of *The Right to Be Lazy*; Mikhail Bakunin and Peter Kropotkin, the major theorists of Russian anarchism; and William Morris, leader and activist of the English Arts and Crafts movement.

Many of these ideas and impulses are distilled in Wilde's famous 1891 essay "The Soul of Man Under Socialism", written immediately after reading Kropotkin. Wilde's essay provokes us into examining our assumptions about what matters most in life. We tend to assume unthinkingly that our primary concern in life should be with what is useful to us, and that beauty is mere embellishment or indulgence. Where the useful serves our deepest needs, the beautiful merely caters to our desires and whims.

Wilde asks us to imagine a self and a society governed instead by the primacy of beauty, where the soul-crushing burden of "useful" labour is outsourced to commonly owned machines. Beauty in such a world consists in a person or thing "being what it is", in manifesting its singular personality. Under socialism, the human personality "will not be always meddling with others, or asking them to be like itself. It will love them because they will be different" (2007, p. 1046).

The value of a person in such a society would consist not in how much she's like everyone else but how much like herself. Socialism as Wilde conceives it will foster the conditions under which singular individuals live side by side, without resentment or rivalry. The angry, dissident spirit is an effect of a society which will not let its members become who they are. "The note of the perfect personality", says Wilde, "is not rebellion, but peace" (p. 1046).

Far from being the enemy of society, in this vision ataraxia becomes its very basis. A "faculty of indifference", a slothful disinclination to dictate to others how they should be, helps us cultivate creative boldness, a fearless and joyful self-expression which is Wilde's very definition of beauty. In abolishing the tyranny of the useful and the "relentless repetition" of labour, we clear the way for the reign of useless beauty over our daily lives.

Things haven't turned out as Wilde had hoped, at least not yet. In this age of "strivers and skivers", the popular fantasy is of a parallel society of welfare cheats and layabouts enjoying easy lives at the expense of our hard ones. The tyranny of the useful seems as entrenched as it's ever been. A unique personality is more a marketing tool than an expression of beauty; "be what you are" sounds more like an advertising slogan than a spur to social and individual transformation.

Wilde's socialist society was an aesthetic one, meaning that art alone, in his view, could express the unconstrained uniqueness of the human person. In our neoliberal society, art has become a means of buying and selling human uniqueness as a commodity like any other. Where Wilde anticipated a world of proliferating slackers doing whatever they wanted, our world is one in which would-be slackers are under compulsion to go wherever the Job Centre tells them.

Under such conditions, making a claim for art as authentic and spontaneous self-expression seems naive. Almost none of us live in a world that nurtures such spontaneity. The majority of artists are stuck between the rock of financial self-sacrifice for the sake of creative time and the hard place of sacrificing creative time to financial necessity. A minority can make a living from their art, while a tiny fraction of that minority is made wealthy by the inflation of their prices to obscene levels, fuelled by the status of art as the ultimate speculative commodity, frequently yielding profits that dwarf those of other sectors.

Far from contesting the tyranny of the useful, art today has become its great ally, put to the task of enhancing brands, adorning corporate boardrooms, and boosting investment portfolios. How, then, is an artist meant to defy such uses of her work? The German artist Maria Eichhorn offered a memorable answer to this question in her 2016 show at London's Chisenhale Gallery, "5 weeks, 25 days, 175 hours".

The show opened with a one-day symposium, featuring lectures and discussions of the ideas and questions it raised. The following day, a sign was placed outside the gallery entrance:

> For the duration of Maria Eichhorn's exhibition, *5 weeks, 25 days,*
> *175 hours*, Chisenhale Gallery's staff are not working. The gallery and
> office are closed from 24 April to 29 May 2016. For further informa-
> tion please visit www.chisenhale.org.uk.

Eichhorn's "exhibition" put the gallery's entire staff on five weeks' fully paid leave, during which no phone calls were taken and all emails were deleted. Staff were requested to do no work relating to their roles at the gallery throughout the duration of the show (or no-show).

Eichhorn wasn't the first artist to have made art out of a refusal to display anything. Robert Barry's 1969 exhibition in Amsterdam consisted of a sign on the gallery's locked door reading, "During the exhibition the gallery will be closed", while in his Los Angeles show of 1974 Michael Asher removed the partition wall between the gallery's empty exhibition space and its office, exposing its everyday operations to the public.

But the emphasis of Eichhorn's show was markedly different. The previous two artists placed the focus on the viewer's desire, thwarted by Barry and gratified by Asher, to see the very spaces blocked off to him. Eichhorn, in contrast, drew our attention to the gallery being closed because the staff were "not working".

In so doing, she channels Wilde's utopian spirit. The symposium prior to the gallery closure spent a good portion of its time detailing the huge volume of administrative labour and fundraising activity that goes into the gallery's survival. Eichhorn's gesture orchestrated a break into this painful labour of survival, using the funds raised for the show to release its staff from work. The gift of their freedom, and the implicit plea for the value of not working, became the invisible content of the show. For those five weeks, she realised in practice what Wilde envisioned in theory: the human being, liberated from the everyday tyranny of labour, could be experienced as what he is rather than what he does or has. We can imagine how the staff might have used or wasted their freed-up time, but we cannot see it or make an image of it to display and sell. The staff, in other words, were released from the bonds of action and into the freedom of being.

We don't get to see what the staff did with their free time. A display of images of the staff sleeping, strolling in the park, watching daytime TV, or falling into massive existential self-doubt would extract a product from their freedom and so compromise it. On the terms set by Wilde, it is a work of art precisely because there is nothing to see, because it isn't a thing to put in a gallery for others to visit. It suspends art as we know it, a discrete commodity produced to be circulated and looked at, in order to get us to imagine life itself as art—that is, life no longer in thrall to the labour of survival.

For Wilde, life and art could only be worthy of themselves when released from instrumental bonds, when they became ends in themselves rather than the means to something else (money or fame). This is impossible as long as art consists of objects made to buy and sell. Eichhorn is the latest in a long chain of modern artists who have asked how it is possible, if at all, to produce a work of art that wouldn't immediately be commodified. In 1961, the Italian artist Piero Manzoni produced a series of cans containing, so he claimed, his own shit (the claim can only be verified by opening the tin, thereby destroying its market value). The last auction of one of the Manzoni cans, in 2016, fetched around £250,000.

Manzoni showed the alchemy whereby the art market turned waste into gold. Eichhorn's alchemy is different, taking funding that would ordinarily be put to work in the forms of curation, publicity, security, administration, and public education, and transforming it into an unexpected and abundant gift of free time. Those five weeks, twenty-five days and 175 hours are taken out of the circuit of productivity and purpose; from the perspective of work and profit, they are wasted. But this wasted time is alchemised by the work into the immaterial gold of non-work, giving us a glimpse of the world as it might look if left to the slackers.

Is psychoanalysis an ally of the slacker in us, or does it seek to discipline and "cure" the non-working self? There are good reasons to suspect psychoanalysis of being on the side of work. "Work", indeed, is one of the preferred synonyms of the psychoanalyst to describe the clinical process of seeing a patient and the gradual change it seeks to effect. And amplifying the qualities of pain and difficulty, one often hears the analogy made between this process and that of antenatal labour and birth, as though the emergence of a new and different self couldn't be authentic if it wasn't also excruciating.

And then there are the desired results of psychoanalytic work. Freud identified "love and work" as the ideals of life and analysis alike, suggesting the ultimate aim of the process was to lift inhibitions on the energy we would want to invest in a productive and purposeful life. In mid-twentieth-century America, this conception of analysis drove its medicalisation. In functioning as the dominant paradigm of psychiatry, it was pressed into the service of society's needs, its primary curative aim being the integration of the patient into the workplace and sanctioned forms of social and family life. In the "ego psychological" tradition that dominated American psychoanalysis during this period, the essential clinical task was conceived as "strengthening the ego", seat of active and rational selfhood, against the incursions of the unconscious and its debilitating conflicts.

Work, with its predictable routines and tasks, is perhaps the most reliable means of strengthening the ego. Like all regular work, psychoanalytic work has something of this predictability, the "relentless repetition" of which Arendt speaks. One of the most difficult demands of clinical practice, at least for me, is the simple maintenance of its routines—beginning and ending the sessions at the appointed times with the same individuals, being no more or less available and attentive to each of them for one session than you were the previous session or will be the next. Of course, the professional requirements of punctuality and consistency are hardly exclusive to psychoanalysis. But in psychoanalysis good timing is not merely a means to the end of efficiency, but a source of therapeutic value, a way for a patient to experience a reliability and regularity that might never have been previously enjoyed. Perhaps because it's a clinical necessity and ethical obligation, the repetitiousness of psychoanalytic routine can feel peculiarly burdensome.

Paradoxically, the purpose of this labour is to protect a space for non-labour, a temporary suspension of the working self and its effort of organised, logically sequential thinking. The assurance of the constancy of the space and time of the session licenses a certain slackening of the mind, a mode of speaking—and, indeed, of not speaking—which doesn't need to know what it's saying or where it's going.

In today's accelerated culture, most of daily life is experienced in drive mode, seeking the fastest and most direct route from one task to the next (though it's worth recalling that driving often gets mired in congestion). The psychoanalytic session releases us from this purposive mode, ushering us into a time of aimlessness, a movement through thoughts and feelings and words directed less towards getting somewhere in particular than to cultivating curiosity about the mind itself.

Walking, suggests Frédéric Gros, is a kind of non- or even anti-work. Work privileges doing over being, the single-minded action over a more diffuse receptivity. One works to produce, whereas in conventional economic terms walking is "time wasted, frittered away, dead time in which no wealth is produced (2014, p. 89). It isn't a coincidence that the experience of watching *Slacker* most immediately evoked in me a long and lackadaisical walk.

The reverse side of the aim-oriented tendency of psychoanalysis is its insinuation into a person's daily life of designated periods of time freed from the imperative to do or say anything in particular. Certainly one addresses one's inhibitions, frustrations, guilt, shame, inadequacy, and other forms of suffering, but the curative force of a session lies not in finding the most effective solution to these problems, but in rousing the kind of interest in, and intimacy with, our own minds that daily life typically blocks off. In this sense, it is another way of cultivating idiorrhythmy, of slowly discovering the pace and style of one's own particular walk.

This is why, especially when seen from the perspective of more time-limited, quick-fix psychotherapies, it is so often accused of frittering away time, with failing to turn a psychic profit with sufficient quickness and efficiency. Psychoanalysis, in this view, doesn't get anywhere, is talk for the mere sake of it. Which is not altogether wrong, but misses the point nonetheless: in one way or another, a patient comes to psychoanalysis to be relieved of the pressure to produce, to formulate a solution, to get somewhere. It offers the experience, as Winnicott hints, of discovering the layer of pure being buried under the surface of daily doing.

For as long as I could remember, each of Jerome's three weekly sessions had brought dispatches of some new outrage perpetrated against his dignity and intelligence by one or other venal, vulgar colleague at his accountancy firm. Listening to him, I'd catch myself wondering caustically how on earth, given the chronic and pervasive mediocrity of its personnel, it got any business at all, let alone serviced the massive roster of corporate clients it boasted.

Filled with his cold rage and hate, the room quickly turned airless, sticky. At first, and without realising it, I survived his contempt by letting myself become infected with it. I quickly learned to expect some tirade against the ignorance and sycophancy of the junior and senior partners promoted over his head. "They haven't a fucking clue," he'd say in a tone of theatrically hopeless exasperation, to which I'd once, early on, replied in a tone of spiteful impatience, "No. It's lucky they have you." His comeback, after several minutes of freezing me out, was merciless: "If your clinical ability is on a par with your wit, I'm wasting my time here."

It was a useful if harsh bit of instruction. With a different patient, my response might have presented a gently ironic mirror to his self-regard and the self-hatred it concealed. But Jerome was too attuned to its tone of scratchy one-upmanship, and duly punished me for it. He hardly needed me to point out his attitude of enraged superiority; he had to live with it every minute of the day.

No, what he needed now was precisely the opposite: a place to bring his hate, to spew it unsparingly until he could trust it wouldn't provoke my retaliation. And so for six, ten, twelve, eighteen months, I took in his contempt and disgust towards his work, his colleagues, towards the wife who so quickly lost patience, the young children who demanded the one thing he couldn't offer—his happiness—and towards his analyst, who just sat there "listening to my tedious bullshit with practically nothing to say".

For close to three hours a week, I inhabited a world peopled by cocks and arseholes, bitches and harridans and brats, a world of sadistic enslavement, of gratuitous meanness and disrespect, of perpetual demands and failed communication. I could find little to say beyond some variation on how difficult it must be to live in a world so bereft of joy or love or fulfilment.

In spite of his regular swipes at me, I had the sense he was helped by the assurance of someone knowing how unrelievedly lousy it felt to be him.

As the story of his childhood emerged, it became difficult to imagine how it could have been any other way. His father, manager of a local retail franchise, transmitted nervous disdain for the imaginative precocity and intellectual curiosity of his youngest son. What kind of kid stayed home to draw and listen to music, when he could be out cheering the local non-league football team with his dad, sister, and brother?

His father's distance found its mirror image in his mother's proximity. He would feel her peer over his shoulder at the picture he was drawing, and half needily, half resentfully await its pronouncement as a masterpiece. Frustrated by her premature exit from formal education, she lived her son's schooling as though it were her own second chance. At a certain point, Jerome told me, he no longer knew whose homework he was doing or whose piano he was practising.

His father looked askance on this alternative couple, more puzzled than concerned, perhaps relieved they'd both found someone who seemed to make them happy. Jerome thus lost the last line of defence against the intrusions of his mother's desire, against her claustrophobic investment in his life. His only refuge during his largely friendless, joyless adolescence was his kitschy fantasies of escaping to Paris to paint in a garret. He would stare longingly at photographs of Cézanne, Matisse, and especially Picasso, placing himself amid the breathless hum of brilliance, agony, absinthe, and women.

The discussion with his mother about college was swift and brutal. "Actually," he'd gathered the courage to tell her, "I want to go to art school." Her laugh in response, he said, was one of the worst moments of his life. "You can paint to your heart's content when you're earning a decent living!" she told him. "I can see now how profoundly I hated her at that point," he told me. So profoundly that his unconscious revenge was to be unhappy for the rest of his life, to spoil her life by spoiling his own. When she told him he should study for accountancy, he simply acquiesced in steely resentment and silent loathing.

She had wanted him to have a life better than hers, a life less blighted by blind compliance and unfulfilled promise. Instead, the two of them had unwittingly colluded to ensure that his life would repeat the very same patterns. She had married a man as unable as her own father to acknowledge the substance of her desire; Jerome, or so he told himself, had married a woman with the very same blind spot. Thus he found himself stuck in an existence whose chief and profoundly perverse pleasure was hating it.

One of the favoured forms of this hate was to sink into fantasies of quitting the firm, coming home to his wife, and telling her gleefully he'd chucked it in, watching her mounting anxiety as he gave his days over to lounging around in assorted hideous Hawaiian shirts, not shaving, going to matinees, getting fat, vaguely contemplating enrolling on a painting course. "I can just see her screaming at me, 'You're a fucking useless waste of space!' and giving her the great Lebowski comeback, 'Yeah, well, that's just, like, your *opinion*, man.'" That would set him laughing uncontrollably for a minute, until he calmed down and stared at the ceiling in eerie silence.

I wondered aloud what might be needed to get him to take his anger and sadness and longing seriously, as opposed to drowning them in trivialising contempt. Wasn't that why he had come to me? He wanted to experience a life set to the rhythm of his own curiosity, shaped by his own desire, and with me he could begin to discover what this might be like. For a few hours a week, he could simply be, without having to do anything. His fantasies of becoming a slacker had for too long served his hate, his image of himself as ridiculous, pathetic; perhaps they could now begin to serve life.

He began to see a couples therapist with his wife and was astounded to hear her say she didn't care what he did, she just wanted him to be happy, or at least not so relentlessly wretched. "But", he had weakly responded, "you and the kids, you need me to support you ..." "You will *not*", she had yelled back, "pin your misery on me and the kids. After all the shit we've put up with, that is one insult too far."

It was a critical intervention, shaking him angrily and lovingly out of his toxically aggressive self-pity and forcing him into a reckoning with his own role in the traumatic loss of his creative and imaginative life. It ushered in a phase of fierce self-reflection in the analysis, in parallel with a new and serious contemplation of the kinds of psychic and external changes he dared to hope for. Then, disaster, cruel and sudden.

In his autobiographical preface to *The Scarlet Letter*, Nathaniel Hawthorne told of the strange coincidence of being abruptly dismissed from the post he'd long hated. "In view of my previous weariness of office," he wrote, "and vague thoughts of resignation, my fortune somewhat resembled that of a person who should entertain an idea of committing suicide, and, altogether beyond his hopes, meet with the good hap to be murdered" (1850, p. 42).

The unfolding of Jerome's story would soon cast the wit of that sentence into severe relief. After years of extravagant fantasies of resignation, he too had the good hap to be murdered. He announced to me flatly one morning that he'd been handed his notice. When he said nothing more, I asked how he was feeling about it. "Intelligent question," he replied. "You must have guessed what a boon it was to my sense of security and self-worth." The old Jerome was, all too literally, back with a vengeance.

Even now, two years on, it is difficult for me to understand why Jerome experienced his dismissal as such a final and irrecoverable blow. The weeks following it saw a fierce surge in the contempt we had been working so hard to understand and transform. Nothing could shift him from the grim conviction that he'd lost all claim on the love and respect of anyone who mattered. When I tried to remind him of the inner transformation he'd begun to experience in the weeks prior to losing his job, he told me dolefully that he'd been a fool to believe all that shit. He was brutally and casually murdering the new self he'd been ushering into being before it could assume real existence.

The analysis had helped free him to imagine a life in which he was licensed to not work, to define himself outside the standards and metrics set by his mother's wishes and spurred by his father's indifference. At forty-four years old, he wouldn't be enrolling in art school and searching Paris Gumtree for a dilapidated garret. But at least the possibility of creative life was no longer being entirely suffocated by cynical self-irony.

Being fired laid waste to these changes in a moment. All that ludicrous guff about painting and living the dream, he declared, had betrayed his mother's dedication to him and confirmed his father's belief in his over-reaching pretention. And I had *encouraged* him to think it.

It seemed he couldn't forgive me. Two weeks later, the first morning after the Easter break and minutes before his session was due to start, I picked up a message on my voicemail. It was Jerome. He wouldn't be coming this morning. He had decided, in fact, that he wouldn't be returning to analysis. He thanked me for my help.

Stung by the sheer coldness of a curt farewell voice message after five years of analysis, I returned his call and told him I thought, after all this time, it was worth coming to discuss his decision and, at the very least, to say goodbye in person. "Sorry, I can't face that … I don't know what it is. I think with me, in the end, nothing works."

I wanted to respond, "OK, but hadn't you started to discover that this desperate zeal for things to 'work' is the problem? What happened to letting things, and you, not work for a while and seeing what unfolded?" But I didn't get the chance. Jerome had replaced the handset, leaving me to listen to dead air.

References

Arendt, H. (1959). *The Human Condition: A Study of the Central Dilemmas Facing Modern Man*. New York: Doubleday Anchor.

Barthes, R. (2012). *How to Live Together: Novelistic Simulations of Some Everyday Spaces*. K. Briggs (Trans.). New York: Columbia University Press.

Cederström, C., & Fleming, P. (2012). *Dead Man Working*. Alresford, UK: Zero.

Cioran, E. M. (1949). *A Short History of Decay*. R. Howard (Trans.). New York: Arcade, 1998.

Epicurus. *The Art of Happiness*. J. K. Strodach (Trans. & Ed.). London: Penguin, 2013.

Gros, F. (2014). *A Philosophy of Walking*. J. Howe (Trans.). London: Verso, 2015.

Hawthorne, N. (1850). *The Scarlet Letter*. Oxford: Oxford University Press, 1990.

Honoré, C. (2005). *In Praise of Slow: How a Worldwide Movement Is Changing the Cult of Speed*. London: HarperCollins.

Independent, The (2010, October 1). Kill the smartphone: The slow fight against the rat race. https://www.independent.co.uk/life-style/kill-the-smartphone-the-slow-fight-against-the-rat-race-2095847.html

Rousseau, J.-J. (1776). *Reveries of the Solitary Walker*. R. Goulbourne (Trans.). Oxford: Oxford University Press, 2011.

Sextus Empiricus. *Outlines of Scepticism*. J. Annas & J. Barnes (Trans.). Cambridge: Cambridge University Press, 2000.

Sloterdijk, P. (2015). *Stress and Freedoms*. W. Hoban (Trans.). Cambridge: Polity Press.

Wallace, D. F. (1996). *Infinite Jest*. Boston, MA: Little, Brown.

Wilde, O. (1891). The soul of man under Socialism. In: *The Collected Works of Oscar Wilde*. Ware, UK: Wordsworth, 2007.

CHAPTER THIRTEEN

Climate crisis: the moral dimension

Sally Weintrobe

My subject is an enduring part of human character, the exception in people. The exception stubbornly clings to a narcissistic form of entitlement, feeling entitled in three main ways:

- I am entitled to believe that I am an idealised version of myself
- I am entitled to whatever I want
- I am entitled to use omnipotent thinking to avoid inner discomfort, especially guilt.

These three supposed entitlements cohere to form a false belief system that operates something like this: "Being me, I am naturally special. I am entitled to whatever I want. Why? Because I am me. No other reason needed. I am entitled to use omnipotent thinking to maintain my belief I am special and so can have anything and everything I want."

A stubborn sense of exaggerated entitlement is key to being an exception, which operates like a kind of inner "refusenik". You might picture a two-year-old in a strop on the pavement, refusing to give way and to fit in.

Here is an example of being an exception. I was at the bus stop, having decided not to take the car to fetch the grandchildren from school to reduce my carbon emissions. It was raining, cold, and windy, and standing there I thought grumpily, "I wish I'd just taken the car!" Next, I imagined my small grandchildren, now grown up, standing right next to me. I was in a bit of bad weather and they were in extreme weather because of climate change. I heard my entitled belief I should not have to face any inconvenience at all. I felt ashamed, embarrassed, and much less of a person than I feel I can be.

I believe I had spontaneously emerged from a layer of disavowal, which is one form of omnipotent (magical) thinking. When in disavowal, I had rearranged things in my imagination such that I had placed my grandchildren far enough away from me to avoid my feeling touched by them. In disavowal, I could know but not really know, with empathy and feeling, what climate change means for them and for others, now and in the future. In that vivid moment at the bus stop, emerging from disavowal, they were back close to me, where they belong. I imaginatively spliced my present world and their future world, each with its weather conditions, together. That way, we were close enough for our eyes to meet, for us all to hear my petulance and for my concern, guilt, and shame to be activated.

Some people say the reason climate change is hard to think about is we cannot see into the future. No doubt feeling my physical discomfort at the bus stop did help me to better imagine their discomfort. But I do not agree that future problems are hard to imagine and think about, and that this is why we do not think about climate change. I have no difficulty imagining my grandchildren in the future, hopefully going to university, having relationships and children of their own. My blind spot was very specific. It was about the effects on them of the climate crisis. It was in this specific regard that I had rearranged my mental furniture such that they were out of my inner sight.

I find the more I think about disavowal, the more peculiar it appears to me. I reach one layer, to find yet another. I think a lot about the climate crisis. I have studied the models of what is predicted to happen if we do not ditch fossil fuels fast. I had taken the bus that day because I am aware I have my own individual carbon footprint and that carbon I am responsible for will stay in the atmosphere for thousands of years. I have thought about the effects of the crisis on my grandchildren. However, somehow, this was with the true climate impact on them bleached out. My thinking had been somewhat disembodied and in the abstract. I had not really tried to picture how they might be feeling and managing in extreme weather.

Disavowal is layered like an onion. Even my thinking about climate change as something in the future involved disavowal. My bus stop example is from 2014, when I already knew climate change is a current, not a future, crisis and that people and animals were already dying. By 2019 things are much worse, as the climate scientists predicted they would be. We know from earth systems scientists that we have already left the clement period of the Holocene and are in the Anthropocene, an age of climate instability. It is easy to write that sentence, but I find it very hard indeed to take in its meaning.

At the bus stop, I had seen more clearly a petulant, entitled, resentful part of myself—my inner refusenik—that was saying to my more concerned caring part, "I'll go along with your carbon reduction actions, but only if I'm not actually inconvenienced." Here, we can see the exception with her stubborn entitlement to be the princess without a pea in her mattress. I suggest the pea here is not so much the literal discomfort of being at the bus stop in wind and rain. Who wants that? I suggest the pea is my moral discomfort. With disavowal I could stay comfortably numb (to use words from a song by Pink Floyd). My grandchildren and their fate were split off. My exception had stepped in front of and eclipsed the person in me who knows carbon is real stuff.

I believe that at the bus stop I experienced a particular crystallisation of conscience, one I felt belonged, and did not belong, to me. I do have a petulant, exaggeratedly entitled side—I recognised this person as me. However, while I could see the entitled brat at the bus stop was me, she also appeared alien to me, and I thought, who is this person? How did I come to think like this? This is not me. I believe my petulance at the bus stop was *also* formed by the culture in which I live. This is neoliberal culture. I will talk later about neoliberalism, its ideology, and the culture it has fostered, but here note that neoliberal culture actively feeds the exception in us, and does so all day long. It encourages us to believe we are special, to idealise ourselves, to believe we should be able to have whatever we want, and that we need not feel guilty about the effects on other people and animals living now and in the future. Neoliberal culture regresses us and leads to what Bion called spiritual drift. I suggest it encourages us to be less than we are, and are capable of being.

I now look in more psychological detail at the part of human character I am calling an exception. If we remember, exceptions essentially feel entitled to be it all, to have it all, and to use omnipotent thinking to avoid feeling guilty about this.

Being an exception

Freud, who studied exceptions, and used the term to describe a psychological state, thought an exception is an ordinary refusenik part of us that lurks in us all. We start out as her or his majesty the baby. Then, reaching the terrible twos, we demand the world sees things our way and obeys our commands. We struggle throughout life to accept our real position, at home, in the classroom, in the playground, at work, and our refusenik can flare up in arguments over inheritances. Surely, we are entitled to the biggest slice of the pie? Surely, we were the most loved? While this kind of entitlement is "narcissistic", not all entitlement is. Indeed, a sense of lively entitlement to a fair share is vital in order to live a meaningful life.

Let us explore further the three core beliefs that exceptions cling to.

I am entitled to see myself as ideal

In reality, no one is ideal, and the world does not revolve round us. Later, I will explore how omnipotent thinking can sustain the illusion it does.

I am entitled to idealised provision

This entitlement fans an avaricious form of greed (see Weintrobe, 2010a). The world and everyone and everything in it are eyed up as just assets to be stripped, only there to aggrandise the self.

I suggest "I want that, so I'll have it, regardless. I'm entitled" has becomes so normalised in our culture that we do not notice our exception speaking when taking the car not the bus, or ordering an item from across the world online, or reaching for that fresh, flown-in food item at the supermarket. Nor do we consciously notice and subject to scrutiny the justifications our exception uses to brush any guilt aside.

I am entitled to use omnipotent thinking

Omnipotent thinking magically "disappears" inner discomfort, restoring a clear conscience so we have no worries. As if. I was using omnipotent thinking at the bus stop. My exception was objecting, "I must have my comfort. It's my entitlement. Never mind the carbon." I could avoid my guilt about driving my car through mentally relocating my grandchildren to a place I called the "future". In effect this was actively "othering" my own grandchildren to avoid feeling guilty about my carbon behaviour. I am highlighting the issue of how omnipotence can use splitting to assuage guilt, aware that the mind can split off mental content in all sorts of ways and for all sorts of reasons.

The caring and the uncaring parts of the self view damage inflicted in radically different ways. The caring part has a more proportionate sense of its own involvement in causing the damage. Because it does not need to "big itself up through self-idealisation", it does not leap to feeling over- (or entirely) responsible for damage. Because not disassociated from feelings, it feels guilty and ashamed at seeing its own implication in the damage. Guilt and shame are highly serviceable useful feelings, as they can trigger the wish to make genuine repairs, where this is possible.

To assess damage, the caring part needs to be able to recognise idealisation. It works hard to de-idealise the self, making it humbler, more aware of needs, dependencies on others, and feelings of love, gratitude, and obligation towards others. The caring self works hard to include the other as like the self, also with needs and entitlements. It experiences loss and is capable of grief and mourning.

The uncaring part sees issues of damage and repair very differently. For this part, "damage" means the phantasy of being ideal is punctured or deflated. "Repairing" the damage means restoring things to the idealised state they appeared to be in beforehand. This is "as if" repair, created through omnipotent thinking. When moral imperfection is noticed in the self, all effort is directed to restoring the self-image as ideally moral. This is "as if" morality, also created through omnipotent thinking.

How might this have applied in my case? As best as I can understand my own inner psychic situation, I readily blamed the oil industry and the neoliberal establishment for the climate crisis, while not sufficiently noticing my own sense of exaggerated entitlement and exceptionalism. The oil industry and the neoliberal establishment are I believe majorly responsible, but was I using their culpability *also* to maintain, "I'm not in any way to blame; it's the system"? If so, that would be omnipotent not rational thinking, also called making a "manic repair". I could wrap up my parcel of culpability and lob it at the oil industry (projection) to block *felt* awareness of guilt about damage I individually cause.

When we are caught up in omnipotent "as if" repairs like this, we are not psychically available for genuine reality-based repairs and for change.

We are caught up in a Laurel and Hardy situation of "Look what a fine mess you've created. No, it's you; no, it's you".

Christiana Figueres, UN climate chief, described a remarkable moving scene at the Paris Climate Talks in 2016 when the block of poorer small nations *who will be the ones to suffer climate effects most directly* were able to move past blaming the global north. The small nations had so much right on their side, but they were able to see the bigger picture and they were able to move past getting stuck in grievance and to mourn. Without that move on their part, Figueres believes the Paris climate accord would not have been reached. (For a discussion of this kind of dehumanising splitting see Weintrobe, 2010b.)

The Exceptions

The exception I have so far introduced is the ordinary exception in us. It is capable of being held in check by a robust caring part. I now introduce a different sort of Exception (capital E). This Exception has seized power and now rules within the psyche, imposing its own hegemony.

To explain the difference between exceptions and Exceptions, I return to the issue of entitlement and turn to John Murray who in 1964 first wrote about entitlement from a psychoanalytic perspective. Quoting Murray,

> Freud in his paper "On Narcissism: an Introduction" begins his approach to the study of the *subject* by his formulation of the two essential characteristics of *schizophrenia* which are not present in health. They are (i) megalomania and (ii) the withdrawal of *libido* from the outside world of people and things, which is then put to work in activating deeply regressive fantasies. In my opinion, his very direct statement, notable for its simplicity, lays the foundation for the understanding of the whole field of severe psychopathologic symptomatology. The fabric of the system is woven out of the warp of the regressive libidinal *fantasy* elements and the woof of the entitle-ment to the regressive world which the narcissistic attitudes provide. Without the interweaving of the two elements the cloth cannot sus-tain into solidity. (p. 478)

Here we can see the difference between what some have termed "normal" and "destructive" narcissism. With normal narcissism, the caring part has the power to contain the exception's sense of narcissistic entitlement. With destructive narcissism, the Exception rules.

In his seminal papers on disavowal, Freud (1940a, p. 139; 1940e, p. 271) traced how a refusenik thinks when she or he takes charge within the psyche. Freud emphasised that in true disavowal (not transitory but held in place in a more organised enduring way) the narcissistic self will find this, that, and the other way to never fit in with and accept the basic facts of life. Freud gave the example of the small boy who sees the girl's genital and, rather than accepting she does not have a penis (and all that might portend for him), scotomises reality and maintains his fantasy view.

I suggest that Murray, by emphasising the importance of entitlement, greatly enriched our understanding of situations where regressive wish fulfilment takes hold. Murray is saying an adamant sense of narcissistic entitlement powers what some have called destructive narcissism and others have called the psychotic part of the self. The entitlement is to the regressive world that omnipotent thinking fashions. Murray is moreover highlighting the way that when narcissistic entitlement becomes powerful enough to adamantly impose its will, psychotic processes hold sway. The issue of narcissistic entitlement is key to understanding situations where the mind has become cleaved from its reality sense.

Rulers who are Exceptions are found throughout human history. Bertrand Russell put it that "The megalomaniac differs from the narcissist ... he wishes to be powerful ... To this type belong many lunatics and most of the great men of history." My example of an Exception powered by narcissistic entitlement is Karl Abraham's account of Amenhotep IV, an Egyptian boy king who lived more than 3,000 years ago (1935, pp. 537–569). Abraham shines a particularly clear light on some of the underlying psychological processes involved with being an Exception.

It would be a misapplication of psychoanalytic method—and sheer bad manners—to claim we can analyse the individual psyche of someone who lived thousands of years ago! Yet, Amenhotep IV's story may help us understand what can happen when the uncaring part takes charge and self-idealisation fuelled by entitlement starts to soar. Abraham wrote his paper not falsely to claim to understand Amenhotep IV, but to make the point that self-idealisation is an enduring part of the human condition. Later, we will see how neoliberal ideology boosts self-idealisation, and undermines whatever holds it in check, in just the way Amenhotep did.

Amenhotep IV believed he was the Sun God Re. Many ancient rulers believed they were deities, but Amenhotep carried things further. He first announced he was son of Re, ordered all signs he had a real father to be obliterated, and arranged to be buried near his mother, commanding that her burial name show no trace of her ever having had any connection with his real father. Next, he announced that he was Re. As Re, he claimed he was the source of all radiance and light in his kingdom.

As Re, Amenhotep IV was caught up in the godlike omnipotent phantasy that he could create the whole world. The world he created was an "as if" psychic retreat of fake reality.

Whereas omnipotent thinking can rustle up an imaginary "as if" pain-free inner world to live inside in an instant, it is entitlement to that world that keeps the regressive thinking going. (Abraham was writing long before Steiner (1993) put forward his ideas on the psychic retreat from reality.) Wanting to "feel special" is common and ordinary, and always involves some self-idealisation. The degree to which we can get trapped in self-idealisation may depend not only on individual personality but on our circumstances in life: how loved we are in reality and what in our environment keeps our omnipotence in check.

When people idealise themselves and use omnipotent thinking, damage they do and others do does not feel quite real to them because they believe they can magically fix things that go wrong. They do not experience a sense of loss.

Neoliberal ideology

My current work is on Exceptionalism within neoliberal ideology. This ideology has powered the neoliberal age (1980s to the present). Neoliberal Exceptions in charge of politics tend to:

- Be self-idealising and superior—including morally superior
- Feel entitled to whatever they want in the short term
- Feel entitled to use omnipotent thinking to assuage their consciences.

Neoliberal ideology was inspired by Friedrich Hayek (Austrian school), developed by economists like Milton Friedman (Chicago school) and James Buchannan (Virginia school), and popularised by writers like Ayn Rand. It gave rise to free market economic theory. While it gradually gained influence after WW2, it was still a relative outrider on the political fringe until the 1980s when it gathered support and was voted into power in Reagan's USA and Thatcher's Britain.

Neoliberal ideology displays the hallmark traits of Exceptionalism: self-idealisation (our ideological position is superior), exaggerated entitlement (we hold dominion and rules and laws do not apply to us), a drift to "as if" omnipotent thinking and "as if" moral quick fixes (we can ignore the climate crisis as it is not real to us; let's leave the Paris Agreement).

Political Exceptionalism is as old as the human hills, as we saw with Amenhotep IV. With its long history, it took on new force from the mid-eighteenth century onwards with industrialisation and colonialism. In the neoliberal age it is threatening our very survival. Neoliberal Exceptions who came to power in the 1980s have acted "as if" the problem of climate change could be addressed just through omnipotent thinking. That way they could continue to see themselves as idealised Exceptions to rules, even the laws of physics.

The idealised self, being ideal, sees itself as all providing. Amenhotep IV thought he could, with the radiant warmth of his rays, light up the whole world. I suggest one version of this phantasy within neoliberal ideology is trickle-down economics, the idea that neoliberals' riches will trickle down. In reality, we have seen increasing trickle up in the neoliberal age, with, as the economist Ha-Joon Chang (2007) has pointed out, rules fixed so the ladder is drawn up behind those in the entitled in-crowd.

I suggest the ideologue Ayn Rand's novel *Atlas Shrugged* (1957) vividly conveys Exceptionalism in its neoliberal form. It might be argued that this novel, widely criticised for the stark crudeness of her style and use of the novel as political propaganda, is a poor example to choose to illustrate neoliberal Exceptionalism. However, admirers of Rand now rule the world. She was thought highly of by Alan Greenspan (for nineteen years chairman of the Federal Reserve Board in the USA), and politicians like Reagan and Thatcher. Trump's cabinet is filled with Randians who include: Mike Pompeo, Rex Tillerson, and Trump himself. Paul Ryan admires Rand too, distancing himself only from her stance on religion (Rand was an atheist). Also, the thinking of Ayn Rand is now on the A level politics syllabus in the UK.

The main character in *Atlas Shrugged*, a businessman, Hank Rearden, defends himself in court against the charge of flouting a government regulation. He appears enraptured with his own superiority and superior creativity, wedded to the idea that he need follow no rules set by others. He argues with passion that he should be able to do whatever he wants to do. He is exaggeratedly entitled and believes he owes nothing to others whom he sees as expectant leeches wanting to suck from him and take from him what he alone created. He is not responsible to or for others, but it is clear he thinks they will be nourished by and benefit from his radiant creativity and largesse. Here he resembles the picture painted of Amenhotep IV who thought he was self-created and that his radiance trickled down and lit everyone up.

Rearden worships his individual freedom, but this is freedom divorced from responsibility to or for others. He shocks with the revealing openness of his position, one normally kept hidden to respect moral probity. Presenting himself as radiantly superior, he hides the ugly underbelly of what is required to maintain Exceptionalism.

It might be asked why is a character like Rearden so appealing? I suggest one reason is that Rearden appeals to the ordinary exception in us all. Which of us does not recognise a wish to be free of, untrammelled by, feelings of guilt and shame; to use omnipotent thinking to rid ourselves of moral conflict and the anxieties that generates?

Neoliberals, driven by the sense of entitlement that powers their Exceptionalism, framed the current global economy along uncaring lines; short-term profit was all, the environment was ignored, no responsibility was taken for damage, and when it was seen "quick fix" omnipotent solutions were offered to make the damage disappear in "as if" ways. My focus is not on neoliberals as such but the Exceptionalism in the ideology they espouse.

Living in a neoliberal economy that takes such little care violates most people's sense of what is right and wrong many times a day, and staying with this knowledge can leave us feeling dispirited and overburdened. Who wants to face the guilt—the ongoing miserable sense of dirty implication—that goes with living in an economic system based purely on short termism and on maximising profit? Who wants to be worrying about the future of the climate system when fetching the grandchildren from school?

While it is not possible to live without causing some damage, the neoliberal globalised economy, increasingly deregulated from frameworks of care, is causing such damage that if it continues unchallenged it will make life on earth not sustainable. I suggest that to know this at a feeling level, especially knowing we are collectively implicated, is to suffer and to live with a sense of great moral injury. Moral injury is knowing that one is caught up in an overarching system in which it is made very difficult to act in ways one feels are decent. Soldiers are currently being diagnosed with moral injury as a consequence of participating in immoral wars. They too describe moments of crystallisation of conscience, when they see that they are caught up in higher order military and political structures that makes it extremely difficult not to violate their moral code (see Puniewska, 2015).

Zigmunt Bauman (2013) pointed out that the "logic of living" within the neoliberal economy conflicts with our basic moral sense. Because of the way in which this economy operates (little investment in infrastructure for renewable energy, licence to pollute, pursuit of ever-decreasing wages and higher profit), ordinary daily activities become fraught with moral dilemmas: Do I take the car or the bus? Do I buy those flown-in, fresh vegetables with a high-carbon price tag? Do I eat that chicken knowing it likely spent a miserable life in an automated intensive rearing operation (neoliberalism's word for a large farm)? Do I buy that book online from a company that employs people on zero-hour contracts? What do I do when nearly everything I see in the supermarket comes in a plastic container or is wrapped in plastic film?

Robert J. Lifton (2014) argued that recently more people have begun to shift from an "unformed" to a "formed" awareness of climate change. Formed awareness, he said, is awareness that climate change is a moral issue. I would add that formed awareness is also awareness that neoliberalism is a deeply immoral system and we are all caught up in it, more or less.

Neoliberal culture

For the new neoliberal economy to function, neoliberals would need to deregulate people's moral sense, so they would not mind so much that the way they were now required to live was immoral and harmful. Bauman had drawn attention to the fact that people *mind* living in immoral ways. It conflicts with caring values. If people did not care, neoliberals in power would not have needed (and still need) to spend trillions on a culture (advertising, mass media, general group culture, and so on) to deregulate existing cultures of care (many of them put in place after the Second World War).

Neoliberal culture would provide people with justifications, language reframing, and manipulation to help them feel less guilty living in the neoliberal economy. It would boost the ordinary exception in people while at the same time undermining their caring part that worked to hold their exception in check. Examples are respect for science and scientific method, government regulations that contain uncare, and social frameworks of care that preserve civility and pluralism. All these have been attacked in the neo-liberal age.

Neoliberal culture grew out of, and would greatly extend, consumerist culture that had begun to take hold with mechanised industrialisation in the early 1920s. Consumerism had grown out of greater understanding of how to appeal to already existing self-idealising tendencies in people. Advertising and marketing were so successful that by the 1960s US culture was being described as the "me" culture (see for example Lasch, 1991).

During the neoliberal era, advertising, mass media, and general group culture worked to achieve a shift in the moral centre of gravity. Advertising now reached ever more people, including children (before Reagan direct advertising to children was banned), and with the digital age came penetration of advertising into ever further areas of life.

Advertisers from early on were adept at stimulating omnipotent identification with idealised figures, mostly celebrities. Omnipotent identification (discussed by Abraham in his paper on Amenhotep IV), is where you falsely believe you can instantly *be* the idealised person you identify with, and also *be* as entitled as you perceive that person to be. It involves stimulating regressive phantasies and entitlement to them and it can operate as a "quick fix" for feelings of envy and exclusion.

Here is an example that involves Edward Bernays, a nephew of Freud who had settled in America. He founded public relations, transformed advertising, and went on to play an important role in public policy.

Bernays boosted omnipotent identification to boost sales. The idea was to tap into the caring reality-based part of people to undermine that part, while at the same time boosting their uncaring part. It sheds light for me on the perennial question of how deliberate and conscious is a regime's attempt to influence people through the culture it promotes. This was deliberate and fully conscious.

George Hill, president of the American Tobacco Company, came to Bernays with a problem, which was that women did not smoke and even if a few smoked secretly, women never smoked in public, which was culturally taboo at the time. How could women be persuaded to take up the habit? That would double the market. Could Bernays help?

Bernays turned to New York psychoanalyst A. A. Brill who suggested he find a way to associate cigarettes with the male penis representing male sexual power. Bernays took up this suggestion and staged an elaborate spectacle at that year's Easter Parade. He persuaded a group of young society women to sit on a float at the parade and all light up their cigarettes together in full view of the public. He had alerted the press, describing the women as suffragettes lighting the torch of freedom.

Bernays was manipulatively drawing associations between the Statue of Liberty with her torch, female freedom, and male power. By persuading young society women to lead the way, he encouraged omnipotent identification with the elite, and he took the sting out of an act of social rebellion by framing the spectacle as in concert with American values: lighting the Liberty Torch, a treasured national icon. He did all this through appealing to women's subjective sense of lively entitlement to be included and to share power, now awakened, given legitimacy and—importantly—shaped and manipulated by Bernays. He changed the culture of smoking and made a lot of money for the American tobacco industry.

His staged event was reported across the press as: "group of girls puff at cigarettes as gesture of 'freedom'." Bernays had made smoking by women socially acceptable with a single symbolic act. He created the idea that if a woman smoked she was more powerful and independent.

There may have been some truth to this idea, as women who took up smoking in public then may have been treated as more powerful and independent in reality. Nonetheless, smoking cigarettes does not make one more powerful and independent, and a belief it does is a false belief.

Bernays and his co-workers tapped into women's desire for more power and into their suffering at not being free and having little power, and he used this to manipulate women, offering them a seductive quick fix, smoking a cigarette, now with all the associations Bernays had attached to that act. With this quick fix women could enter an "as if free" world in which they could forget they had little power; forget they worked in a shop and that society women had more spending power than they did; forget envy of men and envy of the wealthy stoked by unfairness in society; forget that only struggle in the real world would all change this; forget that if they engaged in that struggle they could well face conflicts at home, at work, and within themselves.

Through smoking a cigarette, they could be lured into the "concrete" inner world of the quick fix, in which reality is sidelined (no social difference, no angst, no anger, no inner conflict, no experienced envy of the wealthy class who claimed more entitlement, no feelings of abjection). By inhaling they could inhabit an "as if" world in which they *apparently* achieved their goal of "freedom". The freedom they actually achieved was freedom from the psychic work of facing inner emotional reality and external reality.

Cigarettes are deeply addictive physically. All products used as part of a quick fix "solution" are potentially addictive as they are props in maintaining an idealised wishful view, and in that view nothing is ever enough and more is always craved. Bernays, like Cinderella's prince, was saying this glass slipper is your key to enter my fairy-tale kingdom, where your status can be instantly changed from kitchen girl to queen. Make sure that yours is the foot that fits the shoe. Then you can live the American dream.

The trouble is to maintain the illusion of being the queen in the castle bubble: real experience has constantly to be expunged from self-awareness. Real experience does not fit with the "as if" world of quick fix "thinking".

Bernays' perverse strategy was actively to encourage people to abandon thinking. Inhabiting the "as if" world of false beliefs has a deeply corrosive effect on the capacity to think. It progressively de-moralises people, in other words, it progressively encourages people to become alienated from their moral sense. It attacks people's capacity to care in any genuine way about their true social conditions and those of others.

This new form of hidden persuasion involved "setting free" the inner exception while subtly drawing the caring reality-based part into collusion, thus weakening it through corrupting it. I suggest the most dangerous form of disavowal is the kind that says this kind of persuasion and corruption will not affect *me*. When an entire culture swings to consumerism and its official language becomes consumerist, I believe it takes a certain arrogance to suppose one will not be drawn into the culture. It involves a constant struggle not to be pulled into the culture's perverse framing. Consumerism essentially involves consuming, devouring, taking over, overrunning the caring, reality-based self through a gradual process of corrupting what things truly mean.

The biggest and most perverse reversal of meaning with the smoking advert was of "freedom". America, "land of the free" was beginning a fundamental transformation of what freedom meant. The smoking advert tapped into a deep need for freedom felt by women at the time. It manipulated this need, offering a quick fix that could satisfy the need in a virtual, "as if" way rather than a real way.

American corporations quickly saw the commercial advantage of exploiting Freud's understanding of the power of fantasy and how people can be satisfied with false beliefs and daydreams. Paul Mazur, a Wall Street banker working for Lehman Brothers in the 1930s said,

> We must shift America from a need to a desires culture. People must be trained to desire, to want new things even before the old have been entirely consumed. We must shape a new mentality in America. Man's desires must overshadow his needs. A change has come over our democracy. It is called consumptionism. The American citizen's importance to his country is now no longer that of citizen but that of consumer (1927).

Mazur's point is clear: people must be trained to become insatiable.

Bernays was at the centre of changing a nation's sense of identity. He provided the corporations with psychological theory they could use to great effect. In the 1920s, banks funded department stores across America, built to cater for a rising class with money, and Bernays advised on how to create a new kind of customer who would spend, spend, spend. He created many of the manipulative techniques of mass consumer persuasion we now live with. W. Randolph Hearst employed Bernays to work on his popular women's magazines that were used to advertise the products now in department stores. This enabled Bernays to link his clients' products with celebrities (also his clients), which he also did through product placement in movies. (Hollywood stars now lit up cigarettes as well as the heavens.)

As filmmaker Adam Curtis explained in his British television documentary series, *The Century of the Self* (2002),

> The idea that smoking actually made women freer was completely irrational, but it made them feel more independent. It meant that irrelevant objects could become powerful symbols of how you wanted to be seen by others. Bernays saw that the way to sell was not to say you ought to have this car, but you will feel better if you have this car.... That was Bernays' contribution.

Curtis credits Bernays with contributing in a major way to the "start of the all-consuming self, which has come to dominate our world today". Bernays' thinking and rationale can be seen in my second, much more recent example. This is the L'Oréal advert with the tag line "Because I'm worth it". I suggest it boosts the same psychological mechanisms Bernays boosted with his Easter Parade spectacle: invite omnipotent identification with celebrities, connect to deeper less conscious desires and needs—both caring and uncaring ones—and use this to drive a false belief and a narcissistic sense of entitlement. In the case of L'Oréal, the false belief is that a small cheap tube of hair cream in a plastic container can actually relieve you of feeling not worth it; with smoking it was that a cigarette will help you gain freedom and equality with men. Again, we see the tremendous power of phantasy; how it can provide "as if" satisfactions. When phantasies start to guide behaviour they change the world.

Advertising and branding became ever more sophisticated in the neoliberal age. As the damage caused by the neoliberal economy rose, "greening" (falsely suggesting the product was ecologically sustainable) was increasingly used to quell rising moral unease at buying the product. "As if", fake-perfect, Eden-like worlds were offered to counter awareness that, as Pope Francis (2015) put it, "We are turning our world into a pile of filth." These "as if" worlds were also generated by mass media which, for instance, persistently omitted climate crisis from the news or downplayed its seriousness.

Neoliberal culture offers a collusive deal: move into a bubble-like psychic retreat from reality and you can do the shopping guilt-free. You are an exception and as such entitled to "have a nice day" and not to feel any inner pain, especially guilt and shame.

Feeling entitled to be spared the pain of guilt necessarily treats the caring reality-oriented part of the self as not entitled, not worth it. I believe *that* was part of the pain I registered standing at the bus stop. I saw myself as worth far more than the exaggeratedly entitled falsely "worth it" position I found myself espousing. The caring part measures what it means to be "worth it" and entitled to be worth it differently.

Neoliberal culture has relentlessly encouraged disavowal in the general population, the most serious form being disavowal that neoliberals, supported by the oil industry, are driving rapid the climate crisis and we are colluding. We are all implicated in disavowing the crisis. The subject tends to be dropped from conversations in the media, in our social group discussions, and in general culture, or if admitted, is "normalised" by stripping it of its urgency. (For a discussion of how this plays out in social conversations, see Weintrobe, 2016.)

I believe one of Freud's most fundamental insights and important contributions was his understanding of the power omnipotent thinking has, unless resisted, to change the world inside us and outside us. Walter

Benjamin's depiction of Paul Klee's painting of Angelus Novus vividly conveys our current historical moment. The angel of history is drawn to look fixedly at the past.

> … He sees one single catastrophe, which keeps piling wreckage upon wreckage and hurls it in front of his feet.

I have argued that the *one single catastrophe*, which keeps piling wreckage upon wreckage is the culturally driven upsurge in Exceptionalism (both capital E and small e) during the neoliberal era and the sense of narcissistic entitlement that sustains it. We will only address the climate crisis seriously when we break with neoliberalism and its Exceptionalist mindset and culture. I believe that starts with the pain of seeing that our moral self becomes deregulated when we collude with it.

References

Abraham, K. (1935). Amenhotep IV (Ikhnaton)—a psychoanalytic contribution to the understanding of his personality. *The Psychoanalytic Quarterly, 4*: 537–569.

Bauman, Z. (2013, September 23). Participant on Vetenskapens varld lot 23, stv (Swedish public broadcasting channel). http://www.svtplay.se/video/1480596/del-23

Benjamin, W. Thesis on the philosophy of history. Ninth thesis. In Dark Times blog.

Chang, H.-J. (2007). *Bad Samaritans: The Guilty Secrets of Rich Nations and the Threat to Global Prosperity.* London: Random House.

Freud, S. (1940a). *An Outline of Psycho-Analysis. S. E., 23.* London: Hogarth.

Freud, S. (1940e). Splitting of the ego in the process of defence. *S. E., 23.* London: Hogarth.

Lifton, R. J. (2014, August 24). The climate swerve. *The New York Times.* http://www.nytimes.com/2014/08/24/opinion/sunday/the-climate-swerve.html?_r=2

Murray, J. M. (1964). Narcissism and the ego ideal. *Journal of the American Psychoanalytic Association, 12*(3): 477–511.

Pope Francis (2015, May 24). On care for our common home. [Encyclical letter.] http://w2.vatican.va/content/francesco/en/encyclicals/documents/papa-francesco_20150524_enciclica-laudato-si.html

Puniewska, M. (2015). Healing a wounded sense of morality. *The Atlantic,* July 3. http://www.theatlantic.com/author/maggie-puniewska

Rand, A. (1957). *Atlas Shrugged.* London: Plume Books. Republished London: Penguin, 2007.

Steiner, J. (1993). *Psychic Retreats.* London: Routledge.

Weintrobe, S. (2010a). On runaway greed and climate change denial: a psychoanalytic perspective. Lionel Monteith Memorial Lecture, Lincoln Clinic and Centre for Psychotherapy, London. Published in the annual *Bulletin of the British Psychoanalytical Society* and on www.sallyweintrobe.com

Weintrobe, S. (2010b). A dehumanising form of prejudice as part of a narcissistic pathological organisation. In: E. McGinley & A. Varchevker (Eds.), *Enduring Loss: Mourning, Depression, and Narcissism through the Life Cycle.* London: Karnac.

Weintrobe, S. (2016). [Podcast.] https://www.mixcloud.com/Resonance/frontier-psychoanalyst-ep-3-18-january-2016/

Managing difficult children: psychoanalysis, welfare policy, and the "social sector"

Steven Groarke

The relationship between psychoanalysis and society is best understood in terms of the political rationalities, or modes of governmental thought, operative within a given historical conjuncture. States generate specific types of political rationality and, historically speaking, the important question concerns how and why psychoanalysis became operational in a certain political culture. The question concerns the practice of psychoanalysis and its relation to the emergence of the "social sector" in the late eighteenth and early nineteenth centuries (Donzelot, 1984). My critical starting point is that psychoanalysis has proved useful in providing practical support for this new and intricate "sector". As such, it operates most effectively where the public and the private spheres are diffused among one another; where new welfare policy mechanisms are brought to bear on what we might call the contemporary society of security; and where the problem of government is increasingly formulated in terms of individualising power—including the more precise technical formula of "object relationships".

Psychoanalysis is not confined to the treatment of individuals. It also forms an important part of what Foucault (2007) deemed the modern "art" of government. Foucault's work from the late 1970s, including his lectures at the Collège de France and the Tanner Lectures, provides a critical framework for our discussion of psychoanalysis as a "pastoral" mode of government. Briefly, in the Tanner Lectures, Foucault (1979) provides

241

a useful sketch of "pastorship" as a formation of individualising power. The main proposal in the first of the two lectures is that the pastoral theme (the leader as a shepherd) was raised in classical antiquity—most notably, in Plato's *The Statesman*—only to be called into question as a viable schema of governance. The second lecture takes up the development of the pastoral theme in Christian thought, particularly with respect to self-examination and the guidance of conscience. I don't intend to rehearse the argument in detail here: the important point for our purposes is that within the pastoral context, the welfare relation of modern governance emerges as an irreducible combination of individualising and state power. Foucault (1979, p. 322) formulates the aim of the "pastoral government of the living" in these terms: "to develop those elements constitutive of individuals' lives in such a way that their development also fosters the strength of the state."

This formulation provides a critical perspective for my discussion of psychoanalysis as a type of therapy, but also as a relationship of social welfare. My argument is that psychoanalysis itself forms part of an ongoing struggle concerning the more comprehensive political task of social and personal security. The idea of an *agon* at the heart of the psychoanalytic relationship, starting with the contested meaning of the Freudian interpretation, raises a number of questions: Does psychoanalysis circulate throughout the "social sector" as a transformative, ameliorative, or coercive resource? Does it function to intensify the effectiveness of power? And, does it increase or lower the resistance to social regulation? I intend to demonstrate the inseparability of power and resistance in psychoanalysis, understood as an active form of life conduct as well as a type of therapy.

In approaching psychoanalysis from the standpoint of political technology and social defence mechanisms (Menzies Lyth, 1960), I shall focus on Donald Winnicott's treatment of the "deprived child" in post-war Britain. My main objective is to draw out the extent to which psychoanalysis has become part of the fabric of everyday life, part of "the government of the living", with decidedly mixed results. The Second World War was, of course, decisive for the formation of the welfare state—including historic developments in the welfare of children under the Attlee government of 1945–51. The social democratic framework that was put in place after the war, that is, through a comprehensive set of legislation covering family allowance and national health, national insurance, and national assistance, also made provision for public child care and social work with children. Winnicott's psychoanalytic approach to "deprivation" and "delinquency" emerged in this context.

The single most important factor here was the evacuation of children during the war. Starting with the Government Evacuation Scheme and the social legislation of the immediate post-war period, I shall consider the relationship between psychoanalysis and the social sector on three further counts: the psychoanalytic casework tradition in Britain; the governmental practice of therapeutic management; and the theory of defiance.

Child care legislation after 1945

The profound effect that the evacuation experience seems to have had on Winnicott was evidently shared by the population at large. Almost eighty years later, it remains a particularly traumatic experience in the country's collective memory. The evacuation occurred in two stages: under the fear of imminent air attack in September 1939, when some 750,000 schoolchildren and 542,000 mothers with young children left their homes in the cities; and then again in 1940 when the bombing campaigns became more relentless (Holman, 1995; Isaacs, 1941). The increased visibility of large numbers of working-class families under these circumstances revealed a hidden population of undernourished and maladjusted children—the so-called "skinnies" and "unbilletable" children. The detection of these social and psychological problems was instrumental in the creation of local authority children's departments in 1948. Meanwhile, during the war, local authorities established some 700 children's homes and hostels for children who couldn't settle in ordinary homes and therefore needed special provision.

The category of "special needs" operated implicitly in the management of children for whom Winnicott became responsible when he took on the job of consultant psychiatrist to the Government Evacuation Scheme in Oxfordshire (C. Winnicott, 1980). The appointment laid the foundations for a psychoanalytic theory of care and management that went far beyond psychoanalysis, not only in the wartime hostels, but also in the treatment of the "antisocial tendency" in the aftermath of the war. Clare Winnicott (née Britton), reflecting on the experience of working with her future husband in Oxfordshire during the war, emphasised that "If crises could be met, and *lived through* rather than *reacted to*, there could be easing of tension and renewed trust and hope" (1984, p. 3; italics in original). It is the idea of "hope" that I wish to single out for discussion in this chapter. Winnicott understood difficult children in terms of a particular discourse of hope. As such, he gave full voice to the tension inherent in the institution of psychoanalysis as a mechanism of defence and social regulation, but also as a "potential space" of human freedom, creativity, and contingency.

As I have already suggested, Winnicott found himself engaged with the welfare of children in a particular institutional and historical context, extending from the Second World War and the Government Evacuation Scheme through the 1950s and the period of post-war reconstruction. The "difficult task" of war and the "permanent task" of peace appear inextricably linked in Winnicott's preoccupation with the "antisocial" elements in society. The imperative to restore order and repair social ties in the aftermath of the war, especially in the case of working-class family life, set the agenda for the type of management that he advanced in the case of "deprived" children.

Following the wartime coalition, a Labour government was elected in July 1945 with a clear mandate to implement the recommendations of the Beveridge Report (1942) and to adhere to the democratic principle of social provision. The idea that basic needs were to be met, largely through public provision, extended to social work and other services for children under the jurisdiction of "a single, well-qualified and sympathetic administration" (Holman, 1996, p. 7). The wartime coalition government had set up an interdepartmental committee of inquiry in March 1945 under the chairmanship of Myra Curtis to look at the care of children separated from their parents with the aim of restructuring children's services. The findings and recommendations of the committee were part of a historical reformation of the "social sector" in post-war Britain, which involved a definitive break with the legacy of the Poor Law in the care of children (cf. Heywood, 1978, ch. 5). Consequently, the state became more, not less, involved in the lives of working-class children and their families.

Winnicott, John Bowlby, Susan Isaacs, and Clare Britton were all called upon to give oral evidence to the Curtis Committee. This proved to be a mutual exchange as the committee's terms of reference subsequently provided an important framework for Winnicott's ideas on deprivation and environmental deficiency. The problem of deprivation was highlighted explicitly in the duties of the committee to "enquire into existing methods of providing for children who from loss of parents, or from any cause whatsoever, are deprived of a normal home life with their own parents or relatives" (warrant of appointment of the Curtis Committee, 1946). The committee was charged to consider how best to "compensate" children in a deprived situation. The provision of a "substitute" home background, with sufficiently qualified and trained staff, thus became a matter of central governmental concern. As we shall see, the combined preoccupation with deprivation and compensation (a substitute home), focusing on the provision of social care for children deprived of family life, framed Winnicott's contribution to the governmental strategy of therapeutic management. An early description of "transitional objects", for example, is set out in a lecture that Winnicott gave to the Nursery School Association in 1950, where he linked the assessment of deprivation to ways in which the deprived child "can be compensated for loss of family life".

The committee's report (the Curtis Report) was delivered in September 1946 and emphasised the deleterious effects of insufficient "individual love and care". This was apparently reflected in the behaviour of younger children in care towards visitors, "which took the form of an almost pathological clamouring for attention and petting"; whereas "in the older children, the effect appeared more in slowness, backwardness and lack of response and in habits of destructiveness and want of concentration" (Curtis Report, para. 418). Consequently, the lives of disadvantaged and neglected children became a matter of governmental concern on various counts, not least of all at the point where "habits of destructiveness" presented society with a problem.

The committee did not suggest which governmental department should be responsible for deprived children, only that the administration should comprise a comprehensive and unified service, and while unified central administrative control wasn't a new idea in itself (cf. the Maclean Report, 1918), the recommendation that child care should be based in local authorities as a responsibility of the state, with specially constituted children's committees and qualified children's officers, was nonetheless part of a newly defined horizon of post-war social security and regulated state care. Accordingly, the Curtis Committee's recommendations were taken up and embodied in the Children Act 1948 (which applied to England and Wales and, with some adaptations, to Scotland) in conjunction with the wide-ranging social security legislation of the immediate post-war period.

In addition to the comprehensive administration of child care and the attempt to coordinate under a single responsibility the care of all homeless children, the Act may be seen as particularly noteworthy in terms of Winnicott's approach to the deprived child and the failure of the environment. I shall single out three points here. First, the duty to receive deprived children into care as a voluntary arrangement with the child's guardian was co-ordinated with the duty of undertaking compulsorily the care of a child committed for care or protection by the juvenile courts. The duty of care, therefore, covered youth offenders and child neglect, which was now seen as a major cause of youth offending, under a co-ordinated strategy of state prevention. Second, the legislation was based on the needs of the child, understood to be a citizen with rights, together with the child's need for a relationship of affection. The minister of health, Aneurin Bevan, referred to the latter as the want of "warmth and humanity", which was seen as part of the conditions for maturation and the fulfilment of the child's potential. Heywood (1978, p. 158) echoes Bevan in suggesting that the way in which the Act defined the general duty of the local authority towards the child in care was, perhaps, "unmatched for its humanity in all our legislation". The reference to "humanity" is indicative of the universalist ideology of post-war social welfare. The duty under the Poor Law to the deprived child was geared towards setting the child to work or apprenticing those children whose parents were unable to care for them. By contrast, the post-war legislation stipulated that "[W]here a child is in the care of a local authority, it shall be the duty of that authority to exercise their powers with respect to him so as to further his best interests and to afford him opportunity for the proper development of his character and ability" (Children Act 1948, Section 12:1). Third, the Act augmented the role of the family under increased state supervision, incorporating the family as an agent of socialisation rather than an external object of concern. The strategic aim was no longer confined to removing children from their environment, or "regarding the reception into care as a final break, after which a permanent substitute home must be found" (Heywood, 1978, p. 157). To the contrary, the Act placed on the local authorities a duty to restore children received into care to their natural family: "[T]he local authority shall, in all cases where it appears to them consistent with the welfare of the child to do so, endeavour to secure that the care of the child is taken over either (a) by a parent or guardian, or (b) by a relative or friend of his" (Children Act 1948, 1:3).

The psychoanalytic casework tradition

The new social security legislation established the necessary institutional conditions for psychoanalysis to participate in the life of society. In particular, object relations theory provided an essential frame of reference aimed at the resocialisation of attitudes, habits, and forms of conduct. The making and breaking of "affectional bonds" (Bowlby, 1979) thus marked the contours of a new post-war "social contract" along therapeutic lines. In the case of the deprived child, Winnicott engaged the legislation (under the general heading of therapeutic management) along the related axes of prevention, facilitation, and supervision. In more detail, (i) prevention was deployed as an extrajudicial form of jurisdiction in the case of young offenders as well as neglected children; (ii) facilitation was concerned with the child's basic needs; and, most importantly, (iii) supervision defined a new field of operation in social life, where the "deprived child" was linked to the "problem family" as composite targets of administration. Social work thus extended its reach beyond the judicial apparatus on all three counts, where "difficult children" and "problem families" exposed the administrative inadequacies of the penal system and the judiciary tradition as a whole.

Winnicott's ideas on deprivation/deficiency became operational, primarily through a familial strategy of social government, where the family itself was rendered amendable to social norms by the efforts of psychoanalysis. On the one hand, Winnicott maintained that the family provides "the bridge leading out of parental care (or maternal care) right across into the social provision" (1960, p. 93). On the other hand, he extended the resourcefulness of family life in terms of the so-called "maturational processes", particularly with respect to the mother–infant relationship. The family was privileged on both counts as the model for socialisation, but also as the main source of dissatisfaction and psychosocial pathology, a place where hopes and ambitions are inscribed, "a virtual horizon of successes" as well as "a real origin of failures" (Donzelot, 1980, p. 231) and despair. The risk of personal failure and despair was coupled with the idea of environmental deficiency through a concerted familial strategy, where psychoanalysis provides efficacy, not only by meeting "the standard of familial ambitions", but also by propagating "social norms" (Donzelot, 1980, p. 200).

The psychodynamic model of casework played a key role in this context (Britton, 1950). The duty placed on local authorities to restore children received into care to their natural family emphasised the casework aspect of the new service for the deprived child. Relationships within the family thus came to the fore through the use of casework techniques in local authority children's departments. Clare Winnicott (1955) summarised these techniques in an important paper that was first presented at the United Nations European Seminar for the Advanced Study of Social Casework in 1954. In the paper, she proposed that the "professional relationship" the worker forms with the child, the parents, and the foster parents is "in itself the basic technique" (p. 149). As such, the "object relationship" encompasses the provision of an environmental setting. It provides a means of holding the child, the family, and the fostering situation, as well as integrating internal and external reality by putting into words what the client has in mind.

In a contested field of professional practice comprising collective action, group work, and community work, the psychodynamic model of casework became the authoritative approach to social work in the 1950s (Morris, 1950). This reflected the prestigious position in which psychoanalysis was placed after the war, and those in favour of the approach emphasised the personal response to need (the experience of a relationship) which it was believed casework uniquely provided: "The basis of all casework is the natural human response of one individual to another in some need" (McDougall & Cormack, 1950, p. 16). In practice, this meant meeting the needs that working-class families couldn't manage without assistance and supervision.

The important point is that casework allowed for the articulation of "needs" and "difficulties". It was no longer a case of removing the child from his home environment but of treating environmental deficiency itself as part of "the general situation in the home" (Stephens, 1945, p. 19). Poverty, dirty conditions, overcrowding, undernourishment, and indiscipline were identified as so many "symptoms of disintegration" (Stephens, 1945, p. 19), the response to which involved a comprehensive method of assessment, diagnosis, and treatment. Legislation was in place to support such an approach. Thus, the law was ready to hand but had to be co-ordinated with a more individualising form of governmental provision. The new duty to restore the child to his family emphasised the casework aspect of the Child Care Service and the development of casework techniques "made it possible to consider working with the problem parents with a view to eventual restoration of the child to the family" (Heywood, 1978, p. 157). The individual was the anchorage point here for a more comprehensive undertaking of "attention and study" (McDougall & Cormack, 1950, p. 28). The child, in other words, provided a point of entry for a more wide-ranging strategy of adjustment and adaptation.

The Younghusband Report (1959, p. 179) consolidated the idea of personal, family, and social adjustment as part of the social worker's task in assessing and managing "the disturbance of equilibrium". As such, the model of adjustment allowed for the supervision of families across a whole range of social pathology, including learning disability, poor parenting skills, mental health problems, domestic violence, and alcohol and drug dependency. Against the background of the welfare state and the principle of universal provision, the social worker was employed "to examine the unsatisfied personality needs and the processes which lay behind the problem, and to guide and enable the individual to solve his problem in his own way" (Heywood, 1978, p. 157). Clare Winnicott (1955, p. 149) made the essential link here between casework techniques and "the construc- tive integrating forces in society", pointing out that "the child care worker derives her power ... [from] the love and sense of parental responsibility that exists in society towards children".

How did things work on the ground? How does one go about mobilising society as a type of affectional bond? Together with the accumulated medical, psychiatric, and pedagogic dossiers and the application of various personal- ity assessments, social casework relied on the technique of "life history" as a detailed compilation of the client's childhood and early life. Accordingly, the intrapsychic past came into public view as a register of intimate faults, insecure attachments, patterns of disturbed behaviour, unmet needs, and deviations from the normal paths of conduct and upbringing. As an integral part of the "casework relationship" that social workers formed with their clients (Biestek, 1961; C. Winnicott, 1955), the life history technique repre- sented a composite form of psychodynamic expertise (gained through the newly established training courses for child care residential and field staff) and confessional accounts of family life. What was new here, and particu- larly effective, was the formation of "a process of circularity between the two practices of expertise and confession" (Donzelot, 1980, p. 210). Based on the personal information that caseworkers gained from their clients, the deprived situation emerged as a new object of knowledge. The latter was unified as a governmental figure by the interpretative framework of psycho- analysis, the theories and techniques of which applied simultaneously to the deprived child, failing or deficient parents (problem families), and potential foster parents.

The governmental practice of therapeutic management

Winnicott engaged with developments in the government of deprived children from the standpoint of unconscious hope, inventing a new and dis- tinct field of operation in the tutelary management of the asocial elements in society. Essentially, he proposed that "antisocial symptoms are gropings for environmental recovery and indicate hope. They fail not because they are wrongly directed, but because the child is unconscious of what is going on" (1950, p. 17). Once again, the "environment" mediates the terms of this proposition, insofar as the "antisocial tendency is characterised by an *element in it which compels the environment to be important*" (1956, p. 123; italics in original). The idea that the child "through unconscious drives, compels someone to attend to management" (1956, p. 123) suggests an entirely new way of thinking about social welfare relations. It augments the form and function of liberal government as "the government of the living" (Foucault, 2014). Thus, in conditions of health, the "average expectable environment" accommodates the infant's instinctual reach for life, the object-seeking life drive, whereas on the other hand, things are liable to breakdown in the case of "environmental deficiency" (Winnicott, 1965). Breakdown, however, does not imply unremitting despair or the negation of hope. For Winnicott, while hopelessness remains "the basic feature of the deprived child" (1956, p. 123), the child is nonetheless capable of expressing a deeper sense of hopefulness, that is, through his violent and antisocial behaviour.

The strategic question pivots on the meaning of asocial freedom where, in the case of antisocial or difficult children, there is a shift in governmental focus from "dangerousness" to the welfare "risks" associated with deficiency/deprivation (Castel, 1991). The threat from antisocial elements remains a matter of real concern, but it isn't managed directly by the law or the judiciary tradition of social order. The corruptibility of the environment was more important for Winnicott than the illegality of antisocial acts. At the same time, the emphasis on hope as a primordial phenomenon, something that belongs to the earliest relationship between mother and infant, carried the imperative of social care beyond judicial logic and the attribution of penalties. The matter of treatment couldn't be decided in terms of guilt and innocence. Rather, the primacy of deficiency over culpability allowed for a particular form of management, predicated on the inviolability of individual needs, where the child was seen as inextricably linked to the environment *rather than* his actions.

Winnicott allowed that repressive measures may satisfy the short-term needs of society in policing antisocial elements, as well as providing a degree of satisfaction to society's wish for vengeance. Nevertheless, he consistently maintained that the law could not be relied upon to stand up to the moment of hope. The danger of an anti-society assumed a more pervasive form than criminality. On the other hand, Winnicott (1963, p. 104) was equally convinced that "moral educators" stand on "the wrong side" of a fundamental fault line that divides the deprived child and the object of hope. Moralists of whatever persuasion, including those who aim to teach morals through psychoanalysis, are necessarily at odds with what the difficult child knows in his bones, namely, "that it is *hope* that is locked up in the wicked behaviour, and that *despair* is linked with compliance" (1963, p. 104; italics in original). As the play of hope and despair indicates, the strategy of therapeutic management was directed towards what the child knows on the inside— what Bollas (1987) describes as a type of "unthought" primitive knowledge.

Antisocial symptoms, understood in terms of the inherent unconscious conflict between hope and despair, confirm the extent to which it isn't enough simply to be good according to the law. Law-abiding behaviour is not and cannot be the measure of the matter. On the contrary, violence enters the discourse of political life (in the form of antisocial behaviour) as a vital expression in its own right, rather than a punishable offence or a moral fault. There was certainly no question in Winnicott's mind that difficult children are out of control. He wasn't sentimental about asocial freedom, nor do I wish to play down the harm that one may cause to oneself and others by antisocial acts of violence. The disruptive and damaging nature of antisocial behaviour is real enough. Nevertheless, Winnicott (always the paediatrician) insisted that the child's violent behaviour neither merits nor deserves blame. More than a fatuous plea for leniency, Winnicott advanced a therapeutic argument based on the combination of violence and hope, in which the recourse to punishment was seen as no more effective than the imposition of penance or associated rituals of degradation.

The articulation of violence and hope comprises a significant, albeit contested focus of late modern political culture. Some thirty or forty years before it became a slogan for New Labour, the logic of "social inclusion" was implicit in the strategy of therapeutic management, while the contemporary society of security continues to rely on the policy of "inclusion" as a centrepiece of the welfare relation. Winnicott advanced the strategy on two counts. First, he argued that unlike psychotic patients, the deprived child is sufficiently mature to perceive that "*the cause of the disaster lies in an environmental failure*" (1956, p. 129; italics in original). The theme of failure enters the discourse of government and is rendered amenable to the calculations of the state (i) where the child has received enough to register what is no longer available and (ii) where he reacts to failure in violent and disruptive ways. The violent reaction to failure is possible only so long as despair doesn't get the better of the child. It was, of course, the failing parents as much as deprived children who were the targets for this strategy. The problem of "environmental deficiency" required a governmental response applicable not only to the child population at large but, more importantly, to the family and family life. Winnicott formulated the task under the heading of family welfare: "When we are able to help parents to help their children, we do in fact help them about themselves" (1956, p. 122). Second, further to the theme of failure and its environmental aetiology, Winnicott conceived of therapeutic management as a type of "social provision", rather than psychotherapy: "what these children need is *environmental stability, personal* management, and *continuity* of management" (1948, p. 74; italics in original). In order not to "waste" (1963, pp. 103–105) the potential expressed in the child's disruptive and violent behaviour, it was important to avoid mismanaging the situation by impractical means: "the management of the deprived child is not the provision of psychotherapy … personal psychotherapy is not practical politics" (1950, p. 179). The admission goes to the heart of a long-standing political debate about the limits of psycho-analysis and psychotherapy in the treatment of working-class and socially deprived populations. Management thus operates as a type of political pastoral technique in excess of the analytic situation.

While Winnicott didn't make a case for psychoanalysis as a form of treat-ment, the assessment in favour of management was nonetheless grounded in the authority of psychoanalysis. Starting from the basic psychoanalytic assumption that "*[T]he antisocial tendency implies hope*", Winnicott argued that the treatment in this case was "not psychoanalysis but management, a going to meet and match the moment of hope" (1956, pp. 123–124; italics in original). Again, the environment determines the personal and political stakes in this liberal model of social care, where the problem of "deficiency" is seen as external to the individual and where management is described as a type of "cure by environmental provision" (1956, p. 129).

There were three main reasons why Winnicott thought therapeutic man-agement was the most appropriate way to compensate the deprived child for the loss of family life: first, management provides "the only setting that can deal with [deprived children] adequately as individuals" (1970, p. 223); second, the deprived child brings with him a degraded sense of hope that mitigates against psychotherapy; and third, the total provision of the setting is more likely than other forms of treatment to withstand the destructive ele-ment of hope manifest in the deprived situation. Winnicott recommended the provision of residential management, essentially on the grounds that it provided a reliable basis for meeting the child's need "to experience despair in a relationship" (1956, p. 130). The recommendation went beyond strictly coercive measures, while at the same time advancing the treatment of despair (understood as the negative index of hope) in an institutional setting. The hostel was therefore seen as a place where the child could expect to find "a building, food, clothing, human love and understanding; a timetable, schooling; apparatus and ideas leading to rich play and constructive work" (Winnicott & Britton, 1947, p. 70). Most importantly, if the child's destructive attacks were treated physically and emotionally as unconscious expressions of hopefulness, he may then be in a position to find a place in "the life of the group as an ordinary member" (Winnicott & Britton, 1947, p. 71).

War was the testing ground but not the terminus for this new invention of managed welfare relations. The defining governmental problem continued to revolve around the conduct of personal life and life in society. Residential care wasn't seen simply as a temporary measure for children who were evacuated from their homes during the war. While the strategy was clearly informed by Winnicott's experience of the evacuation hostels, he was nonetheless keen "to relate such problems as were specifically related to the war situation to the corresponding problems of peacetime experience" (Winnicott & Britton, 1947, p. 54). The "peacetime problem of management of the early antisocial case" (Winnicott, 1948, p. 77) was singled out in the aftermath of war. As a general governmental approach to the problem of environmental deficiency, Winnicott (1948, p. 74) recommended therapeutic management for the treatment of two further categories of post-war deprivation: first, "children whose homes do not exist or whose parents cannot form a stable background in which a child can develop"; and second, "children with an existing home which, nevertheless, contains a mentally ill parent". A generation of children whose family life was disrupted by war provided a new body of knowledge with corresponding strategies and techniques that was reckoned to have more than a local and temporary relevance (Lewis, 1954, p. xii).

Development of the theory of defiance

I have stressed the importance of "relationships" in the therapeutic management of difficult children. We can, I think, take this emphasis further and in a more general direction. Psychoanalysis operates in and through the social sector as a *relationship* of power, a strategic game in which the opposing forces of freedom and resistance are always in play. Foucault (1982, p. 211) famously conceived of this game as an *agon* ("the antagonism of strategies") in human social relations, drawing out the Nietzschean as well as the classical connotations of mutual combat, strategic manoeuvres, and permanent provocation. Most notably, in his two-part essay "The Subject and Power", Foucault (1982a, pp. 221–222) points out that "[P]ower is exercised only over free [individual or collective] subjects, and only insofar as they are free … The relationship between power and freedom's refusal to submit cannot therefore be separated … At the very heart of the power relationship, and constantly provoking it, are the recalcitrance of the will and the intransigence of freedom." The matter is decided only by struggle. Again, Foucault (1982b, p. 355) insists that "[I]t can never be inherent in the structure of things to guarantee the exercise of freedom. The guarantee of freedom is freedom."

We can see how the strategy of therapeutic management operates along these lines, where freedom is first and foremost a practice subject to reversals and counteractions. On the one hand, psychoanalysis is employed as part of a wider historical development aimed at mending social bonds and defending society in the post-war period. The danger of an anti-society, under peacetime conditions, is kept in view by the managerial model of social and personal relations. On the other hand, the strategy reveals itself as an endless and open-ended game, part of the practice of freedom played out at the level of anti-society and social order. I propose that the theory of defiance, as Winnicott defined it, is central to this strategic game; that the theory conveys the degree of contestation over the governmental relation; and that defiance demonstrates the extent to which there is no power without a potential refusal or counter-practice.

Winnicott himself does not use the term "defiance", but we can reconstruct the theory of defiance in his work by focusing on his innovative account of violence and hope. The idea of antisocial symptoms as signs of hope was a basic discovery of the "second phase" of Winnicott's work from 1945 to 1959 (Abram, 2008). However, it was not until his late paper on object use that he formulated a sufficiently coherent account of the spontaneous violence of life, with respect to the infant's early destructive urge towards his mother. The radical import of the notions of primordial hope (the act of *hoping itself*) and destructive aliveness consists in their complementarity as the basis of a general theory of defiance. I am proposing, therefore, that we bring together two sets of ideas that emerged at different stages in Winnicott's thinking: the principle of hope (1945–1959) in conjunction with a destructive first principle (1960–1971).

The moment of hope follows a breakdown in the external world; more precisely, a breakdown in the developing tie between mother and infant. Winnicott describes how the child actually experiences "a break in the continuity of the environmental provision" (1963, p. 104). But while the child is left to defend himself against feelings of despair, there are nonetheless signs of hope in terms of an unconscious awareness that something is missing. The child is not seen as entirely deprived of the wherewithal for living. To the contrary, for the child who *experiences* discontinuity, the object world is already available and in place; being has been realised as dwelling; and the child has a sense of being who he is inside his own body. The child is not subject to a feeling of complete emptiness. And yet, while an awareness that something is missing persists, this denotes a world-impoverished state, a situation in which the primordial sense of prenatal possession has been impinged against. Things get stuck for the child between the underlying conviction that "something is available" and the unconscious assumption that "something is missing". An adult patient of mine, who repeatedly found herself in this situation, described being "let in" by her previous therapist, but not from the "inside". She described her first meeting with the therapist which actually took place in the street outside the therapist's consulting room. The patient had arrived early for her initial consultation and met the therapist coming along the street. There are, of course, any number of ways in which one might experience an event like this; for my patient, however, the encounter presented her with a familiar and dreadful internal set-up. Her sense of emotional dimensionality was sufficiently developed to register her intimate proximity to the object, and yet she believed that her right of access had not been recognised. She experienced the awful feeling of being ushered in "from the outside" and, indeed, the belief that she wasn't really and truly in the room occupied a good deal of this patient's analytic treatment with me.

How is the deprived child supposed to find a way out of this situation? Winnicott gave due weight to the child's unconscious assumption of hope: "[A] manifestation of the anti-social tendency in a child means that there has developed in the child some hopefulness, hope that a way may be found across a gap" (1963, pp. 103–104). Hope is what survives destruction in the case of deprived children, but also in the normal, healthy process of primitive development. Winnicott didn't arrive at a fully elaborated account of this process until he set out his views on destructiveness in his paper,

"The Use of an Object and Relating through Identifications" (1971). The final version of the paper, following a rather disappointing presentation to the New York Psychoanalytic Institute in 1968 (Rodman, 2003, pp. 328–329), was published posthumously in *Playing and Reality* (1971) and provides the essential link for the theory of defiance.

The elaboration of what Winnicott (1971, p. 90) calls "an intermediate position" is the central original contribution of the paper. Here, Winnicott posits an early developmental process in the movement from "object relating" (primitive relatedness) to "object usage" (object relationship proper), a process in which the infant destroys his mother. The important point is that the infant can make use of the mother only if she survives destruction by the infant, or actually stands up to his violent attacks on her *as a mother*. Winnicott (1971, p. 90) summarised his argument as follows: the intermediate position "can be arrived at by the individual in early stages of emotional growth only through the actual survival of cathected objects that are at the time in process of becoming destroyed because real, becoming real because destroyed".

Winnicott was intent in this paper on elaborating the intermediate phase, that between primitive relating and object relation in use, in which the primitive emotional process of destruction–survival is at work. This casts the idea of hope in a new light. Hopefulness is discernible in its uses, where usefulness depends on the destruction–survival of the object. However, further to Winnicott's main intentions in this paper, I believe we can bring his ideas about hope and violence together more fully by introducing a primordial sense of hopefulness as part of the developmental process. By introducing the effect of innate hopefulness prior to object relating, I mean to emphasise the use one *hopes to make* of the object as the psychosomatic groundwork of survival. I take it that what we see in the moment of hope—manifest in the act of asocial freedom—is an unconscious recapitulation of the primordial activity of representation (Aulagnier, 2001). The defiant behaviour of difficult children indicates the extent to which the subject can use the object that has survived destruction only where a findable object has been given on the pre-primitive grounds of hope.

By linking the idea of antisocial symptoms, understood as signs of hope, to the theory of destructibility–survivability, we can see that hope precedes destructiveness or, at least, that destruction is oriented primarily towards the *findable* object. Hate, on the other hand, comes later and always involves an intentionality in relation to the object that *has been found*. That we cannot hate what we *hope to find* attests to the fact that life renews itself as life. Winnicott himself made this link in terms of the child's vital instinct to go on looking, albeit in violent and destructive ways, for what he hopes to find: "[L]ooking for something, somewhere, and failing to find it [the child] seeks it elsewhere, when hopeful" (1956, p. 125). The object itself is less important than the hope that goes into looking for it. The child who steals, for example, "is not looking for *the object stolen but seeks the mother over whom he or she has rights*" (1956, p. 125; italics in original). In this case, the child's vital expression of hope has to be met on two levels: first, by allowing for his primordial claim on the maternal body, and second, by acknowledging the reality of the theft.

The child's needs are met on both levels in the phrase, "*This is (not) yours.*" This allows for the possible "change to the reality principle" (Winnicott, 1971, p. 89), but yet without immediate recourse to the negative law of the father (*nom-du-père*), who metaphorically says "no" to the child's desires: "*This is not yours.*" Stealing may be all that the child is able to come up with for the moment. The important point is that, viewed in the context of early deprivation and the intrapsychic degradation of hope, the act of stealing itself cathects internal and external reality. The deprived child who steals is attempting to stay in touch with the object world. Indeed, it is the reality of the world that matters rather than the object as such. Sustaining hope in the findable object, or in the belief that objects may yet be found, is more important to the child than anything he contrives to snatch from the world.

Clare Winnicott gives an example of stealing that allows us to link this argument to social casework with children. A nine-year-old who was settled in a good foster home started stealing money to buy sweets to give to his foster mother. The caseworker's response to the child was aimed at meeting his needs on each of the two levels noted above. On the one hand, she responded by saying, "You want to show [your foster mother] that you love her and you want her to love you." On the other hand, "[T]he worker went on to say that [the foster mother] liked to know the child loved her, but she didn't like the stealing, and nobody liked stealing" (1955, pp. 158–159). The social worker responds to an internal set-up in which adjustments can be made in terms of the reality principle, while at the same time keeping the child's basic needs in mind—including the need for freedom gained through defiance. The case itself demonstrates the extent to which the reach for meaning, understood as a destructive first principle, is directed towards a world that the child hopes will actually stand up in reality: "[T]he child is seeking that amount of environmental stability which will stand the strain resulting from impulsive behaviour" (Winnicott, 1956, p. 125). The social worker thus thanks the child for something that he is not yet in a position to give her and she acknowledges both the gift and its future potential. Something vital is at stake in the child's violent attempt to re-find his capacity to find things, the meaning of which is not predicated on a prohibiting father whose threat represents the law. The oedipal model does not cover the more primitive reach for life manifest in defiant hope. In fact, the use that the child hopes to make of the object "provokes total environmental reactions, as if seeking an ever-widening frame, a circle which has as its first example the mother's arms or the mother's body' (1956, p. 125). Violence aims to test the reality of hope itself and, rooted in the "first example", hope remains available for use insofar as reality is presented to the child in conjunction with his basic needs for spontaneity and freedom. A child who feels his needs aren't being met cannot make useful or meaningful contact with reality. This is evident in the transformation of defiant hope into criminality proper, or conversely in the transformation of defiance into compliance.

Children who wait

The basic concepts of post-war legislation provided a pragmatic framework for the application of psychoanalytic theories and techniques to the welfare of children. Strategies authorised by psychoanalysis were deployed throughout the 1950s as part of a governmental manoeuvre designed to augment social care as an extrajudicial jurisdiction. Winnicott operated within this discursive and institutional context; drawing on his wartime experience, he advanced therapeutic management as a long-term strategy for the treatment of deprived and disruptive children. At the same time, he formulated an innovative theory of unconscious hope based on the idea that a valid future is discernible in the defiant gesture of the deprived child. I have argued throughout the chapter that the "social sector" represents a particular type of governmental thinking under the heading of "welfarism"; the theory of defiance, however, is not confined to a single ideological and political position within the broadly defined domain of post-war political culture. This, at least, is my argument: the theory of defiance presupposes an open-endedness that remains opposed to any practical closure in politics.

Let me explain why I think this is the case. I suggested, some years ago, "[O]nly that which has to be found becomes an object" (Groarke,

2010, p. 221). I see no reason to discard this suggestion. In light of the present discussion, however, I shall advance two further claims—first, that hope is woven into the fabric of our existence and is integral to what being human means; and second, that the object is most vital in its potentiality, that one is enlivened by the object one hopes to find. Taken together, the constitutive nature of hope and the imminent vitality of objects account for the antecedence of hope to the object. In the primary pre-differentiated phase of life, the infant's sense of hopefulness forms part of the goodness of life; and the moment of hope, manifest in the child's defiant gesture, is a re-finding of this inaugural sense of hope.

Psychoanalytic support for the idea of "re-finding" may be found not only in Winnicott, but also in *Three Essays on the Theory of Sexuality* (1905d, p. 222), where Freud states that "[T]he finding of an object is in fact a re-finding of it." This statement applies both retrospectively and prospectively. We discover, in retrospect, that the object has already been found; we find the object later, as it were, by deferred action (*Nachträglichkeit*). The "first object", therefore, is "later completed into the person of the child's mother" (1940a, p. 188). But as well as belatedness, which accounts for the formation and reformation of psychic structure on the oedipal model, I want to draw attention to what goes into looking forward, what Hans Loewald (1962a, 1962b) calls the "inner future". This raises two questions concerning (i) the inaugural reach for meaning and (ii) the role that hope plays in this process. Winnicott's theory of violence and hope throws new light on both questions, with respect to the valid future prefigured in the defiant gesture.

The retrospective–prospective nature of psychic life allows us to treat the breakdown of hope as a transference phenomenon. Our patients present us with varying degrees of conscious and unconscious despair and, if we accept hope as a primordial phenomenon, together with destruction as a vital positive function, then it follows that despair is a primitive expression of psychic disturbance. In this respect, analysis has reached bedrock when the analyst is claimed as the only hope of the hopeless. Similarly, children who wait are at risk of turning hope into an omnipotent disavowal of reality, an extreme idealisation of themselves that is "symmetrical with that of the hoped-for object" (Potamianou, 1997, p. 83). I don't doubt, based on my own analytic experience, that hope can be used in this way as a psychotic defence organisation. Treating perverse hope can feel like an interminable task.

Freud (1930a, p. 79) alerted us to the danger of "killing off the instincts" in the narcissistic act of hopeful waiting, in which hope sacrifices life for the "happiness of quietness". We can think of this as a perverse form of optimism. On the other hand, Winnicott made a strong case for why it is important to credit hopefulness as a vital resource, not least of all where the repetition of traumatising situations acts as a barrier against "psychic silence", preserving the possibility of vitality by "freezing" (Potamianou, 1997, p. 28). The vital significance of waiting becomes palpable with the notion of psychic freezing: "It is normal and healthy for the individual to be able to defend the self against specific environmental failure by a freezing of the failure situation. Along with this goes an unconscious assumption (which can become a conscious hope) that opportunity will occur at a later date for a renewed experience in which the failure situation will be able to be unfrozen and re-experienced" (Winnicott, 1954, p. 281).

We can uphold the case for waiting, understood as an act of hope, on the grounds that the object is findable in the midst of life (*media vita*). Waiting presupposes any number of motives and proceeds towards different ends. Broadly speaking, however, we wait either at odds with life (perverse optimism) or in the name of life. The positive alternative allows for the conviction, cathected by hope, that we are in the midst of life. Life is *given* in the potentiality that hope embodies. As such, the moment of hope intuits a time beyond boundaries which calls for *more life* without necessarily collapsing into psychopathology and the interminable search for limits through repetition. The moment of hope, in other words, is not in itself a pathological organisation or psychic retreat (Steiner, 1993). On the contrary, it reveals something of the search for one's (lost) potential experiences, following a breakdown of the mother–infant relationship at the beginning of life (Ogden, 2014).

And yet I contend that it is not and cannot be for *this* life only that we are given hope. As Paul writes in his First Epistle to the Corinthians: "If in this life only we have hope in Christ, we are of all men most miserable" (1 Cor. 15.19). Together with the goodness of life (the gift that precedes being), the Apostle's statement may be taken as a watchword for the redemptive reach of hope. The fact that we place our trust in something that hasn't happened, something that remains invisible, points to the transcendent nature of hope. Winnicott does not necessarily draw out this aspect of the argument, but it seems to me that by more than a conscious intention to take hold of the future, to find *this* or *that* object, we are gripped in the present by the very invisibility of the findable object. It is important that this is not seen as a negative proposition: the point rather is that the *findable object* remains irreducible to the *found object*. We are moved by the effect of hope, the unconscious sense of hopefulness, as a condition of any hopeful intent whatsoever. Empty-handed as the case may be, we remain full of hope in the midst of life. The metaphor of "groping" towards life seems particularly apposite here.

Approaching matters in terms of the "fusion" (*Mischung*) and "defusion" (*Entmischung*) of the drives, Freud (1926d, p. 125) maintained that so long as we are in the midst of life, we see only alloys between the drives or moments of drive defusion. However, as Winnicott (1968, p. 239) points out (in a brief comment on his paper on object usage), destructive aliveness is manifest as a phenomenon of basic unity prior to the fusion of the drives. In this case, the fundamental "mixture" (*Mischung*), so to speak, consists of primitive agony and unyielding hope—that is, where the mother is sufficiently available to support the infant's *experience* of both despair and hope. The implication is that children who wait in the wake of deprivation present mixtures in various proportions, conscious and unconscious, of hope and hopelessness. The loss of hope marks a return of helplessness (*Hilflosigkeit*), understood as the prototype of the traumatic situation (Freud, 1926d). And yet, unlike the infant who is laid open by a traumatic encounter at the beginning of life, and who is left to bear the irremediable aftermath of catastrophic disillusionment in "a sensation way" (Tustin, 1985, p. 271), the deprived child does not simply clutch at existence. The waiting embodied in the defiant gesture presupposes an expectation of goodness; it feels to the child as if something is within reach and for which it is worth waiting. The child waits on these grounds for the gift that the archaic, pre-object mother made available. Difficult children are not autistic; like Mr Biswas, they have a house in mind and, in the face of disintegrating family situations, attempt to lay claim to their "portion of the earth" (cf. Prologue to *A House for Mr Biswas* (Naipaul, 1961)). The claim signifies, amongst other things, a defiant refusal to be unaccommodated. We could say that difficult children remain essentially *home wanting*, that their want-to-be is kept alive by a defiant claim on their psychic home.

References

Abram, J. (2008). The evolution of Winnicott's theoretical matrix: a brief outline. In: J. Abram (Ed.), *Donald Winnicott Today* (pp. 73–112). Hove, UK: Routledge.

Aulagnier, P. (2001). *The Violence of Interpretation: From Pictogram to Statement*. A. Sheridan (Trans.). Hove, UK: Routledge.

Beveridge, W. (1942). *Report of the Inter-Departmental Committee on Social Insurance and Allied Services* (Beveridge Report), Cmnd. 6404. London: HMSO.

Biestek, F. P. (1961). *The Casework Relationship*. London: George Allen & Unwin.

Bollas, C. (1987). *The Shadow of the Object: Psychoanalysis of the Unthought Known*. London: Free Association.

Bowlby, J. (1979). *The Making and Breaking of Affectional Bonds*. London: Tavistock.

Britton, C. (1950). Child care. In: C. Morris (Ed.), *Social Case-Work in Great Britain* (pp. 167–194). London: Faber & Faber.

Castel, R. (1991). From dangerousness to risk. In: G. Burchell, C. Gordon, & P. Miller (Eds.), *The Foucault Effect: Studies in Governmentality* (pp. 281–298). Hemel Hempstead, UK: Harvester Wheatsheaf.

Curtis, M. (1946). *Report of the Care of Children Committee* (Curtis Report), Cmnd. 6922. London: HMSO.

Donzelot, J. (1980). *The Policing of Families: Welfare versus the State*. R. Hurley (Trans.). London: Hutchinson.

Donzelot, J. (1984). *L'Invention du Social*. Paris: ADD.

Foucault, M. (1979). "*Omnes et Singulatim*": Towards a critique of political reason. In: *Power, Vol. 3, Essential Works of Foucault 1954–1984* (pp. 298–325). R. Hurley et al. (Trans.). London: Allen Lane, 2000.

Foucault, M. (1982a). The subject and power. In: H. L. Dreyfus & P. Rabinow (Eds.), *Michel Foucault: Beyond Structuralism and Hermeneutics* (pp. 208–226). Chicago, IL: University of Chicago Press.

Foucault, M. (1982b). Space, knowledge, and power. In: *Power, Vol. 3, Essential Works of Foucault 1954–1984* (pp. 349–364). R. Hurley et al. (Trans.). London: Allen Lane, 2000.

Foucault, M. (2007). *Security, Territory, Population: Lectures at the Collège de France 1977–1978*. G. Burchell (Trans.). Basingstoke, UK: Palgrave Macmillan.

Foucault, M. (2014). *On the Government of the Living: Lectures at the Collège de France 1979–1980*. G. Burchell (Trans.). Basingstoke, UK: Palgrave Macmillan.

Freud, S. (1905d). *Three Essays on the Theory of Sexuality*. S. E., 7: 123–245. London: Hogarth.

Freud, S. (1926d). *Inhibitions, Symptoms and Anxiety*. S. E., 20: 72–175. London: Hogarth.

Freud, S. (1930a). *Civilization and Its Discontents*. S. E., 21: 57–145. London: Hogarth.

Freud, S. (1940a). *An Outline of Psycho-Analysis*. S. E., 23: 136–207. London: Hogarth.

Groarke, S. (2010). Making contact. *International Journal of Infant Observation and Its Applications*, 13(2): 209–222.

Heywood, J. S. (1978). *Children in Care: The Development of the Service for the Deprived Child* (3rd edn (revised)). London: Routledge & Kegan Paul.

Holman, B. (1995). *The Evacuation: A Very British Revolution.* Oxford: Lion.

Holman, B. (1996). *The Corporate Parent: Manchester Children's Department 1948–1971.* London: National Institute for Social Work.

Isaacs, S. (Ed.) (1941). *The Cambridge Evacuation Survey.* London: Methuen.

Lewis, H. (1954). *Deprived Children: A Social and Clinical Study.* London: Nuffield Foundation.

Loewald, H. (1962a). Internalization, separation, mourning, and the superego. In: *Papers on Psycho-Analysis* (pp. 257–276). New Haven, CT: Yale University Press, 1980.

Loewald, H. (1962b). Superego and time. In: *Papers on Psycho-Analysis* (pp. 43–52). New Haven, CT: Yale University Press, 1980.

Maclean, D. (1918). *Transfer of Functions of Poor Law Authorities in England and Wales* (Maclean Report), Cd. 8917. London: HMSO.

McDougall, K., & Cormack, U. (1950). Case-work in practice. In: C. Morris (Ed.), *Social Case-Work in Great Britain* (pp. 37–61). London: Faber & Faber.

Menzies Lyth, I. (1960). A case-study in the functioning of social systems as a defence against anxiety: A report on a study of the nursing service of a general hospital. *Human Relations, 13*: 95–121.

Morris, C. (Ed.) (1950). *Social Case-Work in Great Britain.* London: Faber & Faber.

Naipaul, V. S. (1961). *A House for Mr Biswas.* London: Andre Deutsch.

Ogden, T. H. (2014). Fear of breakdown and the unlived life. *International Journal of Psychoanalysis, 91*: 205–224.

Potamianou, A. (1997). *Hope: A Shield in the Economy of Borderline States.* P. Slotkin (Trans.). London: Routledge.

Rodman, F. R. (2003). *Winnicott: Life and Work.* Cambridge, MA: Perseus.

Steiner, J. (1993). *Psychic Retreats: Pathological Organizations in Psychotic, Neurotic and Borderline Patients.* London: Routledge.

Stephens, T. (Ed.) (1945). *Problem Families: An Experiment in Social Rehabilitation.* London: Pacifist Service Unit.

Tustin, F. (1985). The rhythm of safety. In: *Autistic Barriers in Neurotic Patients* (pp. 268–285). London: Karnac, 1986.

Winnicott, C. (1955). Casework techniques in the child care services. In: J. Kanter (Ed.), *Face to Face with Children* (pp. 145–165). London: Karnac.

Winnicott, C. (1980). Child care in Oxfordshire. In: J. Kanter (Ed.), *Face to Face with Children* (pp. 127–141). London: Karnac.

Winnicott, C. (1984). Introduction. In: C. Winnicott, R. Shepherd, & M. Davis (Eds.), *Deprivation and Delinquency* (pp. 1–5). London: Tavistock.

Winnicott, D. W. (1948). Children's hostels in war and peace. In: C. Winnicott, R. Shepherd, & M. Davis (Eds.), *Deprivation and Delinquency* (pp. 73–77). London: Tavistock, 1984.

Winnicott, D. W. (1950). The deprived child and how he can be compensated for loss of family life. In: C. Winnicott, R. Shepherd, & M. Davis (Eds.), *Deprivation and Delinquency* (pp. 172–188). London: Tavistock, 1984.

Winnicott, D. W. (1954). Metapsychological and clinical aspects of regression within the psycho-analytical set-up. In: *Through Paediatrics to Psycho-Analysis* (pp. 278–294). London: Hogarth, 1978.

Winnicott, D. W. (1956). The antisocial tendency. In: C. Winnicott, R. Shepherd, & M. Davis (Eds.), *Deprivation and Delinquency* (pp. 120–131). London: Tavistock, 1984.

Winnicott, D. W. (1960). The family and emotional maturity. In: *The Family and Individual Development* (pp. 88–94). London: Tavistock, 1965.

Winnicott, D. W. (1963). Morals and education. In: *The Maturational Processes and the Facilitating Environment* (pp. 93–105). London: Hogarth, 1985.

Winnicott, D. W. (1965). A clinical study of the effect of a failure of the average expectable environment on a child's mental functioning. *International Journal of Psychoanalysis, 46*: 81–87.

Winnicott, D. W. (1968). Comments on my paper "The use of an object". In C. Winnicott, R. Shepherd, & M. Davis (Eds.), *Psycho-Analytic Explorations* (pp. 238–240). London: Karnac.

Winnicott, D. W. (1970). Residential care as therapy. In: C. Winnicott, R. Shepherd, & M. Davis (Eds.), *Deprivation and Delinquency* (pp. 220–228). London: Tavistock, 1984.

Winnicott, D. W. (1971). The use of an object and relating through identifications. In: *Playing and Reality* (pp. 86–94). London: Tavistock, 1974.

Winnicott, D. W., & Britton, C. (1947). Residential management as treatment for difficult children. In: C. Winnicott, R. Shepherd, & M. Davis (Eds.), *Deprivation and Delinquency* (pp. 54–72). London: Tavistock, 1984.

Younghusband Report (1959). *Report of the Committee on Social Workers in the Local Authority and Welfare Services*. London: HMSO.

Index

Made in the USA
Middletown, DE
01 September 2023